SAT* and ACT® GRAMMAR WORKBOOK

Fourth Edition

George Ehrenhaft, Ed.D.
Former English Department Chairman
Mamaroneck High School
Mamaroneck, New York

BARRON'S

Copyright © 2016 by Barron's Educational Series, Inc.

Previous editions copyright © 2014, 2010, 2006 by Barron's Educational Series, Inc., under the title *Grammar Workbook for the SAT, ACT, and More.*

All inquiries should be addressed to:
Barron's Educational Series, Inc.
250 Wireless Boulevard
Hauppauge, NY 11788
www.barronseduc.com

Library of Congress Control Number: 2016933943

ISBN: 978-1-4380-0873-8

PRINTED IN THE UNITED STATES OF AMERICA
10 9 8 7 6 5 4 3 2 1

10%
POST-CONSUMER WASTE
Paper contains a minimum of 10% post-consumer waste (PCW). Paper used in this book was derived from certified, sustainable forestlands.

Contents

Preface: A Greeting from the Author v

Introduction: Grammar Q's and A's   vii

PART I   **GRAMMAR BASICS: AN ORIENTATION / 1**

    Chapter 1 The Words of Grammar: Terms to Know / 3

        The Noun / 3
        The Article / 5
        The Pronoun / 5
        The Verb / 22
        The Adjective / 36
        The Adverb / 41
        The Preposition / 45
        The Conjunction / 48
        Answer Key / 51

    Chapter 2 Sentences / 59

        A Note to the Reader / 59
        Sentence Basics / 59
        Clauses / 62
        Types of Sentences / 63
        Sentence Problems / 64
        Sentence Structure / 74
        Sentence Expression and Style / 77
        Sentence Mechanics: Punctuation and Capitalization / 85
        Answer Key / 92

PART II   **GRAMMAR TESTS / 97**

Chapter 3 Grammar Pitfalls / 99

Chapter 4 SAT Grammar Questions / 109

Answering the Questions / 109
Tests for Practice / 112
Practice Test A / 113
Practice Test B / 127
Practice Test C / 139
Practice Test D / 151

Chapter 5 ACT Grammar Questions / 163

Topics Covered on the ACT English Test / 163
Sample ACT Questions / 164
Practice Test A / 173
Practice Test B / 195

PART III ESSAY WRITING ON THE SAT AND ACT / 219

Chapter 6 Writing a Grammatical Essay / 221

The SAT Essay / 221
How to Earn a High Score / 224
Finding and Analyzing Evidence / 226
Sample Analysis of a Source Text / 227
ACT Writing Test / 231
Evaluating the Essay / 233
Sample Prompt / 235
Write an ACT Essay for Practice / 237

Index / 241

Preface
A Greeting from the Author

Dear Reader,

Most people would rather be stuck in traffic than study grammar. Nevertheless, the book in your hands invites you to cast aside your prejudices and dare to discover the joys of grammar—although some will say "No way!"

If that's what you think, consider the following facts: Good grammar helps you to speak and write well and earn better grades in school. A command of standard English grammar enables you to present yourself as a generally mature and intelligent person. And, if you happen to belong to the millions of college applicants who each year take the ACT, the SAT—or both—knowing grammar virtually guarantees higher scores.

This user-friendly book will acquaint you with grammatical terms and help you answer grammar-related questions on college entrance exams. Moreover, you'll learn to recognize and avoid the most common grammatical pitfalls and see what it takes to compose correct and effective sentences when writing an SAT or ACT essay.

If you currently feel half-clueless about grammar or have grammar skills rusty from disuse, take heart. You probably know more than you think. Be confident that you've made the right move by picking up this book, which starts with grammar basics. Begin by reading . . . no, begin *by studying* Part I, an introduction to essential grammatical terms and concepts. Track your progress by doing the exercises, called "Checkpoints." They'll tell you how your efforts are paying off.

If you are already well-versed in grammar and on the verge of taking the SAT or ACT—or retaking one of them to raise your score—begin with Part II, a collection of the grammatical issues you're most likely to be asked about. It consists of sample SAT and ACT questions modeled after those on the SAT's Writing and Language section and the ACT English Test. Thorough analyses and explanations will help you nail down correct answers on both exams.

Part III takes you deeper into the SAT and ACT with detailed descriptions of the optional essay questions on both tests as well as a guide for writing first-rate essays. It also contains sample essay questions, student-written responses, and evaluations that illustrate what readers look for as they score the essays. Please don't even think of taking either test without reviewing Part III beforehand.

Whatever your purpose or goal, use this guide regularly and often. Keep it by your side as a ready reference. Browse its pages in your spare time or read it intently from cover to cover. Whatever you do, let the book work for you. Let it help you sharpen your skills and build your confidence as a speaker, writer, and test taker.

Meanwhile, I'll keep my fingers crossed and avidly root for your success.

Good luck and best wishes,

George Ehrenhaft

Introduction
Grammar Q's and A's

Why is grammar important? What's all the fuss about?

If you want to send a verbal message to someone, sound grammar helps. Without it, you can never be sure that your words say exactly what you want them to. Ideas shaped in faulty language may be crystal clear to you, but you can never know exactly what they'll mean to somebody else. Using standard grammar increases your chances of accurately getting your message across.

Why do so many people find it hard to learn grammar?

The reason is that it *is* hard. Grammar is a jumble of rules and principles, most of them easy to memorize but tricky to apply because the language doesn't always cooperate. Exceptions to nearly every rule cause no end of trouble and can make smart people feel dumb.

Nevertheless, billions of people—not all of them brilliant—have learned grammar without whining about it and have spent a lifetime enjoying the rewards of speaking and writing standard grammatical English.

What's the difference between "usage" and "grammar"?

Although some people say "usage" when they mean "grammar," and vice versa, the two words are not synonyms. Usage describes actual spoken and written language. "Standard" usage is the level of language embraced by educated, fluent speakers of English. Grammar, on the other hand, is a set of rules that are followed when you speak and write "correctly."

Why do some rules force you to use language that sounds weird?

Because the English language keeps changing, old rules often become obsolete. It's always been correct to say, "*It is I*," but today, "*It is me*" is perfectly acceptable, especially in informal speech. Once upon a time, a question like, "*What's all the fuss about?*" was considered poor English because of a taboo against ending a sentence with a preposition. In the 21st century, however, no one would seriously say, "*About what is all the fuss?*" In short, the rules of grammar bend to fit the circumstances, but sometimes not quickly enough to keep up with our evolving language.

How will studying grammar help on the SAT and ACT?

Here's a fact: You won't be tested on the rules of grammar on either the SAT or ACT. Instead, you'll be asked to locate and correct grammatical errors in sentences and paragraphs. A sense of language—let's call it an "ear" for what is right and wrong—could steer you to the right answers. But that's not enough. Very often, knowledge of the rules can help you find grammatical errors in an instant and answer the questions with the confidence of an expert. Knowing the rules will keep you from making grammatical mistakes as you write your SAT or ACT essay, and an error-free essay will work in your favor when the essay is scored.

Even so, it's possible to answer all test questions on grammar without memorizing countless rules. But knowing many of them can help—a lot.

How does this book differ from other grammar books?

Instead of handing you a long list of grammatical rules to be learned and followed, this book zeroes in on common errors in grammar and usage. It shows you first how to track down everyday mistakes in speech and writing, and then how to fix them.

Part I
Grammar Basics
An Orientation

Chapter 1
The Words of Grammar
Terms to Know

People in every line of work—from bankers to beauticians, from stargazers to gurus—share a language special to their jobs. Grammarians are no exception, which means that you and I can't discuss grammar without using certain words that we both understand. So, what follows is a chapter full of the terms that people need when they talk and write about grammar. Hard-core, essential terms are printed in boldface capital letters like **THIS**. Less crucial words appear in boldface italics like ***this***. Learn the first kind cold. The second kind you can probably muddle through without—at least until you get serious about grammar and start wallowing in the stuff. That's no joke. There are countless grammar lovers out there—and not all of them are kooks.

This chapter on grammar terminology has been pared to the bone—first, to keep you from being overwhelmed, and second, because grammar contains countless mystifying terms that, although nice to know, don't necessarily help you become a more effective user of English.

> **Hint:** Read these pages slowly, digesting a few bites at each reading. Don't get bogged down trying to memorize every detail. Like everything, grammar takes time to learn. Perseverance helps. Expect to go back again and again until you're satisfied that you haven't missed anything.

THE NOUN

NOUNS (Remember: **BOLDFACE CAPS** indicate the most crucial words.) **Nouns** are the names of things, the labels we apply to everything we can see, touch, taste, and feel. They name the places we go (*school, work, the mall*), our means of getting there (*subway, legs, an SUV*), and what we pass by, pass through, and pass over (*the park, downtown, a bridge*) on our way. Nouns name the solid, concrete, tactile words of our language, the infrastructure, so to speak. But they also name:

- people (*Loretta, the mail carrier*)
- activities (*swimming, kissing*)
- concepts (*sportsmanship, love*)
- conditions (*mess, poverty*)
- events (*9/11, prom*)
- groups (*Microsoft, SADD*)
- feelings (*enthusiasm, headache*)
- times (*morning, curfew*)

Some nouns such as *Detroit* and *Hewlett-Packard* are capitalized. Those are **proper nouns** and refer to specific places, groups, things, events, and so on. The nouns that begin with lower-case letters go by the name of **common nouns**.

All the nouns listed above are **SINGULAR**. That is, they name only one person, one place, one thing, one activity, and so forth. By adding either -s or -es you make many nouns **PLURAL**, meaning more than one. Thus, one *woodpecker* becomes two or more *woodpeckers* and a *box* increases in number into as many *boxes* as you can count. Some nouns increase their **number** (a term that refers to singular and plural) with various combinations of letters other than -s or -es. For example: *sky/skies, knife/knives, ox/oxen, child/children, alumnus/alumni, goose/geese,* and *mouse/mice.*

Several nouns are the same in both singular and plural forms, among them: *deer/deer, scissors/scissors,* and *moose/moose,* as well as a handful of nouns with Latin endings, such as *data* and *media,* which are technically plural but have become singular through constant repetition.

English also contains nouns that come only in singular form. These include *news, garbage, happiness, information, physics, air, laryngitis,* and *honesty.*

Identifying singular and plural nouns is usually no problem for native speakers of English, but some people stumble over **collective nouns**, nouns that stand for groups or quantities or masses of things, such as: *family, class, mob, orchestra, jury, team,* and *audience.* Although these nouns name collections of more than one individual, they are still considered singular most of the time, as in "The class is in the gym." When you refer to individuals in a group, however, collective nouns may be used as plurals, as in "The class were divided in their feelings about the poem." This is more common, however, in British English than American English.

Believe it or not, there are many more pretty cool facts to learn about nouns:

- Nouns can be used to indicate possession, as in *Anthony's* nose and the *day's* end.
- A noun (or pronoun) is crucial to almost every complete sentence (more about that later).
- Some nouns look like verbs and are called **gerunds**, but they still function as nouns (more to come on that, too).
- Some nouns are not always nouns. They occasionally change their identities. Take the word *love,* for instance:

> **Susan is the *love*** (noun) **of my life.**
> **I *love*** (verb) **her dearly.**
> **I wrote her a *love*** (adjective) **song.**

These, among many other wonders of English grammar, await you in the pages ahead. For the scoop on verbs, turn to page 22; punctuation, page 85; sentence structure, page 74; and modifiers, page 36. If you're just dying for a sneak preview of these and other intriguing matters, don't hold back. Just turn the pages and go for it!

THE ARTICLE

If you're ever unsure whether or not a word is a noun, here's something to try: Put one of three articles (*the, a,* or *an*) in front of it. If the article + word sounds like a combination you are apt to hear or even use yourself, chances are that the word in question is a noun, as in *the alphabet, a lobster, an egg*. Because you wouldn't say "*the me*," "*a destroy*," or "*an of*," you can be sure that *me, destroy,* and *of* are not nouns, but some other part of speech.

> The label "article" applies to only three English words: *a, an,* and *the.*

An **ARTICLE** is one of the traditional **PARTS OF SPEECH** (see next paragraph). It is a label that applies to only three English words: *the, a,* and *an*—and no others. *A* and *an* are called **indefinite articles** because they are used to refer to nouns that are not clearly specified, as in: *a truck driver, a river, an explosion. The* is called a **definite article** because it refers to more specific, identifiable people, places, or things, as in: *the old truck driver, the Mississippi River, the first explosion.*

PARTS OF SPEECH is a general term that refers to eight types of words, each playing a different role in speech and writing. You've already met the **NOUN** and the **ARTICLE**. The others are the **PRONOUN, VERB, ADJECTIVE, ADVERB, PREPOSITION,** and **CONJUNCTION.** You'll get to know all of them in the pages ahead. You'll also come to see that, in spite of different names, the parts of speech do not live in isolation. Rather, they work together like the instruments of an orchestra, each influencing the other to create a unified and often melodic language.

But wait! There's one missing—the **INTERJECTION**.

Not to worry. Interjections are minor words and phrases, mostly one-word utterances tacked onto or inserted into sentences to heighten emotion or express feelings. *Uh oh!* is an interjection. So are *alas, well, oh, wow, good grief, shhh!, for Pete's sake!, damn!,* and a host of other expressions, including any number of colorful expletives that can't be printed here. Although interjections serve a rhetorical purpose, they hardly matter grammatically. When you write, use them sparingly—with or without exclamation points.

THE PRONOUN

Simply put, a **PRONOUN** is a handy word used as a substitute for another word, usually a noun. Without pronouns, we'd be stuck using the same nouns over and over again, as in this passage:

> **On the way home, Dot sat next to Dan on the bus. Dot didn't say much, but Dot offered Dan a stick of gum. Dot also let Dan use Dot's iPod, which was Dot's way of saying thanks to Dan for helping Dot with Dot's math homework.**

Thank goodness for pronouns! They spare us from mountains of such monotonous repetition. Look how three everyday pronouns transform the passage into something far more readable:

> **On the way home, Dot sat next to Dan on the bus. Dot didn't say much, but *she* offered Dan a stick of gum. *She* also let *him* use *her* iPod, which was *her* way of saying thanks to *him* for helping *her* with *her* math homework.**

Using the pronouns *she, him,* and *her* as substitutes for *Dot* and *Dan* makes all the difference.

Choosing the Correct Pronoun

It would be hard to prove, but adult speakers and writers of English probably use the correct pronoun ninety-nine out of a hundred times. Well, maybe ninety-eight out of a hundred, but still a very high rate of accuracy. Total compliance with the rules of pronoun usage may be out of reach, but you can do your part by knowing how to choose the right pronoun at the right time.

To begin, you should know that faulty pronoun usage occurs most often:

- When pronouns in the wrong "case" are chosen
- When pronouns in the wrong "person" are chosen
- When pronouns fail to agree in number or gender with the noun for which the pronoun is a substitute.
- When the pronoun reference is unclear or ambiguous

The pages that follow explain each of these pitfalls and show you how to avoid them. Along the way, you'll also find *Checkpoints*—places where you can test your understanding of the grammar that governs pronoun usage.

The "case" of pronouns

He, she, and *him,* along with *I, me, her, it, they, them, we, us,* and *you* are called **personal pronouns.** Most of the time, you can depend on your ear to tell you which pronoun to use. For example, because you'd never tell the bus driver, "Let *I* off at the corner," you'd use *me* without even thinking about it.

Unfortunately, pronoun choice isn't always that simple. For instance, which pronoun—*I* or *me*—should complete this sentence?

Philip is a faster runner than _____.

Half the people would probably say *I*, the other half *me.* Which half is correct? Read on, and you'll learn how to figure it out.

Because you can't always depend on which pronoun sounds right, it helps to know that personal pronouns are divided into two separate groups:

> It helps to know that pronouns fall into two groups: *subject* pronouns and *object* pronouns.

Group 1	Group 2
I	me
he	him
she	her
they	them
we	us
you	you

Group 1 words are called **SUBJECT** pronouns and are in the *nominative case*, whereas Group 2 words are called **OBJECT** pronouns and are in the *objective case*. They've been given different labels because pronouns in the nominative case function differently from pronouns in the objective case, and vice versa. Therefore, the word **CASE** refers to the role each pronoun plays in a sentence.

Grammar Basics

1. Subject pronouns are used in two ways: They name the people, places, or things being described, as in this sentence:

> *She* **is weird.**

Or, they name the performer of some sort of action, as in:

> **It was** *he* **who fell into the water.**

In each sentence a pronoun serves as the grammatical **SUBJECT**. (For details about sentence subjects, turn to page 59.) It also happens that the verbs used in both these sentences are forms of the verb *to be*, a fact worth noting because so-called ***being verbs*** (sometimes called ***linking verbs***)—such as *is, was, were, has been, had been, will be,* and so on—are always paired with subject pronouns and never with object pronouns, even when the pronoun is not the subject of the sentence, as in:

> **The only students** (subject of sentence) **who failed the quiz** *were* (verb) **Damon and** *he* (pronoun).

For the record, the pronoun *he* in this sentence functions as a ***predicate nominative***, a term that refers to words that identify, define, or mean the same as the grammatical subject (details about predicates on page 60).

One more thing: *Object* pronouns don't ever belong in sentence subjects, because you may end up saying things like, "*Them* are going to be late" or "*Him* and *me* walked to the diner," usage suggesting that the speaker is, to put it mildly, grammatically challenged.

2. Object pronouns. In contrast to subject pronouns, object pronouns are used to refer to people, places, or things being acted upon:

> **The music carried** *them* (object pronoun) **away.**
> **He asked** *her* (object pronoun) **to text** *him* (object pronoun).

Pronouns that function as receivers of action are called ***objects of the verb***, as in:

> **Terry invited** *him* **to the prom.**
> (*invited* = verb; *him* = object of the verb)
> **The waiter gave** *her* **and** *me* **a menu.**
> (*gave* = verb; *her* and *me* = objects of the verb)

Object pronouns are also used in ***prepositional phrases***—that is, phrases that (as their name suggests) begin with **PREPOSITIONS**, as in:

> <u>between</u> *you* and *me*
> <u>to</u> Sherry and *her*
> <u>among</u> *us* women
> <u>at</u> *us*
> <u>from</u> *her* and *him*
> <u>with</u> *me* and *you*

(For details on prepositions, turn to page 45.)

> Avoid mixing subject and object pronouns in the same phrase, for example: *she and them*.

Using pairs of personal pronouns

You'll never go wrong if you avoid mixing subject and object pronouns in the same phrase, as, for example, in *she and them* or *they and us*. When you're uncertain about which pronouns are used to make a pair, here's what to do: If you know that one pronoun is correct, pick the second one from the same group. If you're not sure of either pronoun, substitute *I* or *me* for one of the pronouns—if *I* seems to fit, pick the pronouns from Group 1; if *me* fits better, use a Group 2 pronoun. For example, decide which pair of pronouns fits the following sentence:

Elvis asked that (*he, him*) and (*she, her*) practice handstands.

If you insert *me* in place of one of the pronouns, you'll get:

Elvis asked that *me* practice handstands.

Because that language comes from another dimension of reality, *I* must be the word that fits. So, pick your pronouns from Group 1:

Elvis asked that *he* and *she* practice handstands.

Pairing a noun and a pronoun

When using a phrase made up of a noun and pronoun, such as *Katya and I, my canary and me, he and Caleb, them and my uncle*, choose the appropriate pronoun as though the noun didn't exist. That's right, ignore the noun and then decide whether you need a subject pronoun or an object pronoun. For instance:

The teacher and (*she, her*) argued about the test grade.

Whichever pronoun you choose, it's going to be part of the grammatical subject of the sentence. Therefore, forget *teacher* and insert *she* or *her*. Because no one ever says "*Her* argued about the test grade," *she* must be the correct pronoun.

Similarly, if the noun/pronoun pair is the object of a preposition, as in "A bond developed between Sarah and (*I, me*)," let the noun and pronoun swap places in the sentence. Then the correct choice becomes perfectly obvious:

A bond developed between Sarah and *me*.

Using pronouns in comparisons

To find the correct pronoun in a comparison that uses *than* or *as*, complete the comparison using the verb that would follow naturally:

Jackie runs faster than *she* (runs).
My brother has bigger feet than *I* (do).
Cora is as tough as *he* (is).
A woman such as *I* (am) could solve the problem.

Noun/pronoun combinations

When a pronoun appears side by side with a noun (*we* boys, *us* women), deleting the noun will usually help you pick the correct pronoun.

> **(*We, Us*) seniors decided to take a day off from school in late May.**
> (Deleting *seniors* leaves <u>We</u> decided to . . .)
> **This award was presented to (*we, us*) students by the faculty.**
> (Deleting *students* leaves *award was presented to <u>us</u> by the . . .*)

Checkpoint 1. CHOOSING PERSONAL PRONOUNS

Circle the correct pronoun in each sentence below.

1. Maya took my sister and (I, me) to the magic show last night.

2. We thought that Maryly and Jorge would be there, and sure enough, we saw (she, her) and (he, him) sitting in the front row.

3. During the intermission, Jorge came over and asked my sister and (I, me) to go out after the show.

4. Between you and (I, me) the magician was terrible.

5. It must also have been a bad evening for (he, him) and his assistant, Roxanne.

6. Trying to pull a rabbit out of a hat, Roxanne and (he, him) knocked over the table.

7. When he asked for audience participation, my sister and (I, me) volunteered to go on stage.

8. He said that in my pocket I would find $10 in change to split between (I, me) and my sister.

9. When the coins fell out of his sleeve, the audience laughed even harder than (we, us).

10. After the show, (we, us) in the audience thought that the magician needed lots of practice before his next performance.

Answers on page 51

Pronoun "person"

Have you ever noticed that everyday conversation is overwhelmingly about a single topic—namely, ***people***? I tell you about myself; you tell me about yourself; we tell each other about someone else. To help sort out who is being talked about, our language conveniently categorizes pronouns—both singular and plural—according to **PERSON**, or more specifically, ***first-person, second-person***, and ***third-person*** pronouns.

First-person pronouns—*I, we, me, us, my, mine, our, ours*. As you see, first-person pronouns are used when the speakers (or writers) talk about themselves, as in

> **I am hungry. Let's have lunch in *our* kitchen. *We* can have leftover pasta salad that *my* sister made yesterday.**

Second-person pronouns—*you, your, yours*—refer to listeners (or readers), as in

> **How much salad would *you* like me to put on *your* plate?**

At times the pronoun *you* refers to people in general. If you said, "Hey, Dad, *you* can now take the ACT digitally," chances are you'd mean *you* in the general sense because not many dads take the ACT these days. If, however, you hear Raymond warn his lab partner Megan, "Don't do it! *You'll* blow up the lab if *you* combine those two chemicals," you can bet that Raymond is referring to Megan herself.

Third-person pronouns—*she, he, it, one, they, him, her, them, his, her, hers, its, their, theirs*—refer to other people and things, both singular and plural. Unlike first- and second-person pronouns, third-person pronouns also indicate *gender*, that is, whether the person or thing is male, female, or neither.

In other words, third-person pronouns convey more information than first- and second-person pronouns and, therefore, can be somewhat trickier to use.

The list of third-person pronouns also includes what are called *indefinite pronouns*, such as *all, any, anyone, each, either, none, nothing, one*, and lots more. Because many indefinite pronouns express the idea of quantity—*both, few, many, several*, and others—it takes some skill and practice to make sure that your pronouns always agree in number and gender with their **ANTECEDENTS**—the words they refer to.

Consistency in pronoun usage

Everyday pronouns come naturally to people who speak English. No one really struggles to choose between male and female pronouns. Likewise, we use singular and plural pronouns without thinking too much about what's right and wrong.

Yet, accurate pronoun usage can become more complex when a sentence calls for the repeated use of one or more pronouns. When you form a sentence cast in the second person, for instance, keep it in the second person. Consistency is the key.

> **INCONSISTENT: When you walk your** (second person) **dog, I** (first person) **must carry a pooper-scooper.**
>
> **CONSISTENT: When you walk your** (second person) **dog, you** (second person) **must carry a pooper-scooper.**

For some reason, the pronouns *one* and *you* tend to be switched more often than others:

> **INCONSISTENT: The more *one* watches television, the more *you* turn into a vegetable.**
>
> **CONSISTENT: The more *you* watch television, the more *you* turn into a vegetable.**

Actually, the guidelines for using the impersonal pronoun are more like suggestions than strict rules. That's why, in all but the most formal writing, you can properly combine the antecedent *one* with *he/she* and *his/her*, as in:

> FORMAL: *One* must take into account *one's* ability to pay.
> LESS FORMAL: *One* must take into account *his* ability to pay.

Pronoun/antecedent agreement in number and gender

> Pronouns and antecedents should agree in number and gender.

Here's a straightforward rule about pronouns and antecedents: Pronouns and antecedents should agree in number and gender. Despite its simplicity, this rule is widely ignored. In fact, the use of plural pronouns to refer to singular antecedents is so common, that flouting the rule has almost become the norm:

> **Everybody** (singular) **is sticking to** *their* (plural) **side of the story.**
> **Anybody** (singular) **can pass this course if** *they* (plural) **study hard.**
> **Neither** (singular) **teacher plans to change** *their* (plural) **policy regarding homework.**
> **If** *someone* (singular) **tries to write a persuasive essay,** *they* (plural) **should at least include a convincing argument.**

Such agreement errors occur because certain antecedents—chief among them *neither, everybody, everyone, nobody, no one, somebody, someone, anybody,* and *anyone*—sound plural. But the fact is they're singular and always have been. In standard grammar, therefore, the sentences should be:

> **Everybody is sticking to** *his* **side of the story.**
> **Anybody can pass this course if** *she* **studies hard.**
> **Neither teacher plans to change** *his* **policy regarding homework.**
> **If someone tries to write a persuasive essay,** *one* **should at least include a convincing argument.**

Note: Some readers and writers object to the custom of using male pronouns even when the gender of the antecedent is unknown, as in

> **Whoever smokes two packs a day should have** *his* **head examined because** *he* **is destroying** *himself.*

To avoid this sort of sexism, they substitute such phrases as *his or her* and *he and she*:

> **Whoever smokes two packs a day should have** *his or her* **head examined because** *he or she* **is destroying** *himself or herself.*

Although politically correct, such phrases plunge perfectly good ideas into wordy and ungraceful sentences. Seasoned writers, therefore, often turn to gender-neutral plural pronouns, as in

> *Those* **who smoke two packs a day should have** *their* **heads examined because** *they* **are destroying** *themselves.*

Or they might dodge the pronoun problem altogether by restructuring the sentence:

> **Smoking two packs a day is a stupid, self-destructive habit.**

Context determines whether the rule for pronoun-antecedent agreement also applies to so-called collective nouns—that is, words like *jury*, *class*, and *family*, which are sometimes singular and sometimes plural:

> **The jury** (singular) **will render its** (singular pronoun) **verdict on Tuesday.**
> **The jury** (plural) **will return to their** (plural pronoun) **homes after the verdict.**

Clearly, a noun that names a whole group is singular (*police*, *family*), but when it refers to its members acting individually, consider it plural, as in:

> **The police had** *their* **photos taken for the newspaper.**
> **After the funeral the family thanked everyone who had sent** *them* **sympathy cards.**

Checkpoint 2. PRONOUN SHIFT AND PRONOUN AGREEMENT

Some of the sentences below contain shifts in pronoun person or errors in agreement between pronouns and antecedents. Make all appropriate corrections in the spaces provided, but revise only those sentences that contain errors.

1. The English teacher announced that everyone in the class must turn in their term papers no later than Friday.

   _____

2. When one is fired from a job, she collects unemployment.

   _____

3. The library put their collection of rare books on display.

   _____

4. Each of my sisters own their own car.

   _____

5. In that class, our teacher held conferences with us once a week.

   _____

6. In order to keep yourself in shape, one should work out every day.

   _____

7. The individual chosen as team captain will find themselves working very hard.

   _____

8. Each horse in the procession followed their rider down to the creek.

   _____

9. The school's chess team has just won their first match.

   _____

10. When one is visiting the park and you can't find a restroom, they should ask a park ranger.

Answers on page 51

Pronoun references

Pronouns should refer unambiguously to their antecedents. Vague or nonexistent references leave readers scratching their heads. Here are three practical tips for avoiding pronoun-reference traps:

- Double-check every pronoun you use to make sure that it doesn't refer to more than one antecedent:

  The teacher, Ms. Taylor, told Tessa that it was *her* responsibility to hand out composition paper.

So, who's responsible? Ms. Taylor or Tessa? It's impossible to tell because the pronoun *her* could refer to either of them. Corrected, the sentence reads:

  Ms. Taylor told Tessa that it was *her* responsibility as the teacher to hand out composition paper.

- Be wary of sentences that contain two or more pronoun references, such as:

  Mike became a good friend of Mark's after *he* helped *him* repair *his* computer.

Huh? Whose computer needed fixing? Who helped whom? The answer lies in a revised sentence:

  Mike and Mark became good friends after Mike helped Mark repair *his* computer.

This is better, but you still can't be sure who owns the computer. One way to clear up the uncertainty is to write more than one sentence:

  When Mark needed to repair his computer, Mike helped *him* do the job. Afterward, Mike and Mark became good friends.

Ah, now it's clear: Mark owns the computer, and Mike pitched in to fix it.

- Watch out for words or phrases that may be mistaken for the antecedent, as in:

  Francisco was taken fishing by his father when he was ten.

Because the words *he* and *father* are almost next to each other, *father* may seem to be the antecedent of the pronoun *he*. But, unless Francisco's father holds a record for being the world's youngest dad, the sentence needs revision:

  When he was ten, Francisco was taken fishing by his father.

By now you probably get the idea: Clear meaning depends on pronouns that refer unmistakably to particular nouns or other pronouns. But you also need to know that in some sentences, pronouns can refer not to single-word antecedents but to a phrase or an entire clause. The pronoun *it* in the following sentence, for example, refers to an eight-word clause.

The storm named Katrina washed the bridge out, which made *it* impossible to get to Mobile on time.

Here, *it* refers to the clause "The storm named Katrina washed the bridge out." In such cases, the pronoun can be a personal pronoun such as *it*, *they*, and *you*, or a **relative pronoun** such as *which*, *that*, and *this*. For details about relative pronouns, see page 16. Be careful when forming such sentences to avoid referring to something too general or too ambiguous, as in:

Homeless people allege that the mayor is indifferent to their plight, *which* has been disproved.

Whoa! What really has been disproved? That people made an allegation against the mayor? That the mayor is indifferent to the plight of the homeless? No one can be sure, because *which* has no distinct antecedent. To eliminate the uncertainty, revise the sentence:

Homeless people allege that the mayor is indifferent to their plight, but the allegation has been disproved.

Checkpoint 3. PRONOUN REFERENCES

The sentences below suffer from faulty pronoun references. Please revise each sentence to eliminate the problem. Use the blank spaces to write your answers.

1. When we teenagers loiter outside the theater on Friday night, they give you a hard time.

   _____

   _____

2. I answered the test questions, collected my pencils and pens, and handed them in.

   _____

   _____

3. Kaylin told Ken that she wanted only a short wedding trip to Florida, which lies at the root of their problem.

   _____

   _____

4. His father let him know that he had only an hour to get to the airport.

   _____

   _____

5. During Ms. Sanchez's time at the school, she walked the halls more than any other assistant principal.

_____

_____

6. Mr. Henry, an ambulance driver, disapproved of war but drove it to the front lines anyway.

_____

_____

7. After the campus tour, Mike told Todd that he thought he'd be happy going to Auburn.

_____

_____

8. Mira's car hit a truck, but it wasn't even dented.

_____

_____

9. Within the last month, Alicia's older brother Pierre found a new job, broke his leg skiing, and got married to Felicia, which made their parents very happy.

_____

_____

10. She wore her new jacket to school, which was black and made of leather.

_____

_____

Answers on page 52

Other Types of Pronouns

Until now, these pages have focused on ordinary, everyday personal pronouns. But guess what? Pronouns also come in a handful of other varieties:

Possessive pronouns
Relative pronouns
Reflexive pronouns
Interrogative pronouns
Demonstrative pronouns

Here's some good news: These types of pronouns, although just as common as personal pronouns in everyday speech and writing, cause fewer grammatical problems.

Possessive pronouns

The *possessive pronouns*—*my, mine, his, her, hers, your, yours, our, ours, their* and *theirs*—true to their name, indicate ownership, as in *my* hair, *your* sister, *his* house, *their* party, and so on. They are in the *possessive case* and always answer the question "whose?"

> **"Whose cat is that?"**
> **"It is *hers* (possessive pronoun)."**
> **"Are you sure?"**
> **"Well, no, maybe it is *theirs* (possessive pronoun)."**

Always write possessive pronouns without **apostrophes**. Don't write *her's, their's, your's,* and don't confuse the possessive pronoun *its* with its look-alike cousin *it's,* a **contraction** meaning *it is.*

Use a possessive pronoun (*my, our, your, his, her, their*) before a **gerund** (a noun that looks like a verb because of its *-ing* ending).

> **Her asking the question shows that she is alert.** (*Asking* is a gerund.)
> **Mama was upset about *your* letting the cat out.** (*Letting* is a gerund.)

Not every noun with an *-ing* ending is a gerund. Sometimes it's just a noun, as in *thing, ring, spring.* At other times, *-ing* words are verbs; in particular, they're **participles** that modify pronouns in the objective case.

> **I hope you don't mind *my* intruding on your conversation.** (Here *intruding* is a gerund.)
> **I hope you don't mind *me* intruding on your conversation.** (Here *intruding* is a participle.)

> **Note:** Frankly, gerunds and participles tend to cause students a good deal of grief, especially at first. But wait. You'll become better acquainted with them later—on page 66 to be exact.

Relative pronouns

Like all other pronouns, *relative pronouns* (*which, that, who, whom, whose,* and *what*) refer to nouns or other pronouns, as in:

> **Those are the dishes *that* I washed yesterday.**

Here the relative pronoun *that* refers to *dishes.* Simple, right? Yes, but that's not quite the end of the story. If you study the sentence some more, you'll see that the word *that* comes before the words *I washed yesterday*—words that describe the dishes. That is, the dishes are not just any old dishes but specifically those dishes that the speaker washed yesterday. Why is that important? Well, for one thing, it helps you use the correct relative pronoun—not always a slam-dunk matter because in everyday English, the relative pronouns *that* and *which* are often used interchangeably. They shouldn't be. Instead, use *that* when the subsequent words define or describe something essential to the meaning of the sentence, as in:

> **Those are the dishes *that* need to be put away.**

On the other hand, use *which* if the words that follow give information that isn't crucial to the meaning of the sentence, as in:

Those dishes, *which* once belonged to my grandmother, need to be put away.

Here, the fact that the dishes once belonged to the speaker's grandmother may be interesting, but the information is not crucial to the main message of the sentence.

You should also know that the words that come after relative pronouns are called ***relative clauses***. Or, put another way, *relative pronouns* introduce *relative clauses*. For example, here are two sentences with their relative clauses underlined:

1. **The store *that* <u>sold used bikes</u> burned to the ground.**
2. **A backpack, *which* <u>Belinda takes to school</u>, was stolen.**

Notice that Sentence 1 contains no punctuation, whereas Sentence 2 uses a comma both before and after the relative clause. Why? Because in the comma-free sentence, the clause is essential to the intended meaning of the sentence. In the other sentence, it's not. How a sentence is punctuated, then, indicates whether the relative clause is essential to the meaning of the sentence.

> Commas precede relative clauses starting with *which* but not before relative clauses starting with *that*.

Sometimes it may be hard to figure out whether or not the clause is essential. Knowing the context makes a difference. Say, for example, that on your way to school this morning your friend Angela told you about last night's two-alarm fire on Locust Street, which damaged several shops and destroyed one of them completely. "Which one?" you might ask. Angela's answer: "The store *that sold used bikes* burned to the ground." The italicized clause is clearly essential to the meaning of the sentence because it answers your question. With regard to Sentence 2, let's say that you're reporting a theft to a police officer who wants to know what had been taken. Your answer: "A backpack, *which Belinda takes to school*, was stolen." In this context, the fact that Belinda takes the backpack to school isn't important to your intent—to answer the officer's question. Therefore, the clause is set off by commas. How a sentence is punctuated, then, will tell you whether the relative clause is essential.

If you're ever torn between choosing *that* or *which*, determine whether the relative clause needs to be punctuated with a comma. If so, use *which*; if not, use *that*. To reiterate: Commas precede relative clauses starting with *which* (or one of the other relative pronouns), but not before relative clauses starting with *that*.

> **Note:** You're not alone if you are puzzled by any of this material on relative pronouns. For one thing, we haven't disussed clauses yet. Moreover, the twists and turns of English grammar can drive some readers nuts. But please don't throw up your hands in frustration—not yet, anyway, because you'll find ample opportunities to work out the kinks in Chapters 4 and 5, where you'll meet actual SAT- and ACT-style grammar questions.

By the way, if you studied grammar in the past, you may have run into the terms *restrictive clause* and *nonrestrictive clause*. These labels are little more than other names for types of relative clauses. Restrictive clauses don't need commas; nonrestrictive clauses do.

Before we move on, one more detail deserves mention: In certain contexts, you can leave out relative pronouns without altering meaning. In the following two sentences, for instance, the bracketed pronoun is optional:

The doghouse [*that*] Duke lives in is in the backyard.
The guests [*whom*] we expected at six o'clock arrived at seven.

It's very common to omit the relative pronoun in everyday speech and informal writing, but not in more formal communication.

Who or Whom?

The notorious *who/whom* question baffles many people. Even more baffling, though, is its reputation as a tough nut to crack. The solution is reasonably simple:

Use the relative pronoun *who* as the grammatical subject of a sentence or as a pronoun that stands for the subject, as in:

Who (subject) **ordered a pizza to go?**
That (subject) **is the woman *who*** (subject stand-in) **ordered it.**

Use *whom* following a preposition or when it functions as the object of a verb, as in:

To (preposition) **whom should this fish be given?**
The detective found (verb) **the thief *whom* he'd been chasing.**

While weighing the use of *who* or *whom*, ask yourself whether the pronoun is performing an action. If so, use *who*. If the pronoun is being acted upon, use *whom*. Also, you can depend on prepositions. They are always followed by *whom*, as in *with whom, in whom, before whom, around whom, between whom,* and so on.

Who, That, or Which?

1. Use *who* and *whom* to refer to people.

2. Use *that* to refer to things, animals, and people, but use *who* when referring to a specific person, as in:

> Use *who* to refer to people, *that* to refer to things, and *which* to refer to things and nonhumans.

This is Corporal Powder, *who* fought in Afghanistan.

Either *who* or *that*, however, may be used for more general references, as in:

Those are the pilots *who* flew the plane./Those are the pilots *that* flew the plane.

Take your pick; both sentences are valid.

3. Use *which* to refer to things and nonhuman creatures, but never to people.

Star Wars movies, *which* began in the 1970's, are still as popular as ever.

Reflexive pronouns

Reflexive pronouns stand out among all other pronouns because they end with *self* (singular form) or *selves* (plural form):

First person—*myself/ourselves*
Second person—*yourself/yourselves*
Third person—*herself, himself, itself/themselves*

Reflexive pronouns refer to the noun or pronoun that is the grammatical subject of the sentence in which they appear:

We will be going to the city by ourselves.

In this sentence, the reflexive pronoun *ourselves* refers to *We*, the grammatical subject. Because both the subject and the reflexive pronoun must be present in the same sentence, reflexive pronouns can't be subjects:

FAULTY: *Myself* **wrote every word of the paper.**
CORRECT: *I* (subject) **wrote every word of the paper by** *myself*.

Nor can they be object pronouns:

FAULTY: Mimi gave M&Ms to Margo and *myself*.
CORRECTED: Mimi gave M&Ms to Margo and *me*.

Reflexive pronouns can also be used for emphasis, to intensify an idea, or to make a strong statement:

You won't believe it, but I *myself* **cleaned out the closet.**
Gilberto *himself* **ate both hot dogs.**

Interrogative pronouns

Interrogative pronouns are often called *question pronouns*. Their name derives from their function:

Q. *What* is their function?
A. To ask questions, make inquiries, and seek information.
Q. *Who* uses them?
A. You and everyone else.
Q. *Which* is better to use, *who* or *whom*?
A. It all depends.
Q. *Whom* must I ask to get a more specific answer?
A. Well, you could ask an English teacher, or you could just turn back to page 18.

And there you have them—*what, who, which,* and *whom*—four of our language's most popular *interrogative pronouns*. Others include *whose, when, where, why,* and *how*. Have you noticed that some of these words are also relative pronouns? In that incarnation, however, they serve a different function.

Demonstrative pronouns

Demonstrative pronouns also get their name from their function: They point, like arrows. *This, these, that,* and *those* point to nouns, phrases, clauses, and even whole sentences. The pronoun *this* points out an object close by in space (*this book,* for example), time (*this year*), and thought, (*this idea of yours*). The pronoun *that,* on the other hand, points to distant objects (*that star, that time, that theory*).

Like other pronouns, demonstrative pronouns need to point to clear antecedents. When a writer or speaker expects too much from the demonstrative pronoun, ambiguity results:

> **The zoo features more than 1,500 mammals, reptiles, and birds kept in tiny cages. In the primate area, eleven species of monkeys, gorillas, and apes live in a small space no bigger than your average schoolroom. All the animals are fed only twice a day, even though some require nourishment several times in 24 hours. *This* bothers me.**

What does *this* refer to? The irregular feeding of some animals? The conditions described throughout the paragraph? It's hard to tell. Fix the problem with a new pronoun and a more specific antecedent:

> ***These*** (pronoun) ***conditions*** (antecedent) **bother me.**

Checkpoint 4. REVIEW OF PRONOUN PROBLEMS

Correct any faulty pronoun usage you find in the following sentences. Some sentences may be correct.

1. My dog Rosie and myself took a long walk in the woods.

   _____

2. Teachers who I like best have a good sense of humor.

   _____

3. When you're specifically instructed to cross only at the light, one should not jaywalk.

   _____

4. The candy bar was split between Stacy and I.

   _____

5. Riley, Dan, and Chloe were swimming in the ocean when suddenly a giant wave appeared and scared him out of his wits.

   _____

6. The book, that once belonged to President Kennedy, was sold at auction for $5,000.

   _____

7. When myself and a friend took the subway, we got lost.

   _____

8. To be a successful musician, one must be so dedicated that you practice your instrument at least six hours every day.

    _____

9. Him and me are planning to go to a show this weekend.

    _____

10. Everyone should put their seat belts on.

    _____

11. To who should I give my change of address form?

    _____

12. The reason early paintings are so often an artist's most interesting work is that it was done with a fresh and youthful perspective.

    _____

13. Amy provided a room with twin beds for him and me.

    _____

14. Anyone with an airline ticket had better confirm their reservation online.

    _____

15. A person which needs to pay for their own health insurance is out of luck.

    _____

16. The meeting was not planned by Fiona and I, so don't blame we girls for its failure.

    _____

17. At the shipyard entrance, the police have been granted great authority. These include stopping any car they wish to, asking them for IDs, patting them down, and arresting suspects without stating their reasons. This policy was put into effect by the Department of Homeland Security.

    _____

18. Of all the teachers which give homework, Ms. Thomas gives the most.

    _____

19. I like Mariah and he the best of all my classmates.

    _____

20. Even though the mountain peaks are among the highest in the world, it had no snow on it last summer.

    _____

Answers on page 52

THE VERB

> Every complete sentence needs a verb.

VERBS are words that name actions: *study, shout, dance, laugh, jab, think, decide, stand, deliver.* The list goes on and on and on. Some people claim that verbs are the most important words in the language. Whether or not that's true, the fact is that every complete sentence needs a verb, and without verbs we'd end up grunting things like:

> **Kobe downtown this afternoon.**
> **When a fire drill?**
> **If you too much pepper, the sauce spicy.**

With verbs we can turn these utterances into sentences that others will actually understand:

> **Kobe *plans to go* downtown this afternoon.**
> **When *will* a fire drill *be scheduled*?**
> **If you *add* too much pepper, the sauce *will taste* spicy.**

In other words, verbs help us communicate with each other.

Not every verb describes an action like shouting, dancing, or laughing. Some simply express a **state of being**. Instead of telling you what the subject does, they tell you what the subject is or was, as in:

> **Carla *is* a fast runner.**
> **The tomato *is* ripe.**
> **Emile *was* out to lunch.**

Notice that state-of-being verbs function much like equal signs in an arithmetical equation: *Carla = fast runner; tomato = ripe; Emile = someone who is out to lunch.*

The verb *is* happens to be a form of *to be*, the basic state-of-being verb. Other forms include *are, am, was, were, will be, has been, have been, had been,* and *will have been.*

Verb tenses

Be thankful for verb tenses. Why? Because they instantly convey vital information about when an action or event took place. Think of the verb *climbed*, for example, as in:

> **Clare *climbed* the ladder.**

Clare, the subject of the sentence, performed an action, and because of the *-ed* ending, signifying **past tense**, you know that Clare climbed the ladder at some time before this moment. On the other hand, if the verb had been *climbs* instead of *climbed*, the *-s* ending, indicating the **present tense**, would have indicated that Clare is climbing the ladder right now, or at least that she climbs it as part of an ongoing routine, as in:

> **Clare *climbs* the ladder whenever she paints ceilings.**

Changing the tense of active verbs often involves changing their endings. But it sometimes also involves adding so-called **helping verbs**, such as *has, had, have, will,* and *will have*. Using various verb endings and helping verbs, English offers six basic tenses to indicate the time that actions take place:

> **PRESENT:** I *cook* pizza every day.
> **PAST:** Whitney *cooked* a pizza yesterday.
> **FUTURE:** Ellie *will cook* a pizza tomorrow.
> **PRESENT PERFECT:** Lucy *has cooked* a pizza every day for the last month.
> **PAST PERFECT:** Lilah *had cooked* so many pizzas she got tired of them.
> **FUTURE PERFECT:** They all *will have cooked* a thousand pizzas by now.

The same six tenses apply to state-of-being verbs:

PRESENT: *is, are, am*
PAST: *was, were*
FUTURE: *will be*
PRESENT PERFECT: *has been, have been*
PAST PERFECT: *had been*
FUTURE PERFECT: *will have been*

Tenses allow us to express time sequences very precisely. Take, for example, the following sentence:

When Susie *walked* (past tense) **into the store she *realized*** (past tense) **that she *had forgotten*** (past perfect) **her wallet at home.**

The two verbs—*walked* and *realized*—indicate that Susie's mishap took place in the past. But the verb *had forgotten* tells us that Susie's act of forgetfulness occurred before her discovery of what she had done. In other words, changes in verb tense can tell us which events happened first, which ones second, and so on.

Meaning determines which tense to use, but someone not tuned in to the purpose of various tenses might say something like:

There was a condo where the park *was*.

The intent of the sentence is probably to say that a condo now stands in a place that once was a park. But what it really says is that the condo and the park were in the same place at the same time—a physical impossibility. Stated more precisely, the sentence should be:

There was a condo where the park *had been*.

Using the past perfect verb *had been* conveys the meaning more accurately: The condo replaced the park.

People use correct verb tenses much, but not all, of the time. To eliminate errors completely, it's essential to know the differences in meaning that each tense conveys.

- Present/Present Perfect: Present tense verbs refer to actions currently in progress; verbs in the present perfect tense refer to actions occurring at no particular time in the past and that may still be in progress.

    Adam *is* (present) **captain of the wrestling team and *has held*** (present perfect) **the job since sophomore year.**

- Past/Past Perfect: Past tense verbs refer to action completed in the past; verbs in the past perfect tense refer to actions completed before some specific time or moment in the past. The past perfect is needed to indicate which action occurred first.

    Before George *arrived* (past)**, Lenny *had killed*** (past perfect) **the rabbit.**

- Future/Future Perfect: Verbs in the future tense refer to actions that will occur in the future; verbs in the future perfect tense refer to actions that will be completed at some time in the future, but before some other action or event.

    Ellie *will arrive* (future) **in San Diego on the 15th, but by that time, Pedro *will have been gone*** (future perfect) **for two weeks.**

A statement about the future can also be made by using either the present tense or the present progressive tense:

The World Series *begins* (present) **next Tuesday.**
The opening ceremony of the Olympic Games *is being televised* (present progressive) **tomorrow morning starting at 5:00.**

These distinctions may strike you as nitpicking—but knowing such subtle differences separates people who use English precisely from those who don't.

Notice how verb tenses affect meaning in the following pairs of sentences:

1. **a.** Benjamin *was* in the army for two years. (Benjamin is no longer in the army.)
   b. Benjamin *has been* in the army for two years. (Benjamin is still in the army.)

2. **a.** Dinner *had been* on the table for two hours. (Dinner is no longer on the table.)
   b. Dinner *has been* on the table for two hours. (Dinner is still on the table.)

3. **a.** A monument *will be erected* at the site of the battle when the general *returns*. (After the general gets back the monument will be built.)
   b. A monument *will have been erected* at the site of the battle when the general *returns*. (A monument will already have been built by the time the general gets back.)

4. **a.** She *has had* no luck in finding her ring. (She is still trying to find her ring.)
   b. She *had* no luck finding her ring. (In the past her search was unsuccessful, but whether she is still looking remains uncertain.)

5. **a.** Jenny *had driven* a delivery truck on weekends. (Jenny used to drive a truck.)
   b. Jenny *has been driving* a delivery truck on weekends. (Jenny still drives a truck.)

Shifting verb tenses

Stay alert for shifts in verb tenses in sentences containing more than one verb. For example, the sentence that follows begins in the past tense but improperly shifts to the present.

SHIFT: **They *biked*** (past) **to the top of the mountain and then *come*** (present) **back down in time to eat lunch.**

CONSISTENT: **They *biked*** (past) **to the top of the mountain and then *came*** (past) **back down in time to eat lunch.**

SHIFT: **By 4 o'clock all the bushes *had been pruned*** (past perfect) **and the grass *was*** (past) **watered.**
CONSISTENT: **By 4 o'clock all the bushes *had been pruned*** (past perfect) **and the grass *had been*** (past perfect) **watered.**

Consistency doesn't require every verb in a sentence to be in the same tense—far from it. But the verbs must accurately convey the relative time that events occurred, as in:

Harris *lost* (past) **a twenty-dollar bill that *has* now *been found*** (present perfect).

This sentence uses two different tenses because it's about two events that occurred at different times—namely, Harris's loss and the finding of the money.

Here's another example:

> **Mike and Hessie *had dated*** (past perfect) **for six months before they *told*** (past) **their parents.**

Because Mike and Hessie dated for half a year before telling their parents, the past perfect tense is needed to show the sequence of events.

More verb tense guidelines

You'll never go wrong if you remember three additional guidelines for using verb tenses:

- Use the present tense for true statements.

> **Thanksgiving *falls*** (present) **on November 23rd this year.**

In fact, use the present tense for true statements regardless of the tense of other verbs in the sentence:

> **Tanisha *had been taught*** (past perfect) **that triangles *contain*** (present) **180 degrees.**

- When a sentence or clause starts with *if*, use the past perfect tense instead of *would have* to express the earlier of two actions.

> When a sentence or clause starts with *if*, use the past perfect tense instead of *would have* to express the earlier of two actions.

> **If Colin *had driven*** (not *would have driven*) **more slowly, he would have made the curve easily.**
> **The ceremony would have been better if Kirk *had been*** (past perfect) **the speaker.**

- Get into the habit of adjusting participles according to the tense of the main verb (for details, turn to the discussion of participles, page 66). When a participle, which usually ends with *-ing*, indicates an action that occurred before the action named by the main verb, add *having*. Then revise the participle to the present perfect or past perfect tense.

> **ORIGINAL:** *Working* (participle) **hard on the essay, Joan hated to reduce the number of words.** (Because Joan worked hard on the essay before she got around to revising it, the participle needs to be changed.)
> **REVISION:** *Having worked* **hard on the essay, Joan hated to reduce the number of words.**
> **ORIGINAL:** *Walking* (participle) **in the woods, Jan spotted a deer.** (Because Jan was walking in the woods at the same time as she saw a deer, no change is needed.)

Checkpoint 5. VERB TENSE

Some underlined verbs in the following sentences are incorrect. Cross out the incorrect verbs and write the correct ones in the spaces provided. Some sentences contain no error.

1. <u>Earning</u> a place in the tournament finals, the team resolved to go home with the championship.

   _____

2. The garage mechanic thinks that at the time of the accident Mrs. Murphy <u>has owned</u> the car for only a week.

   _____

3. For anyone with enough brains to have thought about it, now <u>is</u> the time to work out the solution.

   _____

4. The board chose Kristen Brennan to be the company CEO because she <u>was</u> a high school cheerleader, a philosophy major at Ohio State, a computer programmer, and a factory floor manager.

   _____

5. If the wagon train <u>would have reached</u> Salt Creek in time, the massacre would have been prevented.

   _____

6. The aircraft controller <u>expects</u> to have spotted the plane on radar before dusk last night.

   _____

7. The family already <u>finished</u> dinner when the doorbell rang.

   _____

8. First he built a fire, then dragged a log over to use as a seat, and finally <u>collected</u> enough wood to burn all night.

   _____

9. Rose kept the promise she <u>has given</u> to Charles last year in India.

   _____

10. When he talks with Horatio, Hamlet <u>began</u> to suspect foul play in the kingdom.

    _____

11. As they drove to Vermont, they <u>had stopped</u> for lunch at Burger King.

    _____

12. The trooper pulled him over and <u>gives</u> him a speeding ticket.

    _____

13. <u>Working</u> all year to improve her writing style, Debbie finally got a story published in the paper.

   _____

14. Zoe had taken an SAT course for six months before she <u>learns</u> how to solve that kind of problem.

   _____

15. That night at the show we met many people we <u>saw</u> that afternoon.

   _____

16. The current governor <u>lived</u> in the mansion at the present time.

   _____

17. <u>Seeing</u> the film of *War and Peace*, I know that Pierre falls in love with Natasha.

   _____

18. After the drought hit eastern Africa, the Somalis <u>began</u> to suffer.

   _____

19. Spring <u>came</u> before summer.

   _____

20. Greta does so well in her practice runs that she <u>had decided</u> to train for the New York Marathon.

   _____

Answers on page 53

Verb forms

You already know that verbs in the present tense regularly end in *-s* or *-es* (*runs/rushes*), and past tense verbs regularly end in *-d* or *-ed* (*smoked/shouted*). Which ending to use is generally governed by who is performing the action. If the performer(s) of the action is *I* or *we* (first person), you use one form; if the action is performed by *you* (second person) or *he, she,* or *they* (third person), you use another form. The form is also determined by the number (singular or plural) of the subject. The following chart shows various verb forms in the present, past, and perfect tenses.

	Singular	*Plural*
First person		
Present tense	I scream	we scream
	I wash	we wash
	I eat	we eat
Past tense	I screamed	we screamed
	I washed	we washed
	I ate	we ate
Present perfect/ past perfect tense	I have/had screamed	we have/had screamed
	I have/had washed	we have/had washed
	I have/had eaten	we have/had eaten

	Singular	*Plural*
Second person		
Present tense	you scream	you scream
	you wash	you wash
	you eat	you eat
Past tense	you screamed	you screamed
	you washed	you washed
	you ate	you ate
Present perfect/	you have/had screamed	you have/had screamed
past perfect tense	you have/had washed	you have/had washed
	you have/had eaten	you have/had eaten
Third person		
Present tense	he/she/it screams	they scream
	he/she/it washes	they wash
	he/she/it eats	they eat
Past tense	he/she/it screamed	they screamed
	he she/it washed	they washed
	he/she/it ate	they ate
Present perfect/	he/she/it has/had screamed	we have/had screamed
past perfect tense	he/she/it has/had washed	we have/had washed
	he/she/it has/had eaten	we have/had eaten

Most verbs change very little between tenses and persons or when shifting between singular and plural. For example, an *-s* is usually added when the verb changes from first or second person to third person:

First/second person: *I talk, you talk*   Third person: *he/she/it talks*

Another common pattern is the addition of an *-ed* when a verb shifts from present to past in the first, second, and third person:

Present tense, first/second/third person: *I talk, you talk, he/she/it talks*
Past tense, first/second/third person: *I talked, you talked, he/she/it talked*

Such changes follow a fairly consistent pattern from verb to verb. But some verbs—called ***irregular verbs***—refuse to conform. They change in ways that defy logic and include such common verbs as *sleep/slept, ride/rode, swim/swam, is/was, are/were, go/went, catch/caught,* and so on. Native speakers of English learn to use irregular verb forms as they learn to talk, although the various forms of some verbs, such as *to lie* (to recline) and *to lay* (to put or to place), remain a lifelong mystery for some.

English contains hundreds of irregular verbs. Here are a few dozen:

IRREGULAR VERBS

Present Tense	Past Tense	Perfect Tense (Add *have, has,* or *had*)
awake	awoke	awakened
bear	bore	borne
beat	beat	beaten
begin	began	begun
bid (to command)	bade	bidden
bite	bit	bitten
break	broke	broken
bring	brought	brought
burn	burnt *or* burned	burnt *or* burned
burst	burst	burst
catch	caught	caught
choose	chose	chosen
come	came	come
creep	crept *or* creeped	crept *or* creeped
dive	dived *or* dove	dived
dream	dreamt *or* dreamed	dreamt *or* dreamed
drink	drank	drunk
dwell	dwelt *or* dwelled	dwelt *or* dwelled
eat	ate	eaten
flee	fled	fled
fling	flung	flung
freeze	froze	frozen
go	went	gone
hide	hid	hidden
lay (to put or place)	laid	laid
lead	led	led
lend	lent	lent
lie (to recline)	lay	lain
lie (to tell an untruth)	lied	lied
ring	rang	rung
rise	rose	risen
shine	shone *or* shined	shone
shrink	shrank *or* shrunk	shrunk *or* shrunken
sing	sang	sung
sink	sank	sunk
slay	slew	slain
speak	spoke	spoken
spit	spit *or* spat	spit *or* spat

spring	sprang	sprung
steal	stole	stolen
strive	strove *or* strived	striven *or* strived
swear	swore	sworn
swim	swam	swum
tear	tore	torn
tread	trod	trod *or* trodden
wake	woke *or* waked	waked *or* woken
wear	wore	worn
write	wrote	written

Checkpoint 6. VERB FORMS

Fill in the blanks with the correct verb form. If in doubt, refer to the list of irregular verbs above.

1. eat   They haven't _____ out in months.

2. caught   The umpire said that Reggie had _____ the ball before it touched the ground.

3. swim   They _____ across the lake in less than an hour.

4. drink   All the soda had been _____ by the end of the dance.

5. go   Crystal had already _____ home by the time Cher arrived.

6. lay   After the burial, his widow _____ a wreath on his gravesite.

7. shine   The sun _____ all day.

8. shrink   When he put on the sweatshirt, he noticed that it had _____.

9. sing   The four of them have already _____ two songs.

10. slay   In the story the king was relieved when Theseus _____ the Minotaur.

11. steal   They concluded that the computer had been _____ over the weekend.

12. strive   All summer the crew _____ to finish the job in time.

13. awake   The sound of the smoke alarm had _____ the whole family.

14. wear   By Sunday the visitors had _____ out their welcome.

15. break   Dawn had just _____, and the floor was cold under my feet.

16. dive   No sooner had the submarine _____ than the destroyer appeared on the horizon.

17. creep   Last night the cat burglar _____ up the fire escape.

18. fling   After flunking the test, Zack _____ his math book out the window.

19. swear   Although they been _____ to secrecy, someone leaked the news to the press.

20. lead   John Wesley Powell _____ the expedition down the Green River in 1869.

Answers on page 54

The Infinitive

The basic form of all verbs is the ***infinitive***, consisting of the verb and the word *to*, as in *to fly*, *to wander*, and *to twitter*. You can usually recognize an infinitive by putting the word *to* in front of it. If the *to* fits, chances are you've got an infinitive. If the combination makes no sense, as in *to carried*, *to shrunk*, and *to eating*, you can bet that the verb is in some other form.

Surprisingly, the infinitive form of a verb sometimes functions as a noun:

To shop (infinitive) **is the purpose of Annie's existence.**

Here the infinitive is the subject of the sentence. Infinitives can also function as adjectives and adverbs, too, but we'll get into that later.

The Subjunctive

Technically, the ***subjunctive*** is not a separate verb form. Rather, it's called a *mood*. Regardless of the label, though, you should know how it works because verbs change when sentences are cast in the subjunctive. The subjunctive should be used to express a condition contrary to fact, usually in sentences beginning with *if, as if,* or *as though*:

If I were (not *was*) **rich, I'd buy myself a sailboat.** (The sentence is contrary to fact because I am not rich.)

Use the subjunctive, too, in statements expressing a wish:

I wish I were (not *was*) **wealthy enough to buy a sailboat.**

In each instance, the singular verb *was* has been changed to *were,* as though the subject were (not *was*) plural.

The subjunctive is also used to convey a sense of doubt:

If only the bus were (not *was*) **uncrowded, we could find a seat.**

Finally, the subjunctive is used to make a recommendation, a request, or a demand:

The lawyer insisted that her client be (not *should be*) **released on bail.**

An Encouraging Word to the Reader from the Author

Having read this far, you've passed through a dense thicket of information about grammar. If some of it is confusing or even impenetrable, take heart. The truth is that it's less complicated than it may seem. So don't give up. The chapters ahead are designed to help to clear up what may now be a total muddle in your mind.

Subject-Verb Agreement

SUBJECTS and verbs must agree. That is, they must make a match, like a nut and a bolt. A mismatch occurs when a singular subject is used with a plural verb, or vice versa. That's why phrases like *the books was* and *the book were* are nonstandard usages. You should also know that this rule applies not only to sentence subjects and verbs—a topic discussed in detail on pages 59–61—but to all pairs of nouns and verbs, wherever they appear in a sentence.

Matching a subject and a verb poses few problems when the two are close or next to each other in a sentence. But, inconveniently, certain language constructions can obscure the connection and raise questions about their relationship:

Q. What happens when a clause or phrase falls between the subject and the verb?

A. Ignore the intervening words. Most of the time they have no bearing on the relationship between the subject and verb.

> MISMATCHED: *Delivery* (singular subject) **of today's newspapers and magazines *have been delayed*** (plural verb).

The prepositional phrase *of today's newspapers and magazines* blurs the relationship between subject and verb. The plural noun *magazines* has misled the speaker into using a plural verb.

> MATCHED: *Delivery* **of today's newspapers and magazines *has been delayed***.

Also keep in mind also that common intervening words and phrases such as *in addition to*, *along with*, *as well as*, and *including* do not affect the number of the noun or the verb:

> *One* (singular subject) **of his paintings, along with several sketches, *is*** (singular verb) **on display in the library.**

Q. What should be done when the subject is composed of more than one noun or pronoun?

A. Nouns joined by *and* are called ***compound subjects*** and need plural verbs.

> The ***picture and text*** (compound subject) ***go*** (plural verb) **inside this box.**
> Several ***locust trees and a green mailbox*** (compound subject) ***stand*** (plural verb) **outside the house.**

Compound subjects thought of as a unit need singular verbs.

> ***Green eggs and ham*** (compound subject) ***is*** (singular verb) **Reggie's favorite breakfast.**
> **Their** *pride and joy* (compound subject)**, Samantha,** *was* (singular verb) **born on Christmas Day.**

Singular nouns joined by *or* or *nor* need singular verbs.

> **A Coke** *or* **a Pepsi** *is* **what I thirst for.**

When the subject consists of a singular noun and a plural noun joined by *or* or *nor*, the number of the verb is determined by the noun closer to the verb.

> **Either** *a pineapple* (singular noun) **or** *some oranges* (plural noun) *are* (plural verb) **on the table.**
> **Neither the** *linemen* (plural noun) **nor the** *quarterback* (singular noun) *was* (singular verb) **aware of the tricky play.**

> A subject made up of singular and plural nouns joined by *or* or *nor* requires a verb that agrees with the closer noun.

When a subject contains a pronoun that differs in person from a noun or another pronoun, the verb agrees with the closer subject word.

> **Neither Meredith nor** *you are* **expected to finish the job.**
> **Either he or** *I am planning* **to work late on Saturday.**

When the subject is singular and the predicate noun is plural, or vice versa, the number of the verb is determined by the subject.

> **The** *bulk* **of Wilkinson's work** *is* **two novels and a collection of poems.**
> *Two novels and a collection of poems are* **the bulk of Wilkinson's work.**

Q. How do you handle subject words that may be either singular or plural?

A. It depends on how they are used. When a collective noun is used in its singular sense, use a singular verb. Likewise, when a collective noun is used in its plural sense, use a plural verb (see page 4 for details on collective nouns).

> **The** *majority* (singular) *favors* (singular) **a formal senior prom.**
> **The** *majority* (plural) *have* (plural) **their tickets for the boat ride.**

Q. What if subject words are singular but sound plural?

A. The names of books, countries, organizations, certain diseases, course titles, and other singular nouns may sound like plurals because they end in "s," but they usually require a singular verb.

> **The** *news is* **good.**
> *Measles is* **being wiped out all across the country.**
> **The** *World Series is* **played in October.**

Q. What about subjects that consist of indefinite pronouns?

A. Indefinite pronouns like *everyone, both,* and *any* pose a special problem because a correct match depends on the sense of the sentence (for details, see page 11).

> *Some* **of the collection *is* valuable.** (*Some* is singular because it refers to collection, a singular noun.)
> *Some* **of the bracelets *are* fake.** (*Some* is plural because it refers to bracelets, a plural noun.)
> *None* **of the ice cream *is* left.**
> *None* **of the people *are* going to be left behind.**

Q. How do you handle sentences in which the verb precedes the subject?

A. No differently. Treat the subject and verb as though they came in the usual order—subject before verb.

> **MISMATCHED: Here *comes*** (singular verb) **my *brother and sister*** (plural subject).
> **MATCHED: Here *come*** (plural verb) **my brother and sister.**

Errors in subject-verb agreement often occur when the writer or speaker loses track of the subject of the sentence. Once the subject is nailed down, however, everything else, including the verb, usually falls into place. So, the key to agreement between subject and verb is no secret: **Identify the subject and keep your eye on it**. If finding the subject perplexes you in any way, you should study "*To find the 'bare bones' of a sentence*" (page 64), a surefire technique for finding the subject of any sentence.

Checkpoint 7. SUBJECT-VERB AGREEMENT

In some of the sentences below, nouns and verbs do not agree. Locate the error and write the corrected version in the space provided. Some sentences may be correct.

1. Brian's talent in acting and singing, two of the most important criteria for getting parts in plays, almost assure Brian that he'll have a role in this spring's musical.

   _____

2. The original play, which tells the story of thirteen young actors who aspire to succeed in show business careers, were one of history's most popular Broadway productions.

   _____

3. At the end of their first year in New York, the close-knit group, regardless of whether they earned stage parts, begin to split up.

   _____

4. On second thought, either Brian or you are going to be the male lead in the play.

   _____

5. Jane and Melissa, who starred in *A Chorus Line* last spring, have decided not to try out for this year's show.

   _____

6. There is many younger kids who will be glad to know that everybody has an equal chance to get a role in the production.

_____

7. This year's admission proceeds from the play is going toward rebuilding the school's gazebo, burned down by vandals last summer.

_____

8. The school paper reports that a committee of students and teachers are going to decide who get a role in the play.

_____

9. Before the administration laid them off, neither the director nor the producer were told that their jobs were in danger.

_____

10. Many teachers and parents claim that new policies in the drama department has had an adverse effect on morale.

_____

11. Reading play reviews printed in the newspaper is a desirable thing to do by everyone who expect to develop a deep understanding of theater arts.

_____

12. Plays, produced both on Broadway and in regional theaters, have always been one of Brian's passions.

_____

13. Arthur Miller, along with his contemporary Tennessee Williams, are among the most impressive playwrights.

_____

14. Katie Green, one of the best pianists in the school, and her brother Gene, who also plays extremely well, has been invited to provide musical accompaniment.

_____

15. Nancy Atkins, along with her friend Sluggo, expect to be in charge of sets.

_____

16. A number of innovative ideas for using the school's new lighting and sound systems have created enormous enthusiasm for the show.

_____

17. Here's the costumes that were used last year.

_____

18. The school board's insistence on high production standards are putting pressure on the stage crew and the production staff.

   _____

19. Members of the school band, in spite of how they all feel about the issue, wants to participate.

   _____

20. According to school policy, there is to be two security guards stationed in the auditorium during each performance.

   _____

Answers on page 55

THE ADJECTIVE

ADJECTIVES are describers. They are the words that describe colors, sizes, and shapes, as well as the look and condition of things, feelings, and other qualities of every imaginable sort. Grammatically speaking, adjectives **MODIFY** nouns, which means they describe or limit them, turning, say, an *ordinary* day into one that is *sunny, boring, momentous, thrilling, wretched, frantic,* or *memorable.* They turn nights *dark* or *starry*, turn friends *loyal* or *hostile*, make food *nutritious* or *greasy*. How many adjectives exist no one can tell, but they give users of English unlimited opportunities for describing people, places, experiences, and things.

> Many adjectives are fickle. Sometimes they're adjectives, and at other times they're nouns.

Not every adjective is so obviously an adjective as *big* or *buxom* or *blissful.* Some adjectives also function as nouns. Take *baseball*, for instance. In the sentence "Baseball rocks," *baseball* is a noun, but in "The baseball game ended with a walk-off home run," *baseball* is an adjective modifying *game.* Incidentally, there are countless nouns, from *absolute* to *zigzag*, that can also serve as adjectives.

Some words neither look nor feel like adjectives. Yet, they belong to the adjective family because in their fashion they act more or less like adjectives. The articles *the, a,* and *an*, for instance, tell you whether a noun is specific (*the train, the olive, the principle*) or nonspecific (*a train, an olive, a principle*). Likewise, such words as *this, that, those,* and *these*, along with other types of pronouns—*his, her, our, their, my, your*—and words like *some, many, much,* and *few*, act like adjectives because they modify nouns, as in:

> *This* **faded shirt is mine.** (The word *this* identifies the shirt: It's not any scruffy old shirt, it's *this* one.)
> *Our* **trip took four hours.** (The word *our* identifies whose trip it was.)

Compound Adjectives

Although single-word adjectives are most common, **compound** adjectives—usually pairs of words such as: *world-famous, so-called, short-term, well-known, poorly organized*—show up frequently in speech and writing. In fact, three, four, five, or even more words can be strung together to make compound adjectives such as *off-the-wall* and *never-to-be-forgotten*. Notice that **hyphens** separate the words in compound adjectives. Don't jump to the conclusion, however, that every compound adjective needs a hyphen. The fact is that compound adjectives that come before the noun they modify usually contain hyphens, and those that follow usually don't:

> **George Clooney is a *world-famous* actor.**
> **Actor George Clooney is *world famous*.**

Adjective Phrases and Clauses

We've seen that nouns and articles assume the role of adjectives. The same goes for phrases and clauses. Take, for example:

> **The snow on the grass melted.**

The noun *snow* is described, or modified, by the phrase *on the grass*, which describes the particular snow that melted. It wasn't the snow on the roof or the snow in Buffalo that melted, but the snow on the grass. Thus, the phrase *on the grass* acts like an adjective.

In the same manner, the italicized phrases in the following sentences serve as stand-ins for adjectives by modifying the underlined nouns:

> **Look at Cyrano, the <u>man</u> *with the six-inch nose*.**
> **The *funniest* <u>joke</u> *ever told* was the topic of my term paper.**
> **The gas <u>pumps</u> *marked "self-serve"* need to be replaced.**
> **A <u>deer</u> *hit by a car* lay on the road.**

If phrases can serve as substitute adjectives, logic dictates that clauses can, too. Indeed, you'd be hard pressed to find many prose passages that don't contain adjective clauses—clauses that typically begin with the relative pronouns *that, which, who, whose,* or *whom* (go back to page 16 for a quick review of relative pronouns). Notice how the italicized clauses in the sentences below modify the underlined nouns:

> **The <u>recording</u>, *which sold more than two million copies*, made Taylor Swift a household name.**
> **The <u>children</u> *who need a time-out* should go directly to the flagpole.**
> **This is the <u>scene</u> *that always makes me cry*.**
> **<u>Most</u> of the battalion, *many of whom came from the Iowa National Guard*, decided to reenlist.**

Comparing with Adjectives

The world is full of people described by the adjective *smart*. But some people are smarter than others, and someone is the smartest of them all—maybe you! In other words, there are degrees of smartness that can be compared with each other.

A unique feature of adjectives is that they come in different forms that allow you to make such comparisons. **Degrees of comparison** are indicated by endings, usually *-er* and *-est*, as in *smarter* and *smartest*, but also by the use of *more/most* and *less/least*, as in *more brilliant, most talented, less gifted,* and *least competent*.

English offers three degrees of comparison: *positive*, *comparative*, and *superlative*.

Positive	Comparative	Superlative
tall	taller	tallest
dark	darker	darkest
ugly	uglier	ugliest
handsome	handsomer *or* more handsome	handsomest *or* most handsome
cool	cooler	coolest
graceful	more graceful	most graceful
prepared	less prepared	least prepared
able	abler *or* more able	ablest *or* most able

As you can tell from this list, you form adjectives in the comparative degree by adding *-er* or putting *more* (or *less*) in front of the positive form. And to form adjectives in the superlative degree, you add *-est* or *most* (or *least*) in front of the positive form. But, as always, there are exceptions, among them: *good/better/best; well/better/best, bad/worse/worst, little/less/least, much/more/most,* and *many/more/most.*

You might also have gathered that *-er/-est* endings apply mainly to one-syllable words (*late/later/latest*). The *more-most/less-least* pattern relates to words of two or more syllables (*more famous, most nauseous, less skillful, least beautiful*). Some two-syllable words follow the guidelines for words of one syllable (*pretty/prettier/prettiest*), although you can also say *more pretty* or *most pretty.*

Here are some additional facts to know about making comparisons:

- Three-syllable adjectives and all adjectives ending in *-ly* use the *more/most* or *less/least* combination (*most luxurious, less comfortable*).

- The comparative degree is used to compare two things.

> **This test was *harder* than that one.** (Two tests are being compared.)
> **The *younger* of my sisters takes dancing lessons.** (The speaker has two sisters.)

- The superlative degree should be used to compare three or more things.

> **This is the *hardest* test we've had all year.** (They've had at least three tests.)
> **Maria's *youngest* sister takes dancing lessons.** (Maria has at least three sisters.)

Don't use *more, most, less,* and *least* in the same phrase with adjectives in the comparative or superlative degrees. For example, avoid phrases like *more friendlier, less prouder, most sweetest,* and *least safest.* Because such phrases make double comparisons, they contain redundancies.

Also, stay alert for several dozen *absolute* adjectives—adjectives whose meaning keeps them from being used to make comparisons. For instance, if you are *dead* or *pregnant,* that's it! You can't be "deader" or "deadest," or "more pregnant" than someone else. The same holds true for such common adjectives as

> Use adjectives in the *comparative degree* to compare **two** things.
>
> Use adjectives in the *superlative degree* to compare **three or more** things.

complete, final, square, full, superior, basic, empty, ultimate, fatal, perfect, and *extreme.* Also, beware of *unique,* a particular troublemaker. By definition, *unique* means one of a kind. Therefore, it makes no sense to say "more unique" or "most unique."

Finally, be mindful of the difference between the adjectives *less* and *fewer.* Use *less* to refer to singular nouns: *less rain, less cocoa, less fighting.* Use *fewer* for plurals: *fewer people, fewer tickets, fewer voyages.* Put another way, reserve *fewer* for things that can be counted: *fewer children, fewer dollars, fewer cans of beans.* And save *less* to refer to nouns that can't or aren't likely to be counted: *less salt, less air,* and *less hostility.* There are exceptions, of course, like *less money.*

Checkpoint 8. COMPARATIVE DEGREE

Find the errors in comparative degree in the following sentences. Write the correct usage in the spaces provided. Some sentences may be correct.

1. Ross is a lot more rich than his brother.

   _____

2. Although James Patterson and David Balducci write thrilling books, Patterson is the best storyteller.

   _____

3. Of all the colleges Bill visited, Pomona stood out as the most unique one.

   _____

4. This is by far the greater tuna-noodle casserole that I have ever eaten.

   _____

5. Ricky is about the forgetfulest person I've ever met.

   _____

6. Of all of Shakespeare's plays, *Hamlet* is the more popular.

   _____

7. Jim couldn't tell who is most stubborn—his sister or his brother.

   _____

8. Both situations were terrible, but Ron first tried to fix the worst of the two.

   _____

9. The climbers would be smart to take the less harder route to the summit.

   _____

10. After weighing the three fish he caught, Parker decided to throw the lightest one back.

   _____

11. Lynne's victory was more sweeter because her opponent had beaten her last year.

   _____

12. Bill's idea was profounder than Al's.

   _____

13. Both I-95 and the parkway will take you to New Haven, but the latter is the fastest route.

   _____

14. Because they received the new flu vaccine, the people are immuner than they were last year.

   _____

15. That was the most unkindest remark I ever heard.

   _____

16. Trust became a bigger issue than either taxes or crime in the election campaign.

   _____

17. Because of the weather, Frankie's team played less games than last year.

   _____

18. Because she felt unsure about her performance, the result was more nicer.

   _____

19. Which is longest—the Mississippi River or the Colorado?

   _____

20. In the autumn, Vermont has prettier colors than most other states.

   _____

Answers on page 56

THE ADVERB

The **ADVERB** is first cousin to the adjective. Both words describe—or modify—other words. Adjectives modify nouns; adverbs modify verbs. By modifying verbs, adverbs tell *how, why, when, where, how much, in what way,* or *to what degree* an action occurred. They answer such questions as *How did the action occur? When did it take place? Where did it happen?* and so on.

> Adverbs answer such questions as How? When? Where? How much? In what way? In what manner?

Dad snored *loudly*.

Here, the adverb *loudly* describes *how* Dad snored: He snored loudly.

Mom *immediately* poked him in the ribs.

Here, the adverb *immediately* tells *when* Mom did something about it: She poked him *right away. (Right away,* by the way, is an **adverbial phrase**—a phrase that functions like an adverb.)

Adverbs not only modify verbs, but also adjectives and other adverbs. Regardless of which words they modify, however, they always answer the same sorts of questions: How? When? Where? How much? In what way? In what manner?

Dad is *completely* unaware of the sounds he makes.

Here, *completely* is an adverb modifying the adjective *unaware.* It tells *to what degree* Dad is aware of his nocturnal snorts and wheezes. In a word, Dad is oblivious.

All through the night, he sleeps *remarkably soundly*.

This sentence contains two adverbs—*soundly* modifying the verb *sleeps,* and *remarkably,* which modifies *soundly,* an adverb that intensifies the depth of Dad's sleep: Dad doesn't just sleep soundly; he sleeps *remarkably* soundly.

Many adverbs come directly from adjectives. Add an *-ly* to an adjective and *voila!* you've got an adverb, as in *slow/slowly, late/lately, regular/regularly, indiscriminate/indiscriminately.* In fact, an *-ly* ending frequently says "Hey, this word is an adverb." But don't bet the farm on it, because plenty of adjectives also end with *-ly* (*lonely, sickly, daily, lovely*), and adverbs themselves come in all sorts of guises, among them:

How?	When?	Where?	How much?	In what way?
bravely	recently	here	exhaustively	extensively
glumly	soon	there	relentlessly	by all means
well	now	nowhere	often	in some respects
without a doubt	off and on	in town	heart and soul	sincerely

Adverbial phrases serve the same purpose as single-word adverbs: They modify verbs, adjectives, and other adverbs:

> **Timothy *is* (verb), *without a doubt* (adverbial phrase), the world's worst waiter.**
> **Not only is he *gruff* (adjective) *beyond belief* (adverbial phrase), but he can't remember what people order.**
> **He treats customers so *discourteously* (adverb) *to begin with* (adverbial phrase) that they flee the restaurant without eating.**

Adverbial clauses also function like adverbs, modifying verbs, adjectives, and adverbs. The italicized adverbial clauses in these sentences modify the underlined verbs:

> *Unless the mail comes before noon*, you <u>will miss</u> the deadline.
> <u>Watch out</u> when you give the news to Brianna *because she is short tempered*.
> Hank, *even though he's old enough to drive*, <u>prefers to ride</u> a bicycle.

Placing adverbs in sentences

Recognizing an adverb when you meet one can help you analyze sentences, but placing it properly into a sentence is far more useful. In fact, where you put an adverb can steer the meaning and intent of a sentence in different directions. For instance, in the following pair of sentences, the placement of the adverb could make a huge difference to a boy named Mike and a girl named Sharon:

> Mike *only* loves Sharon.

Here the adverb *only* modifies the verb *loves*. The position of *only* is appropriate if Mike feels nothing but love for Sharon—no admiration, no awe, no respect, nor any other emotion. But if Mike has but one love in his life, and she is Sharon, then *only* is misplaced. Properly placed, *only* should come either before or after *Sharon*:

> Mike loves *only* Sharon.
> or
> Mike loves Sharon *only*.

Now Sharon knows where she stands with Mike, and if she loves only Mike (or Mike only) maybe they'll live together happily ever after.

Splitting Infinitives

In everyday speech and writing, splitting the two parts of an infinitive with an adverb is a common practice. But it's not good form, especially when the split is unnecessary, because either way the meaning of the sentence is the same:

> SPLIT: It felt creepy *to*, after all this time, *visit* my elementary school.
> UNSPLIT: It felt creepy after all this time *to visit* my elementary school.
> SPLIT: The nurses were trained *to* silently *enter*.
> UNSPLIT: The nurses were trained *to enter* silently.

Even though some guardians of pure English object to splitting infinitives, doing so may occasionally be the most accurate way to express an idea, as in:

> The hikers neglected to thoroughly clean up the campsite.

A version with the adverb inserted before the infinitive fails to deliver the same message:

> The hikers neglected thoroughly to clean up the campsite.

And were you to put the adverb after the infinitive—well, you'd mangle the language but good:

> The hikers neglected to clean up thoroughly the campsite.

Making comparisons with adverbs

Adverbs follow the same pattern as adjectives when they are used to make comparisons. When you compare two qualities, for instance, add an *-er* or use *more* before the adverb. To compare three or more things, add *-est* or use *most* before the adverb.

Which form to use depends largely on syllable count. One-syllable adverbs use *-er* and *-est*:

> **Mitzi drives *fast*.**
> **Mitch drives *faster*.**
> **Mike drives *fastest* of all.**

Adverbs of two or more syllables, including all adverbs with *-ly* endings, use *more* or *most*:

> **Mitzi eats *quickly*.**
> **Mitch eats *more quickly*.**
> **Mike eats *most quickly*.**

Adverbs vs. Adjectives

Most of the time, choosing between an adverb or an adjective is a simple matter. But occasionally it can pose a problem, even when the words are seemingly simple, such as when choosing between *good* and *well*.

A few pages back you learned that adjectives describe, or modify, nouns and pronouns. In the phrase "good book," for example, the adjective *good* modifies *book*. That's easy enough. But *good*, along with some other adjectives, may cause trouble when used after a verb, as in *talks good, drives good, writes good*—all nonstandard phrases.

Yet, *good* is perfectly acceptable after some verbs, called **linking verbs,** such as *look, smell, taste, feel, appear, stay, seem, remain, grow, become*, and all forms of *to be*. Therefore, such phrases as *sounds good, feels good*, and *smells good* are perfectly correct.

The guidelines for using adjectives are generally straightforward. But grammar, being grammar, occasionally throws you curveballs. Here is one of them: Linking verbs are sometimes used as active verbs. For example, *look* is a linking verb when it refers to someone's health or appearance, as in "He looks good in that hat." But *look* becomes an active verb when it refers to the act of looking, as in "Margie looked sadly at her sick cat." In such cases, an adverb (*sadly*) is correct, whereas an adjective (*sad*) is not.

To determine whether the verb is a linking verb or an active verb, substitute a form of *to be* in its place. If the sentence retains its basic meaning, the verb is probably a linking verb. For instance:

> **Zack *climbs* a ladder well./Zack *is* a ladder well.**

Because the second sentence makes no sense, *climbs* is clearly not a linking verb.

> **The sauce *tastes* spicy./The sauce *is* spicy.**

Because the two sentences have essentially the same meaning, *tastes* is a linking verb. Therefore, *tastes* may not be followed by an adverb such as *well, sweetly, weirdly*, and so on. Instead, use whatever adjective suits you: *good, sweet, weird, bland, spoiled*, etc.

Checkpoint 9. USING ADVERBS

Check each sentence for proper placement and use of adverbs. If you find an error, write a correct version of the sentence in the space provided. Some sentences may be correct.

1. The trekkers felt bitterly that they had been abandoned by their guide.

   _____

2. Rover smelled badly after swimming in the swamp.

   _____

3. Of the two sisters, Janie swims most quickly but Marnie dives best.

   _____

4. Lauren felt anxious before her college interview.

   _____

5. No problem, I can do both jobs as easy as pie.

   _____

6. Amy sounded sincere when she apologized to Alberto.

   _____

7. Be sure to proceed slow through the construction zone.

   _____

8. The generalissimo looked down cynical on the people gathered in the plaza below.

   _____

9. This soup tastes badly. Give me another kind, please.

   _____

10. Of the hundred songs I heard on iTunes, I more fully enjoyed "The Stomp."

    _____

11. The coach talked slow about the team's decline during the second half.

    _____

12. José always feels good after a long workout and a hot shower.

    _____

13. At graduation, he mounted the stage happy to pick up his diploma.

_____

14. I expected to early get up this morning, but I lolled around in bed until noon.

_____

15. The wind off the river felt coldly this morning.

_____

16. Diana learned to play the piano good by taking lessons from Mr. Mittler.

_____

17. Has he told you lately that he loves you truly?

_____

18. Jack chose a comfortable place to lie down and slept more comfortable than he did the night before.

_____

19. When the kitten decided to finally eat, it scampered over to the saucer of milk.

_____

20. They felt their way uncertainly along the walls of the dark cave.

_____

Answers on page 57

THE PREPOSITION

A **PREPOSITION** is defined as a word (or sometimes a phrase) that can connect a noun or pronoun to some other piece of a sentence. That's a pretty fuzzy definition, isn't it?

So, let's try to do better. How about this: In your mind's eye, picture a flying airplane and a puffy cloud. The plane can fly *to* the cloud, *through* the cloud, *above* the cloud, *under* the cloud, and so forth. All the words in italics—*to, through, above,* and *under*—are prepositions, serving to show the relative position of one object, the plane, to another, the cloud. (Notice the word *position* within the word pre*position*.) English offers dozens of other prepositions that more or less refer to location, among them: *at, off, between, among, over, beside, near, onto, out, past, toward, with, within, behind,* and *across.*

Another group of prepositions enables you to express the relative time when events took place, among them: *before, after, during, since, until.*

Still other prepositions serve to connect and compare objects and ideas, as in:

He walks *like* a duck, *unlike* Jim, who walks *like* a chicken.
No one is as good *as* you at throwing horseshoes.
Except for Marion, no one at the party wanted to be there.
Because of you, my life is now worthwhile.

> A pronoun serving as the object of a preposition must be in the objective case. Therefore, say "*between you and me*," not "*between you and I*."

You won't find prepositions wandering around on the loose. They are always attached to nouns or pronouns in what are known as **prepositional phrases**: <u>to the country</u>, <u>over him</u>, <u>after the ball</u>, <u>in accordance with</u> her wishes. Grammatically speaking, the noun or pronoun in a prepositional phrase is called the ***object of the preposition***, which means, in terms of pronouns at least, that you must use the objective case. (Remember that pronouns fall mainly into two cases—the nominative and the objective. Turn to page 6 to refresh your memory.) Therefore, "*between* (preposition) you and *I*" is incorrect. (*I* is a nominative case pronoun.) Instead use "*between* you and *me*." (*Me* is a pronoun in the objective case.)

NONSTANDARD: The toll collector argued *with* Harry and *I*.
STANDARD: The toll collector argued *with* Harry and *me*.

Take note of these four additional issues involving prepositions:

• **When to use *like* and when to use *as***

Like is a preposition used for making comparisons. Because *like* introduces a prepositional phrase, it must be followed by a noun or pronoun, as in:

Barney looks *like* my dog.
My dog looks *like* me.

(*Like* can also be a verb, a noun, an adjective, or an adverb—but that's a matter that needn't concern us now.)

As—along with its chums *as if* and *as though*—is a **conjunction.** (A discussion of conjunctions comes up next.) *As* introduces clauses and is followed by a verb, as in:

Alice does *as* her father says.
Do *as* I say, not *as* I do.

When you are uncertain whether to use *like* or *as*, look for a verb. If a verb follows, you'll know that *as* is the word to use. For instance:

Every day the child acts more *like* her mother (no verb).
He acts *as if* he *had seen* (verb) Elvis alive.

In comparisons the verb may sometimes be left out to avoid wordiness. So stay alert for usages in which the verb is optional, as in:

Melissa loves the city as much *as* I (do).

- **When to use *between*; when to use *among***

Use *between* to refer to anything split into two or divided by two, such as the trail mix that Barbie split *between* Ken and herself. Use *among* for a division by more than two, say, the seven famished hikers who divided a bag of Doritos *among* themselves. Also:

> **Among the three of us, we ought to figure out the solution.**
> **We should probably choose between Sam's and Kathy's answers.**

- **Ending a sentence with a preposition**

English teachers have fought hard to keep students from ending sentences with prepositions. It's a losing battle, however, because the rule often forces you to use odd-sounding language, as in:

> **After the test, we had many things *about* which to talk.**

You'd probably raise some eyebrows on the school bus if you talked like that. In the 21st century, it's far more natural to say

> **After the test, we had many things to talk *about*.**

Yet, you should respect the restriction against sentence-ending prepositions whenever possible. A reasonable rule of thumb to follow is to avoid sentence-ending prepositions, unless by so doing you'll end up sounding phony or pompous.

- **The idiomatic use of prepositions**

Many words go hand in hand with certain prepositions. That's why *wait for the bus* is standard English, whereas *wait on the bus* is not. Yet, you can *wait for a table* or *wait on a table*, depending on whether you intend to eat lunch or serve it. In short, there is no consistent logic to explain why certain words go with certain prepositions. Customary English idiom simply obliges you to choose your prepositions with care.

> **NONSTANDARD: Maude stepped *in* a puddle.**
> **STANDARD: Maude stepped *into* a puddle.**
> **NONSTANDARD: I sympathize *on* your loss.**
> **STANDARD: I sympathize *with* your loss.**

Keep in mind, among many others:

agree *to* (a thing), agree *with* (a person)
angry *at* (a thing), angry *with* (a person)
compare *to* (for illustration), compare *with* (to examine qualities)
concern *in* (be interested), concern *for* (troubled), concern *with* (involved)
concur *in* (an opinion), concur *with* (a person)
differ *from* (things), differ *with* (a person)

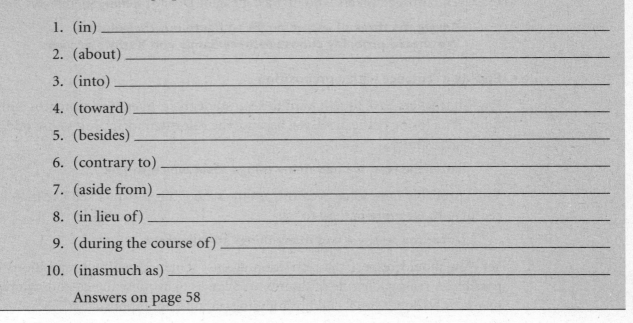

Checkpoint 10. PREPOSITIONS AND PREPOSITIONAL PHRASES

In the spaces below write a short sentence that includes the preposition in parentheses. In each, underline the prepositional phrase and circle the object of the preposition.

1. (in) _____

2. (about) _____

3. (into) _____

4. (toward) _____

5. (besides) _____

6. (contrary to) _____

7. (aside from) _____

8. (in lieu of) _____

9. (during the course of) _____

10. (inasmuch as) _____

Answers on page 58

THE CONJUNCTION

CONJUNCTIONS work hard but earn little credit. They are the glue that ties words, phrases, and clauses together. And the conjunction that does more gluing than any other is the word *and*, as in ham *and* eggs, Romeo *and* Juliet, and yesterday *and* today. Notice that the previous sentence began with this very hardworking conjunction. In formal speech and writing, it's best to avoid starting a sentence with *and* or its close companion *but*, but in more casual communication it's done all the time. But don't do it too often, because it can get monotonous.

Both *and* and *but* belong to a group of seven *coordinating conjunctions*. The others are *or, yet, for, nor,* and *so*, easily remembered using the acronymn BOYFANS. Coordinating conjunctions get their name from their function—joining equivalent words, phrases, and clauses.

Please pick up some bread *or* rolls (two nouns) **for dinner.**
So close, *yet* so far (two phrases).
I love you, *but* you don't love me (two clauses).

> A coordinating conjunction that links two or more independent clauses results in a compound sentence.

A coordinating conjunction that links two or more clauses results in a *compound sentence* consisting of coordinated ideas of more-or-less equal rank (the next chapter explains the ins and outs of *compound* and other types of sentences). If the ideas in a compound sentence seem unrelated or are otherwise mismatched, the choice of conjunction could be at fault, but more than likely the ideas themselves may be at odds with each other:

My sister got married *and* she wolfed down a peanut butter and jelly sandwich.

C. Edward Good, *A Grammar Book for You and I . . .Oops, Me!*, Capital Books, 2002, p. 150.

In spite of rumors to the contrary, getting married and gobbling up a PBJ sandwich are not equivalent or connected actions, so unless the sentence was meant as a joke, a revision is in order.

How to fix the incongruity shouldn't be a problem, provided you employ another kind of conjunction, called a ***subordinating conjunction***, which allows you to link two seemingly unrelated ideas in a single sentence.

> ***After*** **getting married, my sister wolfed down a peanut butter and jelly sandwich.**

> Subordinating conjunctions help you to link two disparate ideas in a single sentence.

By using the subordinating conjunction *after*, the sentence now makes slightly more sense, however surreal.

For another example, say that you wanted to convey what seem like two unrelated facts: 1) Jody rushed to school, and 2) Jody put on mascara.

The link between these two statements can be quickly clarified with a subordinating conjunction. Let's use *while*:

> ***While*** **she rushed to school, Jody put on mascara.**

Or the sentence might have been stated:

> ***While*** **she put on mascara, Jody rushed to school.**

In each sentence the less important idea—that is, the *subordinate* idea—is contained in the subordinate clause—the part of the sentence that starts with a subordinating conjunction. Such conjunctions are often used to tie ideas together. Notice how the word *however* functions in this pair of sentences:

> **Some people oppose raising the minimum wage, claiming that it will increase unemployment.** ***However,*** **many economists dispute this argument.**

The subordinating conjunction—also called an adverbial conjunction—creates a logical link between the two sentences. Some other common subordinating (or adverbial) conjunctions are *although, as if, as though, because, before, if, in order to, since, so that, that, though, unless, until, when, whenever, where, whereas, wherever,* and *whether*. It's useful to keep in mind that subordinate clauses, also called ***dependent clauses***, cannot stand alone as complete sentences. In other words, they depend grammatically on ***independent clauses*** . . . but let's leave the nitty-gritty of clauses alone for now. Details are on deck.

A third type of conjunction, called a ***correlative conjunction,*** comes in pairs: *neither-nor, either-or, whether-or not, both-and, not only-but also*. Some pairs are almost inseparable. You'll rarely find *either* without *or* or *neither* without *nor*.

> **I'll** ***either*** **go for a walk** ***or*** **go to sleep when I get home.**
> ***Neither*** **rain** ***nor*** **sleet will keep me from seeing you tonight.**
> **Lucy excels in school** ***not only*** **as a student** ***but also******** **as an athlete.**

*In this sentence, *also* is optional.

Because correlative conjunctions can't swap partners, avoid *either-nor* and *neither-or* combinations.

Checkpoint 11. CONJUNCTIONS

Underline the conjunctions in the sentences below. Then name the type of conjunction by writing (COO for "coordinating," SUB for "subordinating," ADV for "adverbial," and COR for "correlative" in the space that follows. Some sentences may contain no conjunctions.

1. Without a doubt, the abandoned bike was neither new nor in good condition.

    _____

2. Still and all, I think we should buy it, fix it up, and sell it for a profit.

    _____

3. Although it's expensive, there is a strong market out there for used bikes.

    _____

4. Not only can we make lots of money, but we will learn about the business.

    _____

5. We don't yet have all the skills we need. Consequently, our venture will be a little risky.

    _____

6. But since you have the tools and I have the space for a bike repair shop, we can be equal partners.

    _____

7. We have no experience, yet I think we ought to try.

    _____

8. So that we can avoid conflict, we should decide ahead of time who has the final say in making important decisions.

    _____

9. Whatever happens, though, we must be prepared for failure because most small businesses fold within a year.

    _____

10. Whether or not we end up doing this, the thought of starting a business is exciting but also a little intimidating.

    _____

Answers on page 58

ANSWER KEY

Page 9, Choosing Personal Pronouns

1. me — Because "my sister" and the speaker received the action (they were taken to the show), use the object pronoun.

2. her, him — Object pronouns are needed because the pair (*her* and *him*) were being acted upon; they were being seen.

3. me — Because the speaker received the action (they were being asked), use the object pronoun.

4. me — The phrase *you and me* is the object of the preposition *between*.

5. him — The pronoun *him* is the object of the preposition *for*.

6. he — The phrase *Roxanne and he* is the subject of the sentence. Therefore, use the subject pronoun *he*.

7. I — The pronoun *I* is part of the subject of the sentence.

8. me — The phrase *me and my sister* is the object of the preposition *between*.

9. we — Choose the pronoun that would be used if the final verb had been included (*harder than we laughed*).

10. we — *We* is the subject of the sentence.

Page 12, Pronoun Shift and Pronoun Agreement

1. . . . his term paper — The antecedent *everyone* is singular; the pronoun *their* is plural.

2. . . . one collects — The switch from *one* to *she* is a shift in pronoun person. (This is not an error in informal writing and speech.)

3. . . . its collection — The antecedent *library* is singular; the pronoun *their* is plural.

4. . . . owns her own car — The antecedent *each* is singular; the pronoun *their* is plural.

5. No error

6. . . . you should — The switch from *you* to *one* is a shift in pronoun person. (This is not an error in informal writing and speech.)

7. . . . himself — The antecedent *individual* is singular; the pronoun *themselves* is plural.

8. . . . its rider — The antecedent *each horse* is singular; the pronoun *their* is plural.

9. . . . its first match — The antecedent *team* is singular; the pronoun *their* is plural.

10. . . . one can't, one should — The switch from *one* to *you* is a change in person; also, the antecedent *one* is singular and the pronoun *they* is plural.

Page 14, Pronoun References

These are only suggestions. Your sentences may eliminate pronoun reference problems just as effectively as these.

1. When we teenagers loiter outside the theater on Friday night, the manager gives us a hard time.

2. I took the test and handed it in after collecting my pencils and pens.

3. The root of their problem is that Kaylin told Ken that she wanted only a short wedding trip to Florida.

4. Bob had only an hour to get to the airport, and his father told him so.

5. During her time at the school, Ms. Sanchez walked the halls more than any other assistant principal.

6. Mr. Henry disapproved of war, but he drove his ambulance to the front lines anyway.

7. After the campus tour, Mike said to Todd, "I think I'll be happy going to Auburn."

8. Mira hit a truck, but her car wasn't even dented.

9. Within the last month, Alicia's older brother Pierre made his parents very happy by finding a new job and marrying Felicia. But he also broke his leg while skiing.

10. She wore her new black leather jacket to school.

Page 20, Review of Pronoun Problems

1. . . . and *I*	Reflexive pronouns may not be used as the subject of a sentence.
2. . . . *whom* I like	Use *whom* when it functions as the object of the verb.
3. . . . *you* should	Sentences cast in the second person should remain so throughout.
4. . . . Stacy and *me*	Use the objective case when the pronoun is the object of a preposition.
5. . . . scared *them* . . . *their*	Plural pronouns are needed for plural antecedents.
6. . . . *which* once	Use *which* to refer to nonessential information in a relative clause.
7. When *I* . . .	Reflexive pronouns may not be used as the subject of a sentence or a clause.
8. . . . *one* practices *one's* or . . . *you* must . . .	Sentences cast in the third person should remain so throughout. Informally, a switch from *one* to *he/she practices* and *his/her instrument* is acceptable. Another possibility: Cast the whole sentence into second person (*you . . . your*).

9.	*He and I*	Use subject pronouns in the subject of a sentence.
10.	. . . *his* seat belt	Use singular pronouns to refer to singular antecedents.
11.	To *whom* . . .	Use *whom* in a prepositional phrase.
12.	. . . *they* were done	Plural pronouns are needed for plural antecedents.
13.	No error	
14.	. . . *his* reservation	Use singular pronouns to refer to singular antecedents.
15.	. . . person *who* . . . *his* own	Use *who* to refer to people. Use singular pronouns to refer to singular antecedents.
16.	. . . and *me*, . . . *us* girls	Use the objective case when a pronoun is the object of a preposition and when a pronoun is the object of the verb.
17.	*This* includes . . . asking *occupants* for IDS	Use singular pronouns to refer to singular antecedents. Pronouns require specific antecedents.
18.	. . . *who* give	Use *who* to refer to people.
19.	. . . and *him*	Use an object pronoun when it functions as the object of the verb.
20.	. . . *they* had . . . on *them*	Plural pronouns are needed for plural antecedents.

Page 26, Verb Tense

1.	Having earned	A participle describing an action that occurred before the action of the main verb must include *having* plus the present or past perfect form of the verb.
2.	had owned	The past perfect tense refers to actions completed in the past before some other past action.
3.	No error	
4.	had been	The past perfect tense refers to actions completed in the past before some other past action.
5.	had reached	When a sentence or clause starts with *if*, use the past perfect tense to express the earlier of two actions.
6.	had expected	The past perfect tense refers to actions completed in the past before some other past action.
7.	had finished	The past perfect tense refers to actions completed in the past before some other past action.
8.	No error	
9.	had given	The past perfect tense refers to actions completed in the past before some other past action.

10. begins	The same tense is used to describe events occurring at the same time.
11. stopped	The same tense is used to describe events occurring at the same time.
12. gave	Sentences cast in one tense should remain in that tense unless a shift in time has occurred.
13. Having worked	A participle describing an action that occurred before the action of the main verb must include *having* plus the present or past perfect form of the verb.
14. learned	Past tense verbs refer to action completed in the past.
15. had seen	The past perfect tense refers to actions completed in the past before some other past action.
16. lives	Present tense refers to actions and conditions currently in progress.
17. Having read	A participle describing an action that occurred before the action of the main verb must include *having* plus the present or past perfect form of the verb.
18. No error	
19. comes	Use present tense to express common truths.
20. has decided	The present perfect tense refers to actions occurring at no particular time in the past and that may still be in progress.

Page 30, Verb Forms

1. eaten
2. caught
3. swam
4. drunk
5. gone
6. laid
7. shone or shined
8. shrunk
9. sung
10. slew
11. stolen

12. strove or strived

13. awakened

14. worn

15. broken

16. dived

17. crept

18. flung

19. sworn

20. led

Page 34, Subject-Verb Agreement

1. talent . . . assures

2. play . . . was

3. group . . . began

4. No error

5. No error

6. are . . . kids

7. proceeds . . . are

8. committee . . . is, who gets

9. neither . . . was

10. policies . . . have had

11. everyone . . . expects

12. No error

13. Miller . . . is

14. Katie and Gene . . . have been invited

15. Nancy Atkins . . . expects

16. number . . . has created

17. Here are the costumes . . .

18. insistence . . . is

19. Members . . . want

20. there are to be . . . guards

Page 39, Comparative Degree

1.	. . . a lot richer	*More rich* may be acceptable in some contexts, but ordinarily add *-er* to one-syllable adjectives in the comparative degree.
2.	. . . the better	Use adjectives in the comparative degree when comparing two things or people.
3.	unique *or use* most unusual	*Unique* is an absolute adjective that cannot be used in making comparisons.
4.	. . . greatest	Use the superlative degree to compare more than two things.
5.	. . . most forgetful	Use *more/most* with three-syllable adjectives.
6.	. . . most popular	Use the superlative degree to compare more than two things.
7.	. . . more stubborn	Use adjectives in the comparative degree when comparing two things.
8.	. . . the worse	Use adjectives in the comparative degree when comparing two things.
9.	. . . less hard	Avoid making redundant double comparisons.
10.	No error	
11.	. . . was sweeter	Avoid making redundant double comparisons.
12.	. . . more profound	Use *more/most* with most two-syllable adjectives.
13.	. . . the faster	Use adjectives in the comparative degree when comparing two things.
14.	. . . more immune	With many two-syllable adjectives, use *more/most*.
15.	. . . most unkind	Avoid making redundant double comparisons.
16.	No error	
17.	. . . fewer games	Use *fewer* when comparing countable things.
18.	. . . was nicer	Avoid making redundant double comparisons.
19.	. . . is longer	Use adjectives in the comparative degree when comparing two things.
20.	No error	

Page 44, Using Adverbs

1. . . . felt bitter
    Felt is a linking verb and must be followed by an adjective instead of an adverb.

2. . . . smelled bad
    Smelled is a linking verb and must be followed by an adjective instead of an adverb.

3. . . . more quickly, . . . dives better
    Use words in the comparative degree when comparing two things.

4. No error

5. . . . as easily as
    In spite of how silly it sounds to say it, *as easily as pie* is grammatically correct because *do* is an active verb that should be modified by an adverb. But everyday English idiom makes *as easy as pie* perfectly acceptable.

6. No error

7. . . . proceed slowly
    Because *proceed* is an active verb, it is modified by an adverb.

8. . . . looked . . . cynically
    In context, *looked* is an active verb and, therefore, must be modified by an adverb.

9. . . . tastes bad
    Tastes is a linking verb and must be followed by an adjective.

10. . . . most fully
    Use the superlative degree (*most*) when comparing more than two things.

11. . . . talked slowly
    Because *talked* is an active verb, it is modified by an adverb.

12. No error

13. . . . stage happily
    Because *mounted* is an active verb, it is modified by an adverb.

14. . . . to get up early
    Splitting the infinitive leads to an awkward expression.

15. . . . felt cold
    In context, *felt* is a linking verb and must be followed by an adjective.

16. . . . piano well
    Because *play* is an active verb, it is modified by an adverb.

17. No error

18. . . . slept more comfortably
    Because *play* is an active verb, it is modified by an adverb.

19. . . . finally decided to eat
    The split infinitive is unnecessary.

20. No error

Page 48, Prepositions and Prepositional Phrases

Your sentences will no doubt be different from these, but each one should illustrate the proper use of prepositions.

1. A theme *in* the poem "Richard Cory" is envy.

2. The poem is *about* a man whom others admire from a distance.

3. The poet doesn't go *into* the details *of* Cory's life.

4. Cory's attitude *toward* the people is distant and aloof.

5. *Besides* wealth, Cory had good looks and good breeding.

6. But *contrary to* the people's perception, Cory was a troubled man.

7. *Aside from* his appearance, Cory was a mystery to them.

8. *In lieu of* getting to know him, people held him up as an icon.

9. *During the course of* the poem, the reader cannot suspect its shocking ending.

10. *Inasmuch as* you may someday read the poem, I won't tell you how it ends.

Page 50, Conjunctions

1. neither . . . nor (COR)

2. and (COO), and (COO)

3. Although (SUB)

4. Not only . . . but (COR)

5. so (SUB) or (ADV)

6. But (COO), since (SUB) or (ADV), and (COO)

7. yet (COO)

8. So that (SUB) or (ADV)

9. Whatever (SUB) or (ADV), because (SUB) or (ADV)

10. Whether (SUB) or (ADV), or not (COR), but (COR)

Chapter 2

Sentences

> **A Note to the Reader**
>
> You are about to plunge into a chapter on the grammar of sentences, a subject that requires you to absorb many facts, rules, and, of course, numerous exceptions to the rules. So, please take your time. Don't let it weigh you down. Read a couple of pages, then read them again. Underline key ideas, take notes. Circle anything that puzzles you and return to it later for further study.
>
> Here's another idea: Skim the chapter to see what it contains. Then go on to the grammar questions in Part II of this book. Come back to this chapter whenever you need help in solving a particular problem or want to clarify a point of grammar. In other words, use these pages as a handy resource, a place to visit again and again for answers to your questions.

SENTENCE BASICS

A **SENTENCE** is a group of words that begins with a capital letter and concludes with an end mark of punctuation, usually a period. Most of the time, it also conveys a more or less complete thought. That's a handy description of a sentence, but honestly, it doesn't tell the whole story. There is much more to know about a creature that takes innumerable forms and shapes and can perform an endless variety of functions. A simple definition just won't do.

For one thing, when talking about sentences, you're obliged to use grammatical terminology. In fact, it's almost impossible to say something intelligent about sentences without referring to *nouns, verbs, prepositions*, and the other parts of speech introduced in Chapter 1.

With that in mind, let's begin with a surprising fact: Did you know that the longest sentence in the world will never be written? That's because a sentence can go on indefinitely. The shortest sentence, on the other hand, is probably a single letter—the answer to a question such as, "Is your name spelled with a *J* or a *G*?" Some might argue that a letter of the alphabet doesn't qualify as a sentence because sentences must consist of two parts, a **SUBJECT** and a **PREDICATE**. They may have a point.

A sentence must have at least a subject and a predicate verb. Without both parts, an utterance is technically not a sentence.

There's no doubt, though, that the simplest *subject* of a sentence is a noun or pronoun, and the simplest *predicate* is a verb.

Ophelia (subject) **wept** (verb)**.**
She (subject) **wailed** (verb)**.**
Push (verb)**!** (In this sentence the subject *you* is implied. Spelled out, the sentence is *You push!*)

It goes without saying that sentences are rarely as short and simple as these examples. In fact, a sentence subject can contain any number of words that modify the noun or pronoun, as, for example, in *poor, broken-hearted, miserable, troubled, pitiful, pathetic Ophelia.* Furthermore, a string of nouns or pronouns can also make up the subject, as in:

Snow, sleet, and freezing rain (subject) **poured down on the city.**
He and she (subject) **are engaged to be married.**

Phrases that contain neither nouns nor pronouns can also be the subject of a sentence. A verb, for example, when it functions as a noun, as in:

To eat (subject consisting of the infinitive of a verb) **like a pig is the sole purpose of Matt's existence.**

To identify the grammatical subject of a sentence, look first for the verb. Then ask who or what is performing the action described by the verb, and chances are you'll have found the subject.

Jack **ran away with Jill.** Who ran? Jack did. Therefore, Jack is the subject.
The *mail* **arrived late this afternoon.** What arrived late? The *mail.*
There were *cars* **parked illegally.** What was parked? *Cars.*

The subject usually comes before the verb, but not always, as in "There in the middle of the room stood *Papa.*" Who stood? *Papa.*

Although this method of finding the subject works much of the time, some sentences refuse to yield their subjects so easily. Then you need to employ additional steps, detailed on page 64.

Predicates are easy to identify because they consist of everything in a sentence that isn't the subject. They can be just a single verb, or a verb accompanied by any number of additional words (italicized in the following sentence) that tell you something about the subject. Predicates can ramble off in all different directions, giving you more details than you need or maybe even want to know.

Ophelia (subject) *wept* (verb) *without stopping for two hours this afternoon, then all through dinner and into the evening until her boyfriend Hamlet sent her a text to apologize for thoughtlessly calling her a moron.*

Regardless of its length or complexity, a sentence must have at least a subject and a predicate verb. Without a subject and verb, you might have an utterance of some kind—even one that communicates a profound thought—but technically, it's not a sentence.

The following are examples of non-sentences:

NO SUBJECT: Reminded me of the troubles they had building the Panama Canal.

NO VERB: A ship with three red smokestacks and a weight of 20,000 tons.

NO SUBJECT AND NO VERB: Too cold, overcooked, and tasteless.

With the addition of the missing ingredient, each of these nonsentences becomes a fully formed complete sentence:

A *video* (subject) on YouTube reminded me of the troubles they had building the Panama Canal.

A ship with three red smokestacks and a weight of 20,000 tons *docked* (verb) at Pier 44 last night.

Chef Marcus (subject) *served* (verb) vegetable soup that was too cold, overcooked, and tasteless.

Objects—Direct and Indirect

The predicates of some sentences contain *objects*—nouns that name the things being acted upon. Objects, in other words, don't perform actions, but rather have actions done to them. Let's say, for instance,

Gloria kissed Mike.

Gloria is the subject, the one doing the kissing. *Kissed* is an action verb, and *Mike* is the object of the verb because he was lucky enough to receive Gloria's kiss. Mike, the recipient of the action, is the ***direct object***.

Let's now assume that after being kissed, Mike returned Gloria's affection:

Mike gave Gloria a hug.

Mike is the subject of the sentence. It's true that Gloria received the hug, but in this sentence she has been turned into the ***indirect object***. The *direct object* is *hug*, the thing that Mike physically gave.

Confusing? Well, maybe, but look at it this way:

Mike gave a hug to Gloria.

An *indirect object* is the thing or person for whom or to whom something is given—in this case, Gloria. The *direct object* is the thing actually given—the hug.

The following sentence illustrates the point in another way:

Mike bought Gloria a card for Valentine's Day.

Here, *card* is the thing that Mike bought, making it the direct object. *Gloria*, as the secondary receiver of the action, is the indirect object.

Between you and I, most people get along in the world without ever distinguishing between direct and indirect objects. To speak and write correctly, however, it helps to know about *objects*—not only objects of the verb, but also objects of prepositions. *Otherwise, you might not have noticed the grammatical blunder in the first phrase of this paragraph.*

CLAUSES

A **CLAUSE** is part of a sentence that contains a subject and a verb. By that definition, a *clause* sounds strangely like a sentence, and to a point, it *is* a sentence—but even though some clauses are complete sentences, others are not. Those that are full-fledged sentences go by the name of *independent clauses* (or **main clauses**), which can stand alone, strong and grammatically perfect. The others are called *dependent clauses* because they depend for their meaning and grammatical validity on independent clauses. Without an independent clause, they would be *sentence fragments*—that is, incomplete sentences.

> Some clauses are complete sentences; others are not.

To illustrate, here is a complete, independent sentence with its subject and verb italicized:

> *Chuckie chewed* a wad of bubble gum.

Now, let's add a dependent clause:

> Because he was nervous, Chuckie chewed a wad of bubble gum.

The new clause contains a subject (*he*) and a verb (*was*), but by themselves that subject and verb don't make a sentence. The clause "because he was nervous" is a fragment, a piece of a sentence. On its own, it lacks grammatical status, which can be achieved only by attaching it to an independent clause.

Dependent clauses serve various functions. They can serve as nouns, as adjectives, and even as adverbs. When they act like nouns, they are called *noun clauses*; when they act like adjectives, they go by the name *adjective clauses*, and so on.

Noun clauses often begin with words such as *that, which, who, whom, when,* and *whatever.* They can be the subject of a sentence, the object of a preposition, or the object of a verb, among other things.

> Some clauses are complete sentences; others are not.

> Using different types of clauses can help you develop a more interesting style of writing and speaking.

> **Whoever chews gum regularly** can develop strong jaw muscles. (*Whoever chews gum regularly* is the subject.)
> **Over time, Chuckie discovered** *that he was a gum addict.* (*That he was a gum addict* is the object of the verb *discovered.*)

Adjective clauses often begin with the relative pronouns *who, whom, whose, which,* or *that.* Like single-word adjectives, they modify nouns and pronouns.

> **The bag** *that held Chuckie's gum supply* **was plastic.**

The clause "that held Chuckie's gum supply" modifies the noun *bag.*

> **Chuckie had paid the woman** *who sells bags full of gum* **two dollars for it.**

The clause "who sells bags full of gum" modifies *woman.*

Adverbial clauses start with such words as *although, because, while, since, as, as though, unless, so that,* and many other subordinating conjunctions. They modify verbs, adjectives, and adverbs.

> *If Chuckie had known the effects of gum,* **he would not have started chewing.**

The clause "if Chuckie had known the effects of gum" modifies the verb *would not have started.*

Frankly, knowing the names and characteristics of various types of clauses won't take you far in this world. But a variety of clauses can help you develop more interesting and varied styles in speech and writing—well, that's a fact worth remembering!

TYPES OF SENTENCES

Although every sentence has a main clause, not every sentence has a dependent clause. ***Simple sentences***, for example, have only one clause containing a subject and a verb. Even if you add modifiers and objects galore, it remains a *simple* sentence. Take the following two sentences. In spite of the difference in their length, both are *simple* sentences:

> **Berkeley admitted Sarah.**

> **Situated on the eastern side of San Francisco Bay, Berkeley, the University of California's flagship institution, admitted Sarah as a freshman starting next semester, not only to the delight of Sarah herself but to the satisfaction of her family, teachers, and friends.**

Leave aside the jumble of miscellaneous information crammed into the second sentence. In the end, you're still left with a simple declarative sentence: *Berkeley admitted Sarah.*

Compound sentences are made up of at least two simple sentences joined by a conjunction, such as *and, but, so,* or any of the other conjuctions discussed in Chapter 1:

> **Berkeley admitted Sarah, and she was delighted.**

What is noteworthy about compound sentences is that they give more or less equal emphasis to the information in each clause. In everyday conversation it's common for people to use fairly lengthy compound sentences, as in:

> **In school yesterday, a water main broke, and we could not take showers in gym, and there was no water to drink, and the toilets could not be flushed, so the principal decided that the situation was unhealthy, and she consulted with the superintendent, and the school was closed before lunch.**

This sentence tells a story without breaking a single rule of grammar. But it's stylistically flawed, because each idea appears in an independent clause, suggesting that no one idea ranks above any other in importance. Clauses of equal rank and structure are called ***coordinate clauses***.

If storytellers want to highlight some details more than others, they would do well to use ***complex sentences***—that is, sentences that contain both a main clause and one or more subordinate clauses:

> **When *Berkeley admitted her,* Sarah was delighted.** (Subordinate clause italicized.)

Here, the cause-and-effect relationship between the two ideas is made clear. This process is called ***subordination***, a simple act of giving prominence to ideas in the main clause and letting secondary, or subordinate, ideas slide into the background.

The structure of some sentences can be still more elaborate. For instance, a sentence that combines elements of both compound and complex sentences is called a ***compound-complex sentence.*** To illustrate:

> ***Sarah was not in the top quarter of her class,* but Berkeley admitted her as a freshman anyway, and she was delighted.**

SENTENCE PROBLEMS
Nonsentences

Partial sentences, called **sentence fragments**, often look remarkably like complete sentences. But looks can be deceptive.

The bike that Blossom often borrowed.

This fragment appears to have all the characteristics of a sentence: It starts with a capital letter and ends with a period. It conveys a complete thought (*Blossom often borrowed the bike* is a complete thought), and it seems to contain a subject (*Blossom*) and a verb (*borrowed*). What makes it a fragment, though, is that *Blossom* isn't the subject. Rather, *bike* is the subject, and the trouble is that *bike* and the verb *borrowed* don't fit together. A bike, after all, is an inanimate object and can't do any borrowing—not in this world, in any case. Clearly, Blossom did the borrowing, but the noun *Blossom* cannot be the subject of the sentence because it is part of the subordinate clause, *that Blossom borrowed*. Therefore, *bike* needs a verb of its own.

The bike that Blossom often borrowed was stolen.

With the addition of *was stolen*, the sentence is now complete.

Sentence fragments often occur when writers fail to distinguish between dependent and independent clauses, when they confuse phrases and clauses, or when they attempt to use verbals as verbs. (See page 66.) To determine whether a sentence is complete, uncover its bare bones. That is, take it apart by eliminating dependent clauses, phrases, and verbals. If what remains does not have a subject and a verb, it's probably a fragment.

> You'll almost never find the subject of a sentence in a prepositional phrase or a dependent clause.

To identify the subject of long sentences may take some doing, but the "bare bones" strategy usually works. Using this approach, you'll strip away everything in a sentence but its subject and verb, a task that may be easier said than done. It's not very formidable, though, if you remember that the grammatical subject can never be in a prepositional phrase, in a dependent clause, or in a phrase that interrupts the flow of the sentence.

To find the "bare bones" of a sentence:

Step 1: Look for prepositional phrases, such as *up the wall, around the corner, to the beach, over the counter*. Cross all of them out. For example, if you were to eliminate all the prepositional phrases in these sentences, only the subject and the verb—the bare bones—would remain.

COMPLETE SENTENCE: In the middle of the night, Abby slept.

Cross out *In the middle* and *of the night*.

BARE BONES: Abby slept.

COMPLETE SENTENCE: Several of the sentences are in the book.

Cross out *of the sentences* and *in the book*.

BARE BONES: Several are.

COMPLETE SENTENCE: One of Frieda's friends is in need of help.

Cross out *of Frieda's friends* and *in need* and *of help*.

BARE BONES: One is.

Step 2: Locate all the dependent clauses—those parts of sentences that contain a noun and a verb but don't qualify as complete sentences because they begin with words and phrases like *although, as, as though, because, before, even though, if, in spite of, regardless of, since, so that, unless, whenever, whether,* and *while*. Other dependent clauses are statements (not questions) that start with *when, where, which, who,* and *what*.

After you delete the dependent clauses in the sentences below, only the main clause—the bare bones—will remain.

COMPLETE SENTENCE: Because she missed the bus, Marnie wept.

Cross out *Because she missed the bus*.

BARE BONES: Marnie wept.

COMPLETE SENTENCE: While he waited for the dentist, Geraldo did his homework.

Cross out *While he waited for the dentist* and *his homework*.

BARE BONES: Geraldo did.

COMPLETE SENTENCE: Tyler helps out whenever he has the time.

Cross out *whenever he has the time*.

BARE BONES: Tyler helps out.

Step 3: Look for and delete interrupters—those parts of sentences that impede the smooth flow of the main idea. Interrupters may be just one word (*however, nevertheless*) or dozens. They're often set off by commas.

COMPLETE SENTENCE: Ava, regardless of the look on her face, rejoiced.

Cross out *regardless of the look on her face*.

BARE BONES: Ava rejoiced.

COMPLETE SENTENCE: The boat, a sleek white catamaran, sank.

Cross out *a sleek white catamaran*.

BARE BONES: The boat sank.

**COMPLETE SENTENCE: Everett, who got ticketed for doing 60 in a
30 MPH zone, paid the fine.**

Cross out *who got ticketed for doing 60 in a 30 MPH zone*.

BARE BONES: Everett paid.

The process of identifying the bare bones of a sentence can be more complex than suggested by these examples. But by carefully peeling away all the sentence parts that cannot contain the subject or the verb, you'll eventually be left with only the subject and the verb.

Verbals

What may further complicate a search for subject and verb is that subjects sometimes look suspiciously like verbs. These so-called *verbals* come in two main forms: *infinitives* and *gerunds*.

- Infinitives: "*To read* books makes life worth living." Here, the infinitive phrase *to read* plays the part of a noun and is the subject of the sentence.
- Gerunds: "*Reading* books makes life worth living." Here, the gerund *reading* (the *-ing* form of the verb *to read*) is the subject of the sentence.

Another type of verbal is the *participle*, also called a *participial phrase*. Instead of acting like nouns, participles play the part of adjectives, modifying the subject.

Having read all day, Hilary was ready to live it up at night.

Here, the participle *having read* modifies *Hilary*, the subject of the sentence. Likewise,

Turning over in his sleep, Jake fell out of bed.

Again, the function of the participial phrase is to describe, or modify *Jake*, the subject.

Dangling Participles

Hurrying to her chem lab, the bell rang.

The participle in this sentence is "*hurrying to her chem lab*." If you look closely at the meaning, however, the sentence says that the bell rang as it hurried to chem lab—not a likely scenario. To fix this so-called "*dangling participle*," the object being modified (in this case the person rushing to lab) must be included in the main clause:

Hurrying to her chem lab, Simone heard the bell ring.

The grammatical subject, *Simone*, is now properly modified by the participle "*hurrying to her chem lab*."

Run-on Sentences

A *run-on sentence* consists of two independent clauses with nothing but a blank space—not a conjunction, not a mark of punctuation—between them:

Birthstones are supposed to bring good luck mine has never brought me any.

To fill the gap between *luck* and *mine*, turn the run-on into a compound sentence by inserting the coordinating conjunction *but*.

Birthstones are supposed to bring good luck, *but* mine has never brought me any.

> "Run-ons" are two or more complete sentences with no punctuation between them.

Note the comma. It's been added because compound sentences require a comma in front of the coordinating conjunction unless the clauses are very short, as in:

Silas drove but I walked.

Another solution might have been to write two separate sentences:

> **Birthstones are supposed to bring good luck. Mine has never brought me any.**

Or you could have used a semicolon, which, in effect, functions like a period.

> **Birthstones are supposed to bring good luck; mine has never brought me any.**

Notice that *mine* is not capitalized in the above sentence. (See page 87 for more on the proper use of semicolons.)

Comma Splices

A variation on the run-on sentence is the comma splice, in which a comma instead of a period or semicolon is used to join, or splice, two independent sentences.

> **Othello was fooled by a disloyal friend, he should have known better.**

Replace the comma with a period and start a new sentence. Or, use a semicolon:

> **Othello was fooled by a disloyal friend; he should have known better.**

Checkpoint 12. CORRECT SENTENCES

Look for sentence fragments, run-ons, and comma splices. Use the spaces to identify the error and write a correct sentence. Some items may contain no error.

1. Although Mara is stressed out about her sore back.

   _____

2. Tim asked for an extension on the assignment, however the teacher turned him down.

   _____

3. My grandmother is 86 years old therefore she walks very slowly.

   _____

4. Many other examples that I could choose to show who I am, many of them not vivid images of memorable moments but everyday aspects of my life.

   _____

5. I wake up, having slept for the four shortest hours of my life, I force open my eyes and I crawl to the shower then my brain begins to function.

   _____

6. For me to believe that the crucial time has arrived when I will leave the protective world of high school and enter college.

   _____

7. The large brown garage door creaks open slowly, out into the morning sunshine a rider on a road bike emerges.

_____

8. "This is the trail we're supposed to follow," said Dan, "if we don't, we may get lost."

_____

9. A biologist working in the field of genetic engineering and involved in the controversy surrounding human cloning.

_____

10. Use the space below to tell one story about yourself to provide the admissions committee, either directly or indirectly, with an insight into the kind of person you are.

_____

Answers on page 92

Faulty Parallel Structure

Parallel structure keeps equivalent ideas in the same grammatical form. Consider this sentence that lists the contents of a student's locker:

> **The locker held a down jacket, aromatic sweatpants, three sneakers, two left-handed gloves, an unused tuna sandwich, a broken ski pole, a hockey puck, six overdue library books, a disposable camera, and a hiking boot.**

Every item listed is an object, each expressed in the same grammatical form: a noun preceded by one or two adjectives. When the student wrote a list of his favorite pastimes, though, the sentence lost its parallelism:

> **I like skiing, hiking, to take pictures, and running.**

The message is clear, but the phrase *to take pictures* is not parallel with the other phrases. To revise it, write *taking pictures*:

> **I like skiing, hiking, taking pictures, and running.**

> Ideas in a series should be grammatically parallel, even when the series consists of only two items.

When you structure the pieces of a sentence in parallel form, you put yourself in the company of world-class stylists. Abraham Lincoln, for one, used parallelism at Gettysburg: "We cannot dedicate, we cannot consecrate, we cannot hallow this ground. . . ." And later, ". . . that government of the people, by the people, and for the people shall not perish from the earth." John F. Kennedy used parallelism in his inaugural speech: "Let every nation know, whether it wishes us good or ill, that we shall pay any price, bear any burden, meet any hardship, support any friend, oppose any foe to assure the survival and the success of liberty."

To apply the essential principles of parallel construction to your prose:

- Express all ideas in a series in the same grammatical form, even when the series consists of only two items:

> Express parallel ideas in the same grammatical form.

> **Her parents objected to the loud music she played and to the late hours she kept.**

Here, parallelism is achieved with prepositional phrases, *to the loud music* and *to the late hours*. Each phrase is followed by the pronoun *she* and the past tense of a verb.

> **After graduation she promised to turn the volume down and to come home earlier.**

Each parallel idea consists of an infinitive followed by a noun and an adverb.

- Use grammatical equivalents to make comparisons and contrasts. When comparing two ideas, for example, express both ideas in phrases, or pair an idea stated in a clause with a second idea also stated in a clause.

> **FAULTY: They are worried more about public opinion than for what the effect of the proposal may be.**

The prepositional phrase *about public opinion* may not be paired with the clause *what the effect of the proposal may be.*

> **PARALLEL: They are worried more about public opinion than about the effect of the proposal.**

Parallelism is achieved by pairing two prepositional phrases.

> **FAULTY: Going out to eat no longer thrills me as much as to cook at home.**

The gerund *going out* should not be paired with the infinitive *to cook*.

> **PARALLEL: Going out to eat no longer thrills me as much as cooking at home.**

Parallelism is achieved by pairing two gerunds: *going* and *cooking*.

- Stay alert for pairs of words that signal the need for parallelism, such as *either/or, neither/nor, whether/or, both/and*, and *not only/but also*.

> **FAULTY: Elena will attend *neither* NYU *or* Columbia.**

Revise by changing *neither* to *either*, or changing *or* to *nor*. Remember to keep the pair of words close to each other in the sentence. If they are too far apart, your sentence may be hard to follow:

> **Cory *both* started on the basketball and the volleyball teams.**

The signal word *both* is too far removed from the parallel phrase, *the basketball and the volleyball teams*. Its placement misleads the reader into thinking that the verb *started* is one of the parallel ideas. Correctly worded, the sentence reads:

> **Cory started on *both* the basketball and the volleyball teams.**

- When an article, preposition, or a conjunction appears before the first in a series of parallel items, repeat the word before the others in the series.

> **UNCLEAR: Our mechanic did a better job on my bicycle than his.**

Did two mechanics work on the same bicycle or did one mechanic work on two different bicycles? To clear up the ambiguity, repeat the preposition *on*, as in:

> **CLEAR: Our mechanic did a better job on my bicycle than *on* his.**

Sometimes repeating both a preposition and an article is necessary:

> **UNCLEAR: Before signing the contract, Tiffany spoke with the president and treasurer of the company.**

Did Tiffany speak with one person or with two? Repeating *with the* helps to clarify the meaning:

> **CLEAR: Before signing the contract, Tiffany spoke *with* the president and *with the* treasurer of the company.**

- Make sure that parallel ideas are logical equivalents.

> **ABSURD: Terry is six feet tall, kind, and a Texan.**

Physical features, traits of character, and place of origin are not logically coordinated.

> **LESS ABSURD: Terry, a six-foot Texan, is kind.**

Still not terribly logical, but at least the revision emphasizes only one of Terry's qualities—his kindness.

> **ILLOGICAL: San Diego's *harbor* is reported to be more polluted than *any city*.**

This sentence is meant to compare pollution in the San Diego harbor with pollution in the harbors of other cities, but it fails to achieve its goal. Instead, it illogically compares San Diego's harbor with a city.

> **LOGICAL: San Diego's *harbor* is reported to be more polluted than the *harbor of any other city*.**

> **ILLOGICAL: Unlike most *cars* on the street, *Ellie* has her Subaru washed almost every week.**

This sentence is intended to compare Ellie's car with other cars on the street, but it manages only to compare Ellie with the other cars, an illogical comparison.

> **LOGICAL: Ellie's *Subaru*, unlike *most cars* on the street, is washed almost every week.**

Checkpoint 13. PARALLEL STRUCTURE

Seek out flaws in parallel structure in the sentences that follow. Write a corrected version of the offending word or phrase in the space provided.

1. Steve likes canoeing, biking, to read good books, and writing.

   _____

2. Smoking is prohibited in many public places because it harms people's health, deprives nonsmokers of clean air, and an offensive, smelly habit.

   _____

3. To endure extreme cold, you need to be well trained in survival tactics as well as in excellent physical condition.

   _____

4. As an actor, Arnold Schwarzenegger is admired more for his body instead of portraying characters.

   _____

5. The accountant found that business was bad during the third quarter, just like Tony.

   _____

6. Owen enrolled in painting, harmony, music appreciation, and to study art history.

   _____

7. On our first day we visited Fisherman's Wharf, the Golden Gate, and rode the cable cars.

   _____

8. The lawyer insisted that her job took more hours than a teacher.

   _____

9. In the speech, the senator accused his colleague of being an ignoramus and too dense to know what was at stake in the legislation.

   _____

10. It has been said that walking is better for you than to jog the same distance.

   _____

Answers on page 92

Active and Passive Sentences

We've already seen that active verbs differ from being verbs. Because active verbs (*leap, launch, laugh*) show movement, they re-create life. Even active verbs that name sedentary activities as *thinking, writing,* and *sleeping* pulse with greater energy than such passive verbs as *is, were,* and *has been.*

In like manner, active sentences—those structured in the ***active voice***—place emphasis on actions and those who performed them:

> **Bruce *yawned* through a performance of *Our Town.***
> **Yolanda *applauded* wildly at the end of the play.**

Is there any doubt in these sentences about who did what?

A passive sentence, one in the ***passive voice,*** on the other hand, puts its emphasis on the receiver of the action or on the action itself. What's more, the performer of the action may be left out altogether:

> **Six weeks were spent preparing for the play.**

Who prepared for the play? From this sentence it's impossible to tell.

> **A new painting was hung in the gallery.**

Similarly, in this sentence whoever hung the painting gets no recognition. To give credit to the performer of the action, the sentences might read:

> **Six weeks were spent preparing for the play by the acting group.**
> **A new painting was hung in the gallery by Carmine.**

These versions contain more information than the originals, but each still emphasizes the action instead of the performer of the action. To turn them into sentences in the active voice, make the actor the subject of the sentence and place it before the verb:

> **The *acting group* prepared for the play for six weeks.**
> ***Carmine* hung a new painting in the gallery.**

Sometimes, of course, passive construction makes a good deal of sense:

> **The hospital was built in 2015.**

What's important here is the construction date of the hospital, not who poured the foundation and put up the building.

> To pep up your prose, use the active, rather than the passive, voice.

In general, however, good writers prefer to use the active voice because most events in life don't just occur by themselves. Somebody *does* something; a person or thing *acts.* Hamburgers don't just get eaten; people cook and then devour them. Marriages don't just happen; couples deliberately go out and get hitched. Goals don't score, salmon don't get caught, wallets don't get lost all by themselves. Because people do these things, writers take advantage of readers' natural curiosity about others and strive to put the performer of the action into the grammatical subject of sentences. By doing so, they eliminate passive verbs and pep up their prose.

Checkpoint 14. PASSIVE CONSTRUCTION

Put the following sentences into the active voice:

1. The backyard was covered by dead leaves.

   _____

2. The crisis in the Middle East was discussed by us.

   _____

3. Friday's quiz was failed because I had been at play rehearsal every night that week.

   _____

4. New York was flown to at the start of our weeklong vacation in Brooklyn.

   _____

5. The great white whale was pursued by Captain Ahab and his crew.

   _____

6. The newspaper is fetched by Fido every morning.

   _____

7. The decision to go to war was made by the president and his advisers.

   _____

8. Dinner was taken out by more than twenty customers on Friday night.

   _____

9. Five of Shakespeare's plays were seen by our group in three days.

   _____

10. Normally, the brain is called on by the body before you do something physical.

    _____

Answers on page 93

SENTENCE STRUCTURE

Most sentences used in everyday speech and writing start with the grammatical subject followed by the verb, as in:

> *Cats* (subject) *fall* (verb) **asleep in about three seconds.**
> *They* (subject) *sleep* (verb) **best after eating and cleaning themselves.**
> *I* (subject) *wish* (verb) **to be a cat in my next life.**

Seasoned writers, however, try to vary the structure of their sentences. Instead of leading off with the subject every time, they may begin with a prepositional phrase, an adverb, an adjective, or some other grammatical unit.

> Good writers try to vary the structure of their sentences.

The following pairs of sentences show how a subject can be shifted from its customary position:

> **BEFORE THE SHIFT: Mike Bennett is one of the most hardworking officers in the Boston Police Department.**
> **AFTER THE SHIFT: Of all the officers in the Boston Police Department, Mike Bennett is one of the hardest workers.**

With the insertion of a pair of prepositional phrases, the subject (*Mike Bennett*) and verb (*is*) have been been moved farther along in the sentence.

> **BEFORE: Mike goes to work each day with great enthusiasm.**
> **AFTER: Enthusiastically, Mike goes to work each day.**

Obviously, the revised sentence begins with an adverb.

> **BEFORE: Many of his fellow officers are less excited about police work than Mike.**
> **AFTER: Yet, many of his fellow officers are less excited about police work than Mike.**

Well, here the subject (*many*) is stated after an opening conjunction.

> **BEFORE: Mike has tried to win the respect of the people in the area he patrols, although not every resident has learned to trust him.**
> **AFTER: Although not every resident has learned to trust him, Mike has tried to win the respect of the people in the area he patrols.**

After starting with a dependent clause, the writer names the subject, *Mike*, and then adds the rest of the sentence.

> **BEFORE: Mike introduced the idea of holding monthly block parties to reduce crime and help the residents get to know each other.**
> **AFTER: To reduce crime and help the residents get to know each other, Mike introduced the idea of holding monthly block parties.**

To revise this sentence the writer begins with a verbal, in this case, the infinitive form of the verb *to reduce.*

> **BEFORE: Three hundred people attended the first party, hoping that it would help to unite their neighborhood.**
> **AFTER: Hoping that it would help to unite their neighborhood, three hundred people attended the first party.**

Aiming to vary sentences openings, the writer starts this sentence with a participle.

> **BEFORE: The police department was impressed by Mike's effort and awarded him a medal for humanitarianism.**
> **AFTER: Impressed by Mike's effort, the police department awarded him a medal for humanitarianism.**

Determined to try something different, the writer begins this sentence with an adjective that happens to sound like a verb because of its *-ed* ending.

Still another variation is the sentence constructed from matched ideas set in juxtaposition:

> **It wasn't that the spirit of a community caught their imagination, it was their imagination that created a community spirit.**

The power of such sentences lies in the balance of parallel clauses. Each clause could stand alone, but together they express the idea more vigorously.

Sentences can be classified not only by their structure but also according to their main purpose. ***Declarative sentences*** predominate in most speech and writing. (Just to refresh your memory, a declarative sentence, such as the one you are now reading, simply makes a statement.) But to ask a question, you use an ***interrogative sentence***, and to make requests or give a command you employ ***imperative sentences.*** (Hold my hand when we cross the street.) Finally, ***exclamatory sentences*** serve to express sudden strong emotions (What nonsense that is!). On occasion you can drive home a point with a single exclamatory word. (Excellent!)

Varying Sentences—A Summary

Use a variety of sentence types: *simple, compound,* and *complex.*
Create variety by starting sentences with:

- A prepositional phrase: *From the start, In the first place, At the outset*
- Adverbs and adverbial phrases: *Originally, At first, Initially*
- Dependent clauses: *When you start with this, Because the opening is*
- Conjunctions: *And, But, Not only, Either, So, Yet*
- Adjectives and adjective phrases: *Fresh from, Introduced with, Headed by*
- Verbal infinitives: *To launch, To take the first step, To get going*
- Participles: *Leading off, Starting up, Commencing with*

Checkpoint 15. SENTENCE STRUCTURE

Rewrite each sentence below according to the instructions given. Try to preserve the original meanings.

1. Mr. Finn assigned a huge amount of homework to his students over the weekend.
   (*Begin with a prepositional phrase.*)

   _____

2. Many nations pollute the world's oceans, dumping garbage, sewage, and other hazardous waste products into the sea.
   (*Begin with a participle.*)

   _____

3. Toxic materials end up in fish, lobsters, clams, and other sea life, and the toxins enter our bodies when we eat seafood.
   (*Begin with a subordinate clause.*)

   _____

4. An increase in natural disasters has been experienced by our planet during the last half century.
   (*Change to active voice.*)

   _____

5. The increase has occurred because people in greater numbers now occupy areas prone to natural disasters, according to the evidence.
   (*Begin with adverb or adverbial phrase.*)

   _____

6. As the population has grown, more people have settled on floodplains, along the seacoast, and cities have been built on subterranean fault lines.
   (*Revise problems in parallel structure.*)

   _____

7. Community groups have increased college scholarship awards, they hope to motivate young people to study harder in school.
   (*Eliminate the comma splice and begin with an infinitive phrase.*)

   _____

8. The American Dream, a popular concept in American culture, with different meanings for different people.
   (*Write a complete sentence.*)

   _____

9. An ideal dream in the movies, on television, and in countless books means finding a good job getting married, having a couple of kids, and owning a home.
(*Begin with an adjective or adjective clause.*)

_____

10. Typical homes in the community have a white picket fence and a two-car garage.
(*Begin with an adverb.*)

_____

Suggested answers on page 93

SENTENCE EXPRESSION AND STYLE

Having ventured 77 pages into the world of grammar, you deserve a pat on the back for your dedication. Congrats! As admirable as your commitment may be, however, the truth is that perfect grammar can take you only so far.

Regular use of grammatical English suggests that you've had instruction in grammar, that you grew up where standard English was commonly spoken, or that you've read a lot. Yet, grammatical language can still be dull, repetitious, wordy, awkwardly expressed, and stylistically flawed in any number of ways. Correct sentences don't necessarily mean that they are good sentences, only that they contain no grammatical mistakes. Recognizing that skill in language consists of more than just knowing and applying grammatical rules, the College Board, the ACT, and others have included test questions on style and expression. They believe that clear, cogent, idiomatic, and graceful expression goes hand in hand with correct grammar, and that to test one without the other begets an incomplete picture of a student's English skills.

The pages that follow discuss sentences that are grammatically correct but stylistically flawed. Some are long-winded; in others the word order—known as **syntax**—is not only ungraceful but downright jarring, like the wrong note in a familiar melody. Some sentences may lack clarity because they suffer from faulty **diction**, meaning poor word choice, or from incorrect **idiom**—using combinations of words or phrases that don't go together in everyday standard English usage. Such sentences are generally described as *poorly written* or *awkward*.

Awkwardness

The adjective *awkward* covers a great many writing weaknesses, including poor grammar and flawed sentence structure. Most often, though, awkwardness occurs when the words sound odd or off kilter. Awkwardness is difficult to define, but you know it when you hear it. Your ear tells you that a phrase or sentence is clunky. No specific rules can explain its defects. It just doesn't sound right.

> Awkward writing is hard to define, but you know it when you hear it.

AWKWARD: Rather than walk, Mr. Perkins drove his SUV to mail his letter owing to the knowledge that the post office closed at 4:30.

The phrase *owing to the knowledge* is grammatically valid, but it's awkwardly expressed. Here's a less clumsy version of the sentence:

> **Rather than walk, Mr. Perkins drove his SUV to mail his letter because he knew that the post office closed at 4:30.**

> **AWKWARD: Even though factual contents were there, the film about Charles Lindbergh's solo flight to Paris seemed like fiction.**

The first clause of the sentence is grammatically okay but its words are cumbersome. A plain, idiomatic choice of words would help:

> **Although it was factual, the film about Charles Lindbergh's solo flight to Paris seemed like fiction.**

Faulty Idiom

An ***idiom*** usually consists of a group of words that seems absurd if taken literally. When you "have a ball," the experience has nothing to do with a spherical object used in basketball or ping-pong. The expression "that's cool" doesn't refer to temperature, and to "bite the bullet" is unrelated to guns. And so on. Such idioms often puzzle speakers of other languages, but to native speakers of English they are as natural as breathing.

Idioms cannot be rationally explained. We say "three-foot ruler" when we mean "three-feet." A building "burns *down*," a piece of paper "burns *up*," and a pot of stew just "*burns*." Both *flammable* and *inflammable* mean the same thing—easily set afire. When you don't understand something, you might say it's "*over my head*," an expression that also means deep in debt. We accept these and many other linguistic quirks because they are simply part of our language. Likewise, native speakers of English say "go *to* the movies" and "arrive *at* the movies." For someone just learning English, though, "arrive *to* the movies" would make perfect sense. But we don't say it because it's not idiomatic English.

With respect to grammar tests, however, the word *idiom* has another meaning. It refers primarily to ***idiomatic usage***—that is, to the selection and sequence of words used to convey a meaning. The italicized words in the following sentence are examples of faulty idiom:

> **The general was unwilling to pay the *price for victory*.**
> **Nancy has a negative *opinion toward* me.**
> ***In regards* to her future, Tina said she'd go to college.**

The meaning of each sentence is clear, but the italicized sections don't conform to standard English usage. Revised, the sentences would read:

> **The general was unwilling to pay the *price of victory*.**
> **Nancy has a negative *opinion of* me.**
> ***With regard* to her future, Tina said she'd go to college.**

To identify faulty idiom you must, to a certain extent, follow your instincts and your ear for language. There are no specific guidelines to help untangle problems in idiom. An awkward-sounding word or phrase may be the only evidence.

> **The First Amendment is invoked *in those times* when journalists are asked to disclose their sources.**

The phrase *in those times* is awkward. Replace *in* with *at*, a preposition that often refers to time—*at* four o'clock, *at* the turn of the century. Or better still, discard the phrase entirely:

The First Amendment is invoked when journalists are asked to disclose their sources.

· Another example:

A knight was faithful to his king, to his church, and to his lady, and he would gladly die in the name of them.

The phrase *in the name of them* is grammatical but unidiomatic.

A knight was faithful to his king, to his church, and to his lady, and he would gladly die in their name.

Perhaps you've noticed that a preposition is often the culprit in unidiomatic usage. In fact, verbs, adjectives, and other parts of speech cause problems, too—but not as often as prepositions do.

Unidiomatic Phrases	*Idiomatic Phrases*
abide with (a decision)	abide by (a decision)
according with	according to
agree to (you)	agree with (you)
angry at (a person)	angry with (a person)
capable to	capable of
comply to	comply with
desirous to	desirous of
different than	different from
differentiate (good and bad)	differentiate between (good and bad)
interest for	interest in
off of	off
plan on doing	plan to do
preferable than	preferable to
respect in	respect for
superior than	superior to
sure and	sure to
try and (fix it)	try to (fix it)
type of a	type of

When you decide whether a phrase conforms to standard English idiom, there are no specific rules to follow. Sorry. Correctness is determined not by logic but by custom—that is, by longtime usage, and by what literate, educated English speakers regard as proper.

A particular problem related to idiom is the ***double negative***. English is a quirky language in some respects because it allows you to use two negative words in a sentence to say something positive, as in:

The halftime performance of the marching band was *not* at all *bad*.

Combining the negative word *not* and the negative word *bad* pays a compliment (however mild) to the marching band.

On the other hand, double negatives meant to express negativity violate standard English usage. Therefore, you mustn't use modifiers such as *never, no,* and *not* with other negative words such as *none, neither, no one, nobody,* and *nothing.*

> **DOUBLE NEGATIVE: The kids are not doing nothing during the winter vacation.**
>
> **REVISED: The kids are not doing anything during the winter vacation.**

Because the adverbs *hardly, scarcely,* and *barely* also qualify as negative words, they should not be combined with other negatives. Instead, replace a negative word with a positive one, as in:

> **DOUBLE NEGATIVE: There are *hardly* no chocolate doughnuts left on the tray.**
>
> **REVISED: There are *hardly any* chocolate doughnuts left on the tray.**

Checkpoint 16. IDIOM

Identify the errors in English idiom in the following sentences. Write revised versions in the spaces provided. Some sentences may contain no error.

1. To die at battle for their religion was considered an honor.

   _____

2. After the ceremony, the newlyweds ascended up the stairs.

   _____

3. I hope that the admissions office will comply to my request for an extension.

   _____

4. Paleontologists say that bronze was used by hardly no primitive people before the advent of iron and tin.

   _____

5. Because of his preoccupation in classical music, Justin bought a subscription to Symphony Hall concerts.

   _____

6. Most rock climbers are lured by either danger and love of adventure.

   _____

7. When Lucy returned home, she felt as though she'd never been away.

   _____

8. The posse went in pursuit after the horse thieves.

   _____

9. The new security system uses electronic eye scans in the identifying of employees.

   _____

10. Work-study programs offer opportunities to both students and the business community.

    _____

11. No new plans were developed in respect to the environment.

    _____

12. Columbus sailed west in search for a way to the Indies.

    _____

13. The wounded marine could not endure that kind of a pain without passing out.

    _____

14. The children were waiting on the bus to arrive.

    _____

15. Generic drugs are not nearly as expensive than brand-name drugs.

    _____

16. Billy Collins is regarded to be one of the most popular contemporary American poets.

    _____

17. To support themselves, artists must often make a choice between teaching and not doing nothing except trying to earn money by creating art full time.

    _____

18. Most people who travel at Thanksgiving prefer driving more than flying.

    _____

19. Because the boat's engine had failed, the sailor was never far away from harm during the storm.

    _____

20. Although Jackie's term paper was neither well written or fully researched, its grade was A+.

    _____

Answers on page 94

Faulty Diction

Faulty diction means faulty word choice. It occurs when *good* is used instead of *well* after a certain verb, or when *where* is used instead of *when*, as in "the time *where* he took the bus to Jersey." The English language offers many other opportunities to choose incorrect words, as discussed in Chapter 1.

Problems in word choice usually occur when writers ignore word connotations, fail to draw fine distinctions between synonyms, or simply don't know the precise meaning of words. For example:

> **The poem contains *illusions* to Greek mythology.**

This sentence contains an error in diction because the writer meant *allusions*.

> **The boys ran *a fowl* of the law when they shoplifted the iPhone case.**

Here the writer confused *a fowl* (a chicken or duck) with the word *afoul*.

> **Another quality common to firefighters is their *reliability* on their fellow firefighters.**

The writer probably intended to use *reliance* but put down *reliability* instead.

You may recall that the pronoun *that* can be used to refer to people as well as to animals and nonliving things:

> **Pedestrians *that* jaywalk put their lives at risk.**
> ***Saving Private Ryan* is the name of the film *that* caused a great deal of controversy when it was shown on network television.**

Sometimes, the choice of words is a toss-up. It's fine to say, "Those are the geese *who* are damaging the grass," but it's also acceptable to say, "Those are the geese *that* are damaging the grass."

Word Alert!

Some words sound alike but are spelled differently. Since third grade you've probably been aware of *to, too,* and *two, there, their,* and *they're,* and the difference between *its* and *it's*. But watch out also for the words listed below. For a variety of reasons they, along with many others, are often used incorrectly:

accept, except	criterion, criteria	precede, proceed
affect, effect	data, datum	principal, principle
allude, elude	discreet, discrete	prophecy, prophesy
allusion, illusion, elision	illicit, elicit	shall, will
already, all ready	imminent, immanent,	simple, simplistic
alumnus, alumna, alumni,	eminent	social, societal
alumnae	imply, infer	suppose, supposed to
ambiguous, ambivalent	incident, incidence	through, threw, thorough,
ascent, assent	led, lead	though
compliment, complement	lie, lay	transitory, transient,
conscience, conscious	like, as	transitional
council, counsel	medium, media	

Wordiness and Redundancies

Sentences need revision when they contain words and phrases that either add no meaning or reiterate what has already been stated. For example:

> **A necessary requirement for applying to many colleges is the autobiographical essay.**
> **An important essential ingredient of a hamburger is meat.**
> **Have you read *Lust for Life*, the biography of the life of Vincent Van Gogh?**

Each of these sentences contains a needless word or phrase. In the first, omit *necessary* because *necessary* by definition implies *requirement*. The phrase *necessary requirement*, therefore, contains a redundancy. In the next sentence, an ingredient described as *essential* must by definition be *important*, so delete the word *important*. And in the last sentence, the phrase *of the life* should be removed because a biography cannot be anything other than the story of someone's life.

> To write effective sentences, omit needless words.

Sentences cluttered with unnecessary words are less effective than tightly written sentences in which every word counts. While paring sentences to the bone, try the following techniques:

1. Look for redundancies.

> **Sal carried a fake, forged ID card.**

The words *fake* and *forged* have essentially the same meaning. To eliminate the redundancy, remove one of the words.

> **Sal carried a fake ID card.**

2. Shorten or eliminate unnecessary clauses.

> **At the party there were forty guests who got dressed up in Halloween costumes.**

Rewriting this sentence can reduce it by half.

> **Forty costumed guests attended the Halloween party.**

3. Recast phrases as single words or eliminate them altogether.

> **She wore a smile on her face.**

Because smiles are worn nowhere else but on one's face, the phrase *on her face* can be deleted without changing the meaning of the sentence.

> **She wore a smile.**

4. Omit needless words.

> **He rapidly descended down the steps.**

This sentence can be improved by editing out the redundancy in the phrase *descended down* (by definition *descended* indicates downward motion) and by choosing more concise words.

> **He sprinted down the steps.**

The word *sprinted* cogently captures the sense of a rapid descent.

Here are two more examples:

> **WORDY: During the months of July and August last summer, I had a wonderful summer vacation.**

Because July and August are the names of summer months, jettison the needless words:

> **TIGHT: Last July and August I had a wonderful vacation.**

> **WORDY: As you continue down the road a little farther, you will be pleased and delighted with the beautiful and gorgeous views of the scenery that you'll be seeing.**

The sentence is heavy with redundancies. Lighten its load by turning the initial clause into a phrase and eliminating redundant ideas:

> **TIGHT: Continuing down this road, you'll be delighted with the beautiful scenery.**

Checkpoint 17. WORDINESS

Revise the following sentences for economy of expression.

1. She constantly irritates and bothers me all the time.

   _____

2. He spoke to me concerning the matter of my future.

   _____

3. Is it a true fact that the ozone layer is being depleted?

   _____

4. I thought that if I didn't take chemistry that I couldn't go to a good college.

   _____

5. Consequently, as a result of the election, the state will have its first female governor.

   _____

6. My father's habitual custom is to watch the sun set in the West.

   _____

7. Parker picked up a brush at the age of ten years old and hasn't stopped painting since.

   _____

8. Research shows that avid sports fans not only suffer fewer depressions, but they are also generally healthier, too, than those not interested in sports.

   _____

9. His field of work is that of a chemist.

   _____

10. For the second time, the cough recurred again.

Answers on page 95

SENTENCE MECHANICS: PUNCTUATION AND CAPITALIZATION

Punctuation

Cracking the punctuation code is not all that difficult. Perhaps the trickiest thing about punctuation rules is knowing where and when to apply them. The following guidelines should help:

Apostrophes

Apostrophes are used in only three places:

1. In contractions, such as *won't, it's, could've*, and *where's*. Use an apostrophe to mark the spot where one or more letters have been omitted. You can also re-create the pronunciation of spoken words by using apostrophes in place of dropped letters. For instance, *goin', ma'm*, or *ma'am* and *o'*, as in *top o' the mornin'*.
2. In plurals of letters, signs, or numbers, as in *A's* and *B's*, the *1960's*, and *10's* and *20's*. This custom is changing, however, and many experts now simplify matters by writing *1960s, Ps* and *Qs*, and so forth.
3. In *possessive nouns* such as the *student's class, women's room,* and in indefinite pronouns such as *anybody's guess*. When the noun is plural and ends in *s*, put the apostrophe after the *s*, as in *leaves' color* and *horses' stable*.

    In a series of nouns showing joint possession, only the last noun receives the apostrophe, as in *Susan and George's house*. If Susan and George had separate houses, the phrase would read *Susan's and George's houses*.

    A few possessive forms use both an apostrophe and *of*, as in *a friend of the family's*; a few others that specify time, space, value, or quantity also require apostrophes, as in *an hour's time, a dollar's worth,* and *at my wit's end*.

Commas

Commas are meant to prevent confusion and misunderstanding. They divide sentences into parts, clarifying meaning by separating groups of words into discrete units. They often signal a pause that helps readers understand text. In some situations a comma is optional. When given the choice, leave it out unless its inclusion would prevent ambiguity.

1. Use a comma to signal a pause, as in:

    NO PAUSE: After brushing his teeth gleamed.
    PAUSE: After brushing, his teeth gleamed.

    A comma is needed here to separate a phrase and a clause, although that sort of separation is not always essential, as in:

    On the desk a letter from the admissions office lay waiting.

Commas are needed after some introductory words and in various forms of address:

Well, you can open it whenever it's convenient.
The letter will be waiting for you at home, *Jimmy*.

2. Use commas to set off words that interrupt the flow of a sentence. For example, commas are required when conjunctive adverbs are inserted between the subject and verb:

Rowan, *regrettably*, was omitted from the roster.
Jennie, *on the other hand*, was included.

Commas are also needed when a subordinate clause containing information not essential to the main clause is embedded in the main clause:

The lost hikers, *who had come from New Jersey*, found shelter in a cave.
The three bikers, *whose map of the course was out of date*, arrived two hours after the winner of the race.

Commas are needed to set off *appositives*—phrases that describe nouns or pronouns—as in:

Samantha Higgins, *the defense counsel*, strode into the courtroom.
The judge, *Mr. Peterson*, arrived late.

Single-word appositives may or may not require commas. It depends on the meaning.

Jill's brother, Pete, lives in Newark.

In this case, Jill has one brother whose name is Pete. But if Jill has more than one brother, and one of them is Pete, the sentence would be written this way:

Jill's brother Pete lives in Newark.

3. A comma is often needed to separate the independent clauses of a compound sentence:

The competition is stiff, but it won't keep Mira from winning.
Stacey better call her mom on Mother's Day, or she'll be in big trouble.

If clauses are very short, however, omit the comma, as in:

He ate a snack and then he fell asleep.

4. Use commas in a series:

Rosie's car needs *new tires, a battery, a muffler, and an oil change*.
It was amazing that Marv could sit through the *long, boring, infantile, and ridiculous* lecture.

> Before the last item in a series, a comma is optional. It can't hurt to put it in, however.

Some writers prefer to skip the comma before the last item in a series. In case clarity may suffer, it can't hurt to put it in. However, avoid using a comma before the final adjective in a series if the adjective is considered part of the noun, as in:

The good news arrived on a sunny, hot, humid summer day.

5. Commas separate parts of addresses, dates, and place names:

Who lives at 627 West 115th Street, New York, NY?
Richard was born on May 27, 1990, the same day as Irene.
Dave has lived in Madison, Wisconsin; Seattle, Washington; and Eugene, Oregon.

Note that, because each item in the last example already contains a comma, semicolons are needed in the series to avoid confusion.

6. When writing dialogue, use commas to separate quotations from attributions:

> John said, "Close the window."
> "I want it open," protested Ben.

When Not to Use a Comma

Don't use a comma between two independent clauses because each clause has a subject and verb and, therefore, can stand alone as a complete sentence.

INCORRECT: Connie's mom got a new job in Baltimore, this means that Connie will be attending a different high school.

The comma after *Baltimore* should be a period that ends the first sentence. For more on **comma splices**, see page 67.

Semicolons

Semicolons are handy when you have written two sentences that are so closely tied to each other that separating them would diminish their integrity. The semicolon, in effect, shortens the pause that ordinarily occurs at the juncture of two separate sentences:

> Jake never stays out this late; his mother worried.
> The momentum was building; she couldn't be stopped now.

One word of caution: Semicolons are substitutes for periods, not for commas. Therefore, use them only to separate independent clauses.

> **INCORRECT: On the test Lucy got a 90; which raised her final average.**

The clause "which raised her final average" is not an independent clause.

> Semicolons are substitutes for periods, not for commas.

> **CORRECT: On the test Lucy got a 90; this grade raised her final average.**

Or use them to avoid confusion in a series in which one or more items contains a comma, as in:

> On his trek, Norwood met Allen, a carpenter from Maine; Dr. Jones, a pediatrician from St. Louis; Jonathan, an airline pilot; and me, of course.

Colons

A *colon* calls attention to the words that follow it. It is useful to introduce a list, add an appositive, or, in certain contexts, introduce a quotation. To illustrate:

> In his work, Whitney uses at least five kinds of saws: table saw, radial-arm saw, keyhole saw, coping saw, and jigsaw.

> During vacation Marty must have set two world's records: sleeping 15 hours out of every 24, and consuming more than two pounds of pretzels a day.

> Think about what Polonius says: "Above all, to thine own self be true."

Use a colon between two sentences if the second sentence explains or summarizes the first. Although no rule says that you must capitalize the second sentence, many writers prefer to do so.

> **My gym class feels like outer space: It goes on forever.**

It's a mistake to use a colon after an incomplete sentence, as in:

> **Three common types of hardwood trees are: maple, oak, and ash.**
> **Lucy's courseload consists of: English, math, chemistry, and social studies.**
> **The paint comes in unusual colors such as: sky-blue pink and strawberry green.**

The colons in these examples spoil the unity of what would otherwise be perfectly good sentences.

Dashes

Nothing attracts attention like a **dash**, sometimes called an *em-dash*. A dash makes readers pay attention because it marks an abrupt change in thought. A dash is used mostly to define or explain a word or idea:

> **Halfway through the speech he lost sight of his purpose—to inform the audience about risky investments.**

By using a pair of dashes, you can insert parenthetical material into a sentence or include a sudden change in thought:

> **The state finally agreed to install a traffic light—why did it take them so long?—at the intersection of Route 35 and Bedford Road.**

Single dashes can combine closely related ideas:

> **The state finally agreed to install a traffic light at the intersection of Route 35 and Bedford Road—Hallelujah!**

But beware. Many editors and teachers claim that dashes don't belong in formal prose, so if you insist on using them, do so sparingly and only when you are convinced that they will most effectively express your ideas.

Quotation marks

Quotation marks usually surround direct quotations, as in:

> **Rita said to Bob, "I'm nuts about you."**

But they don't apply to **indirect quotations**—quotations that convey the sense of what was said without using the actual words. For example:

> **INCORRECT: Bob told Rita "that he would marry her someday."**
> **CORRECT: Bob told Rita that he would marry her someday.**

Quotation marks can also be used to call attention to certain technical or unusual words and phrases, as in:

> **Serena quickly established a reputation as a "counter-blogger."**

Quotation marks enclose the titles of poems, stories, chapter headings, essays, magazine articles, and other short works. Longer works such as novels, plays, films, and magazine titles are underlined when they appear in handwritten essays and italicized when they appear in print.

Avoid using quotation marks to call attention to clichés, trite expressions, or slang terms. Rewrite instead, using fresh, original language.

Finally, quotation marks may enclose words that express the silent thoughts of a character, as in:

Carlos glanced at his watch. "I'm going to be late," he thought.

When a narrative includes both silent thoughts and spoken words, steer clear of this technique to avoid confusion.

In American English, periods and commas are placed inside closed quotation marks. Put question marks and exclamation points outside the quotation marks unless they are part of the quote itself.

"When will the seminar start?" asked Regis.
Do you understand the meaning of the term "Age of Anxiety"?

Question marks

A direct question should be followed by question mark.

How do you get to Lexington Avenue from here?

If the question is worded as a request, however, a question mark usually follows, but not always, as in:

Would you please close the window.

Note that no question mark should appear after an indirect question—that is, after a report that a question has been asked.

She asked me what time it was.

Exclamation points

Exclamation points are terrific for conveying strong feelings. But think of them as a form of shouting, and because readers don't want to be shouted at, use exclamation points sparingly. Good writers, knowing that overuse of exclamation points dilutes the effect of each one, rely on words, not marks of punctuation, to pump up their prose.

"Run!" yelled the crowd as the sprinters neared the finish line.

If an exclamation point is part of a quotation, as above, the quotation mark follows the exclamation point, but if the strong emotion belongs to the writer, the exclamation point goes outside the quotation mark.

As the tsunami approached, we were told, "Relax, it's only a wave"!

Capitalization

> The SAT and ACT never ask questions on capitalization. But correct capitalization definitely counts on the SAT and ACT essays.

Neither the SAT nor the ACT includes specific questions on capitalization. Yet, knowing when (and when not to) capitalize can give you a leg up on both tests, particularly when you write the essay.

In spite of what you may have heard, capitalization isn't totally standardized. But it's not a free-for-all, either. Guidelines are numerous. Even experienced writers regularly check dictionaries and grammar handbooks just to be sure.

Here's a review worth studying:

1. Capitalize first words of sentences, direct quotations, and lines of poetry (most of the time). This *may* include sentences that follow colons, as in "He had all the symptoms of love: He could think of nothing but Cheryl all day long." On the other hand, never capitalize a sentence that follows a semicolon.

2. Capitalize proper nouns and adjectives derived from proper nouns: *Victoria, Victorian; Shakespeare, Shakespearean; France, French dressing* (but not *french fries*, which has become a generic term).

3. Capitalize place names: *North America, Lake Moosilauke, Yosemite National Park, Gobi Desert, Mount Rushmore, Panama Canal, the Arctic Ocean, Times Square, Route 66.* Don't capitalize *north, east, south,* and *west* unless you are referring to a particular region of the country, as in "They went camping in the *West.*" Nor should you capitalize a common noun that is not part of the actual place name: Capitalize *Panama Canal,* but not *the canal across Panama; Moline,* but not *the city of Moline.*

4. Capitalize languages, races, nationalities, religions, and their adjectival forms: *the Hungarian language, Inuit, Catholicism, Argentinian, Hispanic, Islam, Muslim.*

5. Capitalize organizations, institutions, and brand names: *United Nations, Pittsburgh Pirates, Library of Congress, Automobile Club of America, Amtrak, Southwest Airlines, the Internet, Toyota.* Don't, however, capitalize the common noun associated with the brand name, as in *Crest toothpaste* or *Starbucks coffee.*

6. Capitalize titles of people that indicate rank, office, or profession, when they are used with the person's name: *Congressman Kelly, Doctor Dolittle, Coach McConnell, Judge Judy, Lieutenant Lawlor.* Also, the titles of high officials when they are used in place of the official's name, as in the *Secretary General,* the *Prime Minister,* the *Secretary of the Treasury.* Don't capitalize titles when referring generically to the position: *the superintendent of schools, the assistant librarian, the clerk of the highway department.*

7. Capitalize family relationships, but only when they are used with a person's name, as in *Uncle Wesley, Grandma Jones, Cousin Dave.*

8. Capitalize titles of books, plays, stories, articles, poems, songs, and other creative works, as in *The Grapes of Wrath, Hamlet,* "An Occurrence at Owl Creek Bridge," "The World Around Us," "Ode on a Grecian Urn," "Box of Rain." Note that articles, conjunctions, and prepositions of less than five letters are not capitalized unless they appear as the last or the first words in the title.

9. Capitalize names that refer to the Deity and the titles of religious tracts, as in *God, the Gospel, the Torah, the Koran, the Lord, the Prophet.* Also pronouns referring to *Him* or *Her.*

10. Capitalize historical names, events, documents, and periods, as in *Battle of Gettysburg, Alien and Sedition Acts, War of 1812, Bill of Rights, Middle Ages.*
11. Capitalize days of the week, months, and holidays, as in *Monday, May, Mother's Day.* The seasons are not capitalized unless given an identity such as *Old Man Winter.*
12. Capitalize the names of specific courses and schools, as in *History 101, Forensic Science, Brookvale High School, Columbia College.* Although course names are capitalized, subjects are not. Therefore, you study *history* in *American History 101* and learn *forensics* in *Forensic Science.* Similarly, you attend *high school* at *Brookvale High School* and go to *college* at *Columbia.*

Checkpoint 18. CAPITALIZATION

Add capital letters where they are needed in the following sentences.

1. on labor day, bennington county's fire department plans to hold a turkey shoot on the field at miller's pond.

2. the judge gave district attorney lipman a book entitled *the rules of evidence* and instructed her to read it before she ever dared set foot in the court of appeals of the ninth circuit again.

3. our secretary of state greeted the former president of austria at the president ronald reagan airport in washington, d.c.

4. the shackleton expedition nearly met its doom on georgia island in antarctica.

5. for christmas he got a black & decker table saw from the sears store next to the old bedford courthouse.

6. according to georgetown's high school principal, eugene griffiths, georgetown high school attracts students from the whole west coast. at georgetown, students may major in drawing and painting, design, graphics, or sculpture. mr griffiths said, "i attended a similar high school in new england just after the vietnam war."

7. we expect to celebrate new year's eve again this year by streaming a movie of an old broadway musical and by settling down in front of the television with some pepsi and a box of oreos.

8. after traveling all the way to the pacific, the corps of discovery rode down the missouri river going east on their way back to st. louis.

9. This irish linen tablecloth was bought at walmart in the emeryville mall off powell street.

10. on our way to the west we stopped at yellowstone national park in the northwest corner of the state of wyoming.

Answers on page 95

ANSWER KEY

Page 67, Correct Sentences

Although your sentences may differ from these, be sure you have correctly identified one or more errors.

1. *Sentence fragment.* Mara is stressed out about her sore back.

2. *Comma splice.* Tim asked for an extension on the assignment. However, the teacher turned him down.

3. *Run-on sentence.* My grandmother is 86 years old and, therefore, walks very slowly.

4. *Sentence fragment.* Although there are many other examples that I could choose to show who I am, many of them are not vivid images of memorable moments but everyday aspects of my life.

5. *Comma splice and run-on sentence.* I wake up, having slept for the four shortest hours of my life. I force open my eyes, and I crawl to the shower. Then my brain begins to function.

6. *Sentence fragment.* It's hard for me to believe that the crucial time has arrived when I will leave the protective world of high school and enter college.

7. *Comma splice.* The large brown garage door creaks open slowly. Out into the morning sunshine a rider on a road bike emerges.

8. *Comma splice.* "This is the trail we're supposed to follow," said Dan. "If we don't, we may get lost."

9. *Sentence fragment.* Louise is a biologist working in the field of genetic engineering and involved in the controversy surrounding human cloning.

10. No error

Page 71, Parallel Structure

Although your answers may be slightly different from these, they should demonstrate your grasp of parallel structure.

1. Steve likes canoeing, biking, reading good books, and writing.

2. Smoking is prohibited in many public places because it harms people's health, deprives nonsmokers of clean air, and is an offensive, smelly habit.

3. To endure extreme cold, you need to be well trained in survival tactics and be in excellent physical condition.

4. As an actor, Arnold Schwarzenegger is admired more for his body than for his portrayal of characters.

5. Like Tony, the accountant found that business was bad during the third quarter.

6. Owen enrolled to study painting, harmony, music appreciation, and art history.

7. On our first day we rode the cable cars and visited Fisherman's Wharf and the Golden Gate.

8. The lawyer insisted that her job took more hours than a teacher's job.

9. In the speech, the senator accused his colleague of being an ignoramus, too dense to know what was at stake in the legislation.

10. It has been said that walking is better for you than jogging the same distance.

Page 73, Passive Construction

Your sentences may differ from these, but be sure you've used the active voice.

1. Dead leaves covered the backyard.

2. We discussed the crisis in the Middle East.

3. I failed Friday's quiz because I had rehearsed for the play every night that week.

4. We flew to New York to begin our weeklong vacation in Brooklyn.

5. Captain Ahab and his crew pursued the great white whale.

6. Fido fetches the newspaper every morning.

7. The president and his advisers decided to go to war.

8. On Friday night, more than twenty customers took out dinners.

9. In three days our group saw five Shakespearean plays.

10. Before you do something physical, the body normally calls on the brain.

Page 76, Sentence Structure

Your sentences may differ from these.

1. Over the weekend, Mr. Finn assigned a huge amount of homework to his students.

2. Dumping garbage, sewage, and other hazardous waste products into the sea, many nations pollute the world's oceans.

3. Because they end up in fish, lobsters, clams, and other sea life, toxic materials enter our bodies when we eat seafood.

4. Our planet has experienced a sharp increase in natural disasters during the last half century.

5. Evidently, the increase has occurred because people in greater numbers now occupy areas prone to natural disasters.

6. As the population has grown, more people have settled on floodplains, along the sea-coast, and in cities built on subterranean fault lines.

7. To motivate young people to study harder in school, community groups have increased college scholarship awards.

8. The American Dream, a popular concept in American culture, has different meanings for different people.

9. Idealized by the movies, television, and countless books, the dream consists of finding a good job, getting married, having a couple of kids, and owning a home.

10. Typically, homes in the community have a white picket fence and a two-car garage.

Page 80, Idiom

1. in battle

2. ascended the stairs

3. comply with

4. hardly any

5. preoccupation with

6. either danger or love

7. Correct

8. in pursuit of

9. to identify employees *or* in the identification of employees

10. Correct

11. with respect to

12. in search of a way

13. that kind of pain

14. for the bus

15. as expensive as

16. regarded as one

17. not doing anything

18. driving to flying

19. far from harm

20. neither well written nor fully researched

Page 84, Wordiness

Answers may vary.

1. She constantly bothers me.

2. He spoke to me about my future.

3. Is it true that the ozone layer is being depleted?

4. I thought that without chemistry I couldn't go to a good college.

5. The voters elected the state's first female governor.

6. My father habitually watches the sun set.

7. Parker hasn't stopped painting since picking up a brush at age ten.

8. Research shows that avid sports fans suffer fewer depressions and are generally healthier than those not interested in sports.

9. He is a chemist.

10. The cough recurred twice.

Page 91, Capitalization

1. On Labor Day, Bennington County's fire department plans to hold a turkey shoot on the field at Miller's Pond.

2. The judge gave District Attorney Lipman a book entitled *The Rules of Evidence* and instructed her to read it before she ever dared set foot in the Court of Appeals of the Ninth Circuit again.

3. Our secretary of state greeted the former president of Austria at the President Ronald Reagan Airport in Washington, D.C.

4. The Shackleton expedition nearly met its doom on Georgia Island in Antarctica.

5. For Christmas he got a Black & Decker table saw from the Sears store next to the old Bedford Courthouse.

6. According to Georgetown's high school principal, Eugene Griffiths, Georgetown High School attracts students from the whole West Coast. At Georgetown, students may major in drawing and painting, design, graphics, or sculpture. Mr. Griffiths said, "I attended a similar high school in New England just after the Vietnam War."

7. We expect to celebrate New Year's Eve again this year by streaming a movie of an old Broadway musical and by settling down in front of the television with some Pepsi and a box of Oreos.

8. After traveling all the way to the Pacific, the Corps of Discovery rode down the Missouri River going east on their way back to St. Louis.

9. This Irish linen tablecloth was bought at Walmart in the Emeryville Mall off Powell Street.

10. On our way to the West, we stopped at Yellowstone National Park in the northwest corner of the state of Wyoming.

Part II
Grammar Tests

Chapter 3
Grammar Pitfalls

This chapter describes twenty-four problems in grammar and usage—two dozen English language pitfalls that show up repeatedly on the SAT and ACT. No matter which test you take, you can count on being asked one or more times about the points of grammar illustrated by the first ten pitfalls. After that, there's less likelihood of a question, but not much less. The best way to prepare yourself, therefore, is to become familiar with all two dozen pitfalls and learn what to do about them.

24 Grammatical Pitfalls

1. Using an incompatible subject and verb
2. Shifting verb tenses
3. Using an incorrect verb form
4. Disregarding parallel structure
5. Using the wrong relative pronoun
6. Using a mismatched pronoun and antecedent
7. Making an ambiguous pronoun reference
8. Making a faulty comparison
9. Connecting sentences with commas
10. Using unrelated sentence parts
11. Misusing colons, semicolons, and commas
12. Misplacing modifiers
13. Dangling participles, a.k.a. dangling modifiers
14. Writing incomplete and run-on sentences
15. Shifting pronoun person
16. Choosing the wrong pronoun
17. Misusing coordinate and/or subordinate clauses
18. Wordiness
19. Using faulty idiom
20. Misusing adjectives and adverbs
21. Mixed sentence construction
22. Shifting noun and pronoun numbers
23. Using awkward language
24. Shifting from active to passive sentence construction

To Make the Most of This Chapter

As you read each "INCORRECT" sentence, try to identify the error and make the correction **before** reading the explanation.

Frankly, if you can identify all twenty-four errors right off the bat and can explain which rule of grammar they've broken, you probably don't need this book. Life is too short to waste time studying principles of grammar and usage that you've already mastered. So, instead of studying these pages, take your dog for a stroll or go see a movie. Or better yet, tutor a friend who can't tell a pronoun from a preposition.

Instructions:

Identify faulty grammar in each of the incorrect sentences and paragraphs. Then decide how to fix it.

PITFALL 1: **Using an incompatible subject and verb**

INCORRECT: Tony's talent in chess and weight lifting prove his mental and physical strength.

Explanation: The word *talent*, the subject of the sentence, is a singular noun. The verb *prove* is plural. Therefore, the subject and verb fail to agree. Correct the error by changing *talent* to *talents* or *prove* to *proves*.

CORRECTED: Tony's *talent* (singular noun) in chess and weight lifting *proves* (singular verb) both his mental and physical strength.

or

Tony's *talents* (plural noun) in chess and weight lifting *prove* (plural verb) both his mental and physical strength.

For details on **subject-verb agreement**, turn to page 32.

PITFALL 2: **Shifting verb tenses**

INCORRECT: On Interstate 80, a trooper pulls me over and gave me a speeding ticket.

Explanation: The verb *pulls* is in the present tense, but the verb *gave* shifts the action to the past tense. Correct the inconsistency either by changing *pulls* to *pulled* or *gave* to *gives*.

CORRECTED: On Interstate 80, a trooper *pulled* (past tense) me over and *gave* (past tense) me a speeding ticket.

or

On Interstate 80, a trooper *pulls* (present tense) me over and *gives* (present tense) me a speeding ticket.

For details on **shifting verb tenses**, turn to page 24.

PITFALL 3: **Using an incorrect verb form**

INCORRECT: After dinner, busboys clear the table and blowed out the candles.

Explanation: The past tense of the verb *clear* is *cleared* and the past tense of *blow* is *blew*. Therefore, the sentence includes an incorrect verb form. Correct the error by changing *clear* to *cleared* and *blowed* to *blew*.

CORRECTED: After dinner, busboys *cleared* the table and *blew* out the candles.

For details on **faulty verb forms**, turn to pages 27–30.

PITFALL 4: **Disregarding parallel structure**

> INCORRECT: **Many sports fans think that pro athletes are spoiled, earn too much money, and selfish.**

Explanation: Items in a series should be stated in the same grammatical form. That is, the way each item is phrased should be parallel to all the others. The words *spoiled* and *selfish* are adjectives, but *earn too much money* is a verb phrase. Correct the error by changing the verb phrase to an adjective.

> CORRECTED: **Many sports fans think that pro athletes are spoiled, overpaid, and selfish.**

For details on **faulty parallelism**, turn to page 68.

PITFALL 5: **Using the wrong relative pronoun**

> INCORRECT: **The doctor first treated the passengers which were most severely injured in the crash.**

Explanation: The relative pronouns *who* and *that* are used to refer to people; *which* refers to other things.

> CORRECTED: **The doctor first treated the passengers *who* (or *that*) were most severely injured in the crash.**

For details on **relative pronouns**, turn to page 16.

PITFALL 6: **Using a mismatched pronoun and antecedent**

> INCORRECT: **Budget cuts are forcing the library to reduce their hours.**

Explanation: The plural pronoun *their* improperly refers to the singular noun *library*. Because pronouns and their antecedents must agree in number, change *their* to *its* or *library* to *libraries*.

> CORRECTED: **Budget cuts are forcing the *library* (singular) to reduce *its* (singular) hours.**

> or

> **Budget cuts are forcing *libraries* (plural) to reduce *their* (plural) hours.**

For details on **pronoun-antecedent agreement**, turn to page 11.

PITFALL 7: **Making an ambiguous pronoun reference**

> INCORRECT: **The friendship between Joanne and Janie fell apart after she went away to college.**

Explanation: The pronoun *she* appears to refer to either *Joanne* or *Janie*. Because the reference is unclear, replace *she* with the name of one of the women.

> CORRECTED: **The friendship between Joanne and Janie fell apart after *Joanne* (or *Janie*) went away to college.**

For details on **faulty pronoun references** turn to page 13.

PITFALL 8: **Making a faulty comparison**

INCORRECT: **Rosie's score on the SAT was higher than Charlie.**

Explanation: Whoever wrote this sentence intended to compare Rosie's score on the SAT with Charlie's score. Instead, the writer compares Rosie's score with Charlie himself. A totally illogical comparison—don't you think? To correct a faulty comparison, be sure to express in parallel form whatever is being compared.

CORRECTED: *Rosie's score* **on the SAT was higher than** *Charlie's score.*

Or even more simply: *Rosie's score* **on the SAT was higher than** *Charlie's.*

Hint: Here's another way to avoid making a faulty comparison: Write a completely new sentence:

Rosie scored higher than Charlie on the SAT.

For details on **faulty comparisons,** see page 69. For details on **parallel structure,** turn to page 68.

PITFALL 9: **Connecting sentences with commas**

INCORRECT: **The concert on Saturday night was terrific, we got home very late.**

Explanation: This construction is made up of two independent sentences joined, or "spliced," by a comma. Correct the error by using a period and capital letter between the sentences, or replace the comma with a semicolon.

CORRECTED: **The concert on Saturday night was terrific. We got home very late.**

or

The concert on Saturday night was terrific; we got home very late.

For details on **comma splices** turn to page 67.

PITFALL 10: **Using unrelated sentence parts**

INCORRECT: **Eli Whitney invented the cotton gin, and who did so during the final years of the 18th century.**

Explanation: The first clause of the sentence states a fact about *Eli Whitney*, the grammatical subject. The second clause, beginning with *and*, adds a piece of relevant information but its construction is not grammatically related to the first clause. The phrase *and who did so* is meaningless and out of place in the context. Correct the error by revising the sentence.

CORRECTED: **Eli Whitney invented the cotton gin during the final years of the 18th century.**

For details on **mismatched sentence parts,** turn to Pitfall 21 on page 106.

PITFALL 11: **Misusing colons, semicolons, and commas**

> **1. INCORRECT: The carpenter brought with him his ususal tools; hammer, tape measure, spirit level, and a variety of saws.**

Explanation: A colon, rather than a semicolon, should be used to introduce a list or series.

> **CORRECTED: The carpenter brought with him his ususal tools: hammer, tape measure, spirit level, and a variety of saws.**

> **INCORRECT: The drone worked beautifully. It landed right on the target.**

Explanation: It's perfectly correct to separate two related independent clauses with a period, but when the second sentence literally explains or reiterates the first one, a colon creates a tighter link between them, especially when the writer opts to start the second clause with a lowercase letter.

> **CORRECTED: The drone worked beautifully: it landed right on the target.**

For details on **colons**, turn to pp. 87–88.

> **2. INCORRECT: Lucy wrote a children's story; which her little sister adored.**

Explanation: This construction uses a semicolon instead of a comma to separate an independent clause ("*Lucy wrote a children's story*") and a dependent clause ("*which her little sister adored*"). Because a semicolon serves the same function as a period—to separate two grammatically independent sentences—it may not be used as a comma substitute.

> **CORRECTED: Lucy wrote a children's story; her little sister adored it.**

> **3. INCORRECT: Mr. and Mrs. Bennett sent their son to grammar camp last summer and that's why Newt is so adept at using commas.**

Explanation: This compound sentence consists of two independent clauses, each with a different grammatical subject. Such sentences require a comma inserted before the coordinating conjunction (*and*).

> **CORRECTED: Mr. and Mrs. Bennett sent their son to grammar camp last summer, and that's why Newt is so adept at using commas.**

Compound sentences consisting of a pair of brief, closely related clauses, however, don't need a comma. For example: **At the wedding, Sam played the guitar and his sister sang.**

> **4. INCORRECT: At the time, I could hardly wait to hear singer, Miley Cyrus's new album.**

Explanation: A comma is incorrectly added to the noun phrase "*singer Miley Cyrus's*," a construction that requires no punctuation. Delete the comma.

> **CORRECTED: At the time, I could hardly wait to hear singer Miley Cyrus's new album.**

For details on **semicolon and comma errors**, turn to page 87. Also see **sentence structure**, page 74.

Grammar Tests

PITFALL 12: **Misplacing modifiers**

> INCORRECT: **The house stood on the corner which was painted red.**

Explanation: The words *which was painted red* are meant to describe the house but appear instead to describe the *corner*. The description, called a *modifier* because it changes (i.e., *modifies*) our image of the house, is too far removed from *house*, the noun it intends to modify. To correct the error move *house* and its modifier closer to each other.

> CORRECTED: **The house, which was painted red, stood on the corner.**

For details on **misplaced modifiers**, turn to page 42.

PITFALL 13: **Dangling participles, a.k.a. dangling modifiers**

> INCORRECT: **Running to biology class, the bell rang before Jake arrived.**

Explanation: A *participle* is a verb form ending in *-ing* in the present tense and is used to modify a noun or pronoun. Here, the participle *running* is meant to modify *Jake*, but it modifies *bell* instead, an error that conjures a bizarre image of a bell sprinting down the corridor. Correct the error by moving *Jake* closer to the participle.

> CORRECTED: **Running to biology class, Jake heard the bell ring before he arrived.**

For details on **dangling modifiers**, turn to page 66.

PITFALL 14: **Writing an incomplete sentence**

> INCORRECT: **Sergeant York, a hero of World War I and the subject of a popular movie that starred Gary Cooper.**

Explanation: This string of words is meant to be a complete sentence, but it is only a sentence fragment because it lacks a verb that goes with the grammatical subject, *Sergeant York*. Correct the error by deleting the comma and adding *was* or some other appropriate verb after the word *York*.

> CORRECTED: **Sergeant York was a hero of World War I and the subject of a popular movie that starred Gary Cooper.**

For details on **sentence fragments**, turn to page 64.

PITFALL 14 (CONTINUED): **Running sentences together**

> INCORRECT: **Maria aspires to be a ballerina she practices dancing five hours a day.**

Explanation: This construction is made up of two independent clauses that lack the punctuation needed to signal where the first clause ends and the second begins. Correct the error by separating *ballerina* and *she*. Use a semicolon, or a period and capital letter.

> CORRECTED: **Maria aspires to be a ballerina; she practices dancing five hours a day.**

or

> **Maria aspires to be a ballerina. She practices dancing five hours a day.**

Another solution: Subordinate one clause to the other, thereby creating a single sentence:

Because Maria aspires to be a ballerina, she practices dancing five hours a day.

For details on **run-on sentences**, turn to page 66.

PITFALL 15: **Shifting pronoun person**

> **INCORRECT: If I apply to the state university, you should hear from the admissions office within a month.**

Explanation: The sentence starts out using the first-person pronoun *I*, but then shifts into the second person with the pronoun *you*. Because the use of pronouns should be consistent throughout a sentence, change *you* to *I*.

> **CORRECTED: If I apply to the state university, I should hear from the admissions office within a month.**

For details on **shifts in pronoun person**, turn to page 9.

PITFALL 16: **Choosing the wrong pronoun**

> **INCORRECT: Between you and I, the cafeteria's food is awful.**

Explanation: Pronouns in phrases that begin with a preposition (in this instance, the preposition *between*), must be in the objective case. Because the pronoun *I* is in the nominative case, it is incorrect. Correct the error by changing *I* to *me*.

> **CORRECTED: Between you and me, the cafeteria's food is awful.**

For details on **the case of pronouns**, turn to page 6.

PITFALL 17: **Misusing coordinate and/or subordinate clauses**

> **INCORRECT: During rush hour a truck full of tomatoes turned over on the highway, but it caused a huge traffic jam.**

Explanation: This sentence consists of two coordinate clauses joined by *but*. The word *but* is a poor choice because it ordinarily introduces a contrast or contradictory idea: e.g., He's not a genius *but* he's not a total moron, either. Therefore, the coordinating conjunction *and* should replace *but*.

> **CORRECTED: During rush hour a truck full of tomatoes turned over on the highway, and it caused a huge traffic jam.**

Perhaps an even better solution: Turn one of the coordinate clauses into a subordinate clause, thereby tightening the sentence, as in:

> **When a truck full of tomatoes turned over on the highway during rush hour, it caused a huge traffic jam.**

For details on **faulty coordination and subordination**, turn to pages 48–49.

PITFALL 18: **Wordiness**

> **INCORRECT: Due to the fact that the building is scheduled to be built in the near future, we will revert back to Plan B in the event of a strike.**

Explanation: This sentence is wordy. (Technically, using too many words isn't a grammatical error, but verbosity is so closely tied to effective use of language that it deserves a place on the roster of pitfalls to watch out for.) *Due to the fact that* can easily be reduced to one word: *because*. Similarly, *in the near future* can be expressed as *soon*, and *in the event of* can be reduced to *if*. Also, the phrase *revert back* contains a redundancy, because by definition *revert* means "*to go back*."

> **CORRECTED: Because the building is scheduled to go up soon, Plan B will take effect if a strike occurs.** (This version is but one of many possibilities.)

For details on *wordiness*, turn to page 83.

PITFALL 19: Using faulty idiom

> **INCORRECT: Listening at the radio kept Jerry from falling asleep while driving.**

Explanation: The word *idiom* refers to idiomatic usage—that is, to the selection and sequence of words. In the given sentence, the use of *at* fails to conform to standard English usage. Correct the error by substituting *to* for *at*.

> **CORRECTED: Listening *to* the radio kept Jerry from falling asleep while driving.**

For details on **faulty idiom**, turn to page 78.

PITFALL 20: Misusing adjectives and adverbs

> **INCORRECT: Her father spoke sharp to Terry when she arrived home two hours late.**

Explanation: Because adverbs, not adjectives, modify verbs, the adjective *sharp* is misused. You can tell by asking the question, *How* did her father speak to Terry? The answer: He spoke *sharply*. The adverb *sharply*, therefore, modifies the verb *spoke*. Correct the error by substituting *sharply* for *sharp*.

> **CORRECTED: Her father spoke sharply to Terry when she arrived home two hours late.**

For details on **choosing adjectives and adverbs**, turn to page 43.

PITFALL 21: Mixed sentence construction

> **INCORRECT: Lilah's ambition is to be a lawyer and intends to go to law school after college.**

Explanation: Mixed sentence construction suggests that the writer, in finishing a sentence, ignored how it began. Here, the grammatical subject of the sentence, *ambition*, goes with the verb *is*. But the subject seems to have been forgotten in the second part of the sentence, because the verb *intends* stands without an appropriate subject. Correct the oversight with a compound sentence containing two subjects and two verbs, for example: "Lilah's ambition is to be a lawyer, and she intends to go to law school after college." For an even better sentence, subordinate one of the clauses:

> **CORRECTED: Lilah, who aspires to be a lawyer** (subordinate clause)**, intends to go to law school after college.**

For details on **mixed construction**, turn to Pitfall 10 on page 102.

PITFALL 22: **Shifting noun and pronoun numbers**

> INCORRECT: **Reading to children every day encourages them to grow up as a literate, book-loving adult.**

Explanation: The noun *children* and the pronoun *them* are plural. But the noun *adult*, which refers to both *children* and *them*, is singular. Because both nouns and the pronoun should be consistent in number, delete the *a* and change *adult* to *adults*.

> CORRECTED: **Reading to children every day encourages them to grow up as literate, book-loving adults.**

For details on **shifts between noun and pronoun numbers**, turn to page 10.

PITFALL 23: **Using awkward language**

> INCORRECT: **Although its being informative, the film ignored the basic causes of alcohol abuse.**

Explanation: An awkwardly worded sentence can be grammatically sound but still in need of repair. Revise the awkward phrase "*Although its being informative*" to convey the same meaning in standard English.

> CORRECTED: **Despite its informative content, the film ignored the basic causes of alcohol abuse.** (This version is but one of many possibilities.)

For details on **awkwardness and standard syntax**, turn to pages 77–78.

PITFALL 24: **Shifting from active to passive sentence construction**

> INCORRECT: **Cindy yearns to go to an out-of-state private college, but the tuition is unable to be afforded by her family.**

Explanation: The first clause is written in the active voice because *Cindy*, its grammatical subject, performs the action, *yearns*. The second clause is in the passive voice, however, because its subject, *tuition*, is not the performer of the action. Technically, the sentence is correct, but the shift from active to passive voice is a stylistic weakness that buries *family*, the performer of the action, in a prepositional phrase. Keep the spotlight on *family* by making it the subject.

> CORRECTED: **Cindy yearns to go to an out-of-state private college, but her family can't afford the tuition.**

For details on **active and passive construction**, turn to page 72.

Chapter 4

SAT Grammar Questions

The SAT is a test of verbal and math skills. It takes three hours to complete. One section of the exam—the 35-minute long "Writing and Language Test"—includes questions on English grammar.

> Your mastery of grammar is also tested if you choose to write the optional SAT Essay, administered during a 50-minute block of time following the scheduled 3-hour exam. For details, turn to Part III of this book.

Questions on the SAT's Writing and Language Test pertain to revising and editing the text of four reading passages, one each drawn from the fields of history/social studies, the humanities, science, and careers. Each passage is accompanied by 11 multiple-choice questions—or a total of 44 questions. Of those, 20 relate primarily to problems of writing style, coherence, the sequence and development of ideas, and to vocabulary in context. The remaining **24 questions are devoted specifically to English grammar.**

In other words, grammar, while not a major component of the entire SAT, still counts significantly in determining your verbal score.

ANSWERING THE QUESTIONS

Each question consists of an underlined word or group of words that may need to be corrected. Because the sum of potential grammar problems far exceeds the number of questions on the SAT, you'll need to know far more about grammar than you'll actually use on the test. To prepare, therefore, be sure to review all the so-called pitfalls discussed in Chapter 3.

Every question on the test comes with four possible answers: A, B, C, or D. Your job is to decide which of the four choices best conforms to the conventions of standard written English. Choice A is always "NO CHANGE," meaning, of course, that the underlined segment is correct as it is.

Sample Questions

Here is a handful of sample questions based on sentences selected at random from a variety of 400-to-500-word passages (not reprinted here)—the kind found on the Writing and Language Test.

1. At our country's constitutional convention in Philadelphia, some of the framers' core values, from freedom of speech to a representative form of government, <u>coming from</u> ancient Greek culture.

   (A) NO CHANGE
   (B) they came from
   (C) came from
   (D) they have come from

   Choice C is the best answer because it provides a verb in the past tense to create a grammatically complete and coherent sentence.

   Choice A is incorrect because it is a sentence fragment, resulting from a faulty choice of verbs. The *-ing* verb form may not be used as the main verb in a sentence without a helping verb, as in *was coming* or *will be coming*.

   Choices B and D are wrong because the clause beginning with the pronoun *they* is grammatically unrelated to the previous part of the sentence.

2. After the magnitude 6.7 earthquake, the Red Cross provided food and water as well as care for <u>the injured and comfort to the dying</u>.

   (A) NO CHANGE
   (B) the injured and also comforted the dying
   (C) the injured, they also gave comfort to the dying
   (D) the injured. In addition, comforted the dying

   Choice A is the best answer because it contains a series of accurately punctuated parallel phrases and is a complete grammatical sentence.

   Choice B is incorrect because the phrase beginning with *also* is not grammatically parallel to the two preceding phrases that name the efforts of the Red Cross.

   Choice C is wrong because it contains a comma splice. A period or a semicolon is needed to separate independent clauses.

   Choice D is not the best answer because the construction beginning with "in addition ..." is a sentence fragment.

3. Public transportation in the suburbs and outlying areas is generally not as convenient and reliable <u>as getting around</u> in the city.

   (A) NO CHANGE
   (B) as they are
   (C) as those in
   (D) as it is

Choice D is the best answer because the pronoun *it* agrees in number with its antecedent *transportation* and enables a valid contrast to be made between urban and suburban transportation.

Choice A is incorrect because *transportation* (a noun) is being compared to *getting around* (a gerund), an illogical and, therefore, faulty comparison.

Choices B and C are wrong because the plural words *these* and *those* do not agree in number with their singular antecedent *transportation*.

4.   The Southwest's center for art and music, <u>Santa Fe, an annual destination for visitors by the thousand</u>.

(A) NO CHANGE
(B) Santa Fe, annually attracts thousands of visitors
(C) annually, thousands of visitors flock to Santa Fe
(D) Santa Fe, thousands of visitors flock there every year

Choice B is the best answer because it is a complete sentence containing an independent clause properly modified by the phrase *the Southwest's center for art and music*.

Choice A is incorrect because it lacks a verb for the subject *Santa Fe*, resulting in a sentence fragment.

Choice C is wrong because of a misplaced modifier. The phrase "*center for art and music*" should modify *Santa Fe*, not *thousands*.

Choice D is not the best answer because the clause "*thousands of visitors . . .*" lacks a grammatical relationship with the earlier part of the sentence.

5.   Is it certain that the grand opening of the new high-speed by-pass around the city, scheduled for this weekend, <u>would be</u> delayed at least two weeks?

(A) NO CHANGE
(B) will have been
(C) will be
(D) had been

Choice C is the best answer because the sentence requires a verb in the simple future tense to achieve its purpose—to ask a question about a future event. Choice A is incorrect because in the context the future conditional tense of the verb is incompatible with the purpose of the sentence—to ask a question about a future event.

Choice B is wrong because in the context the verb in the future conditional tense is incompatible with the purpose of the sentence—to ask about a future event.

Choice D is wrong because the past perfect tense of the verb is not appropriate in the context, which requires a verb in the future tense.

TESTS FOR PRACTICE

Note: The passages in the four practice tests that follow are slightly shorter than those on the actual SAT Evidence-Based Writing and Language Test. The actual test also contains questions on writing style, coherence, development, and so forth. In these tests for practice, however, all questions relate specifically to problems in grammar and usage.

During the SAT Writing and Language Test you will have 35 minutes to answer 44 questions—an average of 48 seconds each. Because grammar questions require less reading and generally take less time than questions on organization, sequence of ideas, and writing style, plan to spend no more than 30 seconds on each of the 24 grammar questions on each test. To simulate actual SAT testing conditions, set a time limit of 12 to 15 minutes to complete each practice test.

PRACTICE TEST A

Directions: Carefully read each of the following passages. Each contains underlined and numbered segments that may contain a grammatical usage or mechanical error. To answer each question, choose the alternative that expresses the underlined word or words in standard written English. If you decide that no error exists, choose (A), indicating that NO CHANGE is necessary.

Once you have decided on the answer, fill in the blank space on the answer sheet that corresponds with your choice.

Time limit: 12–15 minutes

ANSWER SHEET

1. Ⓐ Ⓑ Ⓒ Ⓓ   7. Ⓐ Ⓑ Ⓒ Ⓓ   13. Ⓐ Ⓑ Ⓒ Ⓓ   19. Ⓐ Ⓑ Ⓒ Ⓓ

2. Ⓐ Ⓑ Ⓒ Ⓓ   8. Ⓐ Ⓑ Ⓒ Ⓓ   14. Ⓐ Ⓑ Ⓒ Ⓓ   20. Ⓐ Ⓑ Ⓒ Ⓓ

3. Ⓐ Ⓑ Ⓒ Ⓓ   9. Ⓐ Ⓑ Ⓒ Ⓓ   15. Ⓐ Ⓑ Ⓒ Ⓓ   21. Ⓐ Ⓑ Ⓒ Ⓓ

4. Ⓐ Ⓑ Ⓒ Ⓓ   10. Ⓐ Ⓑ Ⓒ Ⓓ   16. Ⓐ Ⓑ Ⓒ Ⓓ   22. Ⓐ Ⓑ Ⓒ Ⓓ

5. Ⓐ Ⓑ Ⓒ Ⓓ   11. Ⓐ Ⓑ Ⓒ Ⓓ   17. Ⓐ Ⓑ Ⓒ Ⓓ   23. Ⓐ Ⓑ Ⓒ Ⓓ

6. Ⓐ Ⓑ Ⓒ Ⓓ   12. Ⓐ Ⓑ Ⓒ Ⓓ   18. Ⓐ Ⓑ Ⓒ Ⓓ   24. Ⓐ Ⓑ Ⓒ Ⓓ

Questions 1–6 are based on the following passage.

A Walk in the Park

Of great interest to social workers and mental health specialists are those periods of moodiness, the doldrums, **[1]** <u>stress; and</u> spells of ill humor that strike almost everyone from time to time. The length and intensity of such episodes **[2]** <u>varies from person to person</u>. Observers have noted that people who dwell in cities seem to be **[3]** <u>at a greater risk</u> of depression and brooding than those living outside urban centers.

To check the validity of that observation, researchers at Stanford University conducted a study of the psychological effects of city life. Among their findings was that residents of cities apparently have a lower risk of psychological problems when they have regular access to a park or other natural **[4]** <u>environment, which have</u> the effect of reducing the level of stress hormones.

Although nature's salutary effects have long been appreciated, the reason it tends to reduce anxiety remains an intriguing question. Stanford's research psychologists, theorizing that blood flow in a certain part of the brain called the subgenual prefrontal cortex might provide an answer, recruited as subjects for an experiment more than three dozen healthy city dwellers. All were asked to fill out a questionnaire designed to reveal the level of their state of mind and sense of well-being. The flow of blood in **[5]** <u>all the subject's subgenual prefrontal cortex</u> was also measured.

The volunteers were then instructed to take a solitary walk outside for ninety minutes, half of them on streets alongside a noisy and busy highway, the others in quiet, leafy areas of the Stanford campus. Upon returning, they again completed the questionnaire and had their brains

1. (A) NO CHANGE
   (B) stress: and
   (C) stress, and
   (D) stress, and,

2. (A) NO CHANGE
   (B) varies among people
   (C) vary person to person
   (D) vary from person to person

3. (A) NO CHANGE
   (B) at great risk
   (C) at the greatest risk
   (D) at more greater risk

4. (A) NO CHANGE
   (B) environment, that has
   (C) environment, in which
   (D) environment that has

5. (A) NO CHANGE
   (B) all the subject's subgenual prefrontal cortexes
   (C) the subgenual prefrontal cortex of each subject
   (D) all the subgenual prefrontal cortexes of the subjects

scanned. The results were not unexpected: Those who walked near the highway showed virtually no change in their state of mind and sense of well-being. In contrast, those who walked in the woods had their mood lifted, their burdens eased, their peace of mind heightened. In other words, the study concluded that the time one spends outside in nature apparently has positive consequences [6] <u>for your mental health</u>.

Questions 7–12 are based on the following passage.

Ice

Back in the 1830's, a well-to-do young Bostonian, Frederic Tudor, had what he hoped would be a bright idea for increasing his family's wealth. Like other affluent families in the northern states, the Tudors long enjoyed the frozen water from the pond of their country estate. They stored blocks of frozen lake water in icehouses. Their two-hundred pound ice cubes would remain marvelously unmelted until the hot summer months arrived, and a new ritual began: ice fragments chipped off the blocks freshened drinks, served [7] <u>to be</u> a coolant of baths during heat waves, and helped in the making of ice cream.

The idea of block ice surviving intact for months without the benefits of artificial refrigeration sounds unlikely to the modern ear. We are used to ice preserved indefinitely thanks to the many deep-freeze technologies of today's world. But ice in the wild is another matter. Unlike an occasional glacier, [8] <u>we assume that a block of ice can't survive longer than an hour in summer heat, much less months</u>.

But Tudor knew from personal experience that a large block of ice could last well into the depths of summer if it was kept out of the sun—or at least it

6. (A) NO CHANGE
   (B) on your mental health
   (C) on one's mental health
   (D) for their mental health

7. (A) NO CHANGE
   (B) as
   (C) like
   (D) for

8. (A) NO CHANGE
   (B) the assumption is that a block of ice can't survive longer than an hour, much less months, in summer heat
   (C) a block of ice, we assume, can't survive longer than an hour, much less months, in summer heat
   (D) our assumption is that in summer heat the survival rate of a block of ice is no longer than an hour, much less months

would last through the late spring of New England. And that knowledge planted the seed of an idea in his mind, an idea that [9] would ultimately cost him his sanity, his fortune, and his freedom—before it made him an immensely wealthy man.

At the age of seventeen, Tudor, along with his brother John, voyaged to the Caribbean. The trip was a disaster. Suffering [10] through the inescapable humidity and heat of the tropics while wearing the stifling clothing of nineteenth-century gentlemen, John fell ill with tuberculosis, which killed him six months later. Meanwhile, Frederic had a radical—some said "preposterous"—idea. If he could somehow transport ice from the frozen north to the West Indies, there would be an immense market for it. Ice, nearly worthless in Boston, would be priceless in Havana and Martinique.

By experimenting with different techniques to keep ice from melting, Tudor discovered that sawdust, cheaply and readily available from New England sawmills, made a brilliant insulator for ice. Blocks layered on top of each other with sawdust between them would last twice as long as unprotected ice. Moreover, he figured out that ice packed in double-shelled containers, with a layer of air between the shells would keep ice intact far longer than it would take to transport it to the Caribbean. At first, the business failed miserably because the citizens of the island didn't know about ice and hadn't a clue about what to do with it. Gradually, however, the people [11] whom try it began to see its it possibilities and spread the word. Soon, sales of ice grew brisk, and fifteen years after his original hunch, Tudor's ice trade finally [12] turned a profit, therefore, when Tudor expanded his business to India and South America, he began to amass a large fortune.

9. (A) NO CHANGE
   (B) ultimately costed
   (C) ultimately costs
   (D) had ultimately cost

10. (A) NO CHANGE
    (B) about
    (C) from
    (D) against

11. (A) NO CHANGE
    (B) whom tries
    (C) that try
    (D) who tried

12. (A) NO CHANGE
    (B) profit, when
    (C) profit, but when
    (D) profit: so, when

Questions 13–18 are based on the following passage.

Stagefright

Although it is pervasive in some lines of work, not a great deal is known about the affliction known as stagefright. Those who experience it range from veteran performing artists to many of us who [13] <u>had</u> rarely, if ever, set foot upon the stage. Recently, in research conducted to determine the causes and consequences of [14] <u>stagefright. Eight</u> hundred college students at the University of Nebraska were asked to identify their three most intense fears from a list that included flying, heights, money problems, enclosed spaces, and speaking in public. By far, speaking to a group in public beat all the other fears, including fear of death.

The symptoms of stagefright are far more evident than its causes, which remain somewhat elusive. Someone facing an audience may experience uncontrollable anxiety caused by the adrenal glands pumping the hormone epinephrine into the bloodstream. [15] <u>As a result</u>, muscles grow tense, sweat glands erupt, the body trembles, the heart pounds, the mouth dries up, breathing becomes labored, and dizziness and nausea may occur.

Not only are such responses similar to those suffered by, say, a primitive man facing a threat from a ferocious animal, [16] <u>but also resemble</u> panic attacks experienced by soldiers about to go into battle for the first time.

Stage-frightened performers report feeling exposed, or as one said, "like a snail having its shell ripped off." Even successful, world-renowned actors, musicians, and dancers believe that anguish grows from their fear of failure, regardless of how often they've successfully completed the same very performance in the past. To cite one [17] <u>example, the film actor, Daniel Day Lewis</u> played the part

13. (A) NO CHANGE
    (B) did
    (C) would have
    (D) DELETE the underlined word

14. (A) NO CHANGE
    (B) stagefright: eight
    (C) stagefright, eight
    (D) stagefright; Eight

15. (A) NO CHANGE
    (B) Similarly
    (C) Besides
    (D) As a matter of fact

16. (A) NO CHANGE
    (B) but also resembling
    (C) also resembling
    (D) but they also resemble

17. (A) NO CHANGE
    (B) example, the film actor Daniel Day Lewis,
    (C) example the film actor Daniel Day Lewis,
    (D) example, the film actor, Daniel Day Lewis,

of Hamlet on stage. Part way through the play he walked out of the theater, scared not by the ghost of his father but by visions of making a fool of [18] himself. He has only acted in movies ever since.

The roster of other famous personalities who suffer from stagefright contains such names as Mel Gibson, Barbra Streisand, and Adele, who claims to puke a lot before going on stage. Also add Carly Simon and Jay Z, who feels "naked" in front of his fans. Even icons of high culture—the late Luciano Pavarotti and Vladimir Horowitz, for instance— endured their personal version of hell before performances. It is also said that both Thomas Jefferson and Gandhi were mortally afraid of public speaking.

Questions 19-24 are based on the following passage.

Eight Glasses of Water

To work well, the human body needs a certain amount of water and other liquids called electrolytes. Fluids in the body are lost through perspiration, urine, bowel movements, and, believe it or not, breathing. If you lose an overabundance of fluids without replenishing them, you may become dehydrated and suffer from weakness, dry mouth, dizziness, [19] you feel nauseous, a fever, and several other unpleasant sensations.

For some time, authorities claimed that good health could be generally assured and dehydration avoided in hot weather by drinking eight glasses of water daily. Research studies, one of them in 2012 by the *Annals of Nutrition and Metabolism*, declared that 66 percent of France's population was not drinking the recommended amount of water per day. [20] Likewise, the journal *Public Health Nutrition*, drew similar conclusions about residents

18. Which choice most effectively combines the two sentences in the underlined segment?
   (A) himself, thereby acting in movies only ever since
   (B) himself, and he has acted only in movies ever since
   (C) himself, and this has caused him to act ever since in movies only
   (D) himself, and ever since this experience, caused him to act only in movies

19. (A) NO CHANGE
    (B) nausea, a fever
    (C) feeling nausea, feverish
    (D) feel nausea and feverish

20. (A) NO CHANGE
    (B) For instance,
    (C) Similar,
    (D) More directly,

of Los Angeles and New York, suggesting that the problem of dehydration had become a virtual epidemic, with millions of people at risk. Lack of a significant fact—that the research leading to these conclusions [21] were paid for by Nestlé Waters, a company in the business of selling bottled water—has raised some doubts about the seriousness of the problem.

In other words, the eight-glasses-of-water-a-day principle is open to question. How the idea got started is not altogether clear, but over half a century ago, the Food and Nutrition [22] Board then an affiliate of the U.S. Department of Agriculture recommended that people drink 2.5 liters of water a day. Their recommendation made headlines, but one important detail had been left out of the agency's report—that close to recommended amount of water was contained in foods, including fruits and vegetables, and beverages of all kinds.

Since then, moreover, no dependable scientific proof has shown that dehydration is a real threat to anyone who drinks less than eight glasses of water a day. The body is equipped with a finely tuned alarm system that tells you to drink liquid long before actual dehydration begins to set in. Real dehydration—the kind that makes you sick because of extreme exercise, sweating, illness, or even the inability to drink—is undeniably a serious condition, but there are no studies literally proving that eight glasses of water a day will help maintain a person's health.

21. (A) NO CHANGE
    (B) have been paid
    (C) were paid
    (D) was financed

22. (A) NO CHANGE
    (B) Board then an affiliate of the U.S. Department of Agriculture,
    (C) Board, then an affiliate of the U.S. Department of Agriculture,
    (D) Board, then an affiliate of the U.S. Department of Agriculture

Nevertheless, adherents of drinking more water are seriously dedicated to their cause. Even the White House, recently [**23**] <u>campaigning in behalf of</u> greater consumption of drinking water, declaring that four out of ten Americans consume less than half of the recommended amount of water every day.

Generalizations about how much water everyone needs, however, do not hold water (*pun intended*). How much water [**24**] <u>an individual</u> should drink depends to a large degree on what they eat, the climate where they live, what they do each day, their size, and how physically active they are.

23. (A) NO CHANGE
    (B) campaigns for
    (C) campaigning for
    (D) campaigned on behalf

24. (A) NO CHANGE
    (B) the people
    (C) people
    (D) a human

ANSWER KEY

1. C	4. B	7. B	10. C	13. D	16. D	19. B	22. C
2. D	5. C	8. C	11. D	14. C	17. B	20. A	23. D
3. A	6. C	9. A	12. C	15. A	18. B	21. D	24. C

Total Correct: _____

SCALE

Correct Answers	Rating
20–24	Superior
15–19	Good
9–14	Fair
0–8	Poor

ANSWER EXPLANATIONS

Note: Although some choices contain multiple errors, only one or two major errors are explained for each incorrect choice.

1. **Choice C is the best answer** because it uses proper punctuation for items listed in a series. In this instance, the items are nouns: *moodiness, doldrums, stress*, and *spells*.

    Choices A and B are incorrect because neither recognizes that the nouns are part of a series. Because a comma is used after *moodiness*, a colon and a semicolon should not be used after *stress*. Choice D is wrong because the comma after and is unnecessary and confusing.

2. **Choice D is the best answer** because the plural verb *vary* agrees in number with its plural subject, *length and intensity*.

    Choices A and B are incorrect because the singular verb *varies* fails to agree with the plural subject, *length and intensity*. Choice C is not the best answer because the omission of the preposition *from* causes the phrase to deviate from standard English idiom.

3. **Choice A is the best answer** because it uses an adjective in the comparative degree to make a logical comparison between two categories of people.

    Choice B is incorrect because it fails to include an adjective that completes the comparison between two groups of people. Choice C is wrong because it improperly uses an adjective in the superlative degree to compare two groups of people. (Such adjectives are meant for comparing three or more things.) Choice D is not the best answer because the intensifier *more* creates a redundancy with an adjective in the comparative degree. Omit *more* or change *greater* to *great*.

4. **Choice B is the best answer** because it uses commas to properly punctuate a nonrestrictive clause—*i.e.*, a subordinate clause not essential to the meaning of the sentence.

    Choice A is incorrect because the plural verb *have* fails to agree in number with the singular subject, *park*. Choice C is wrong because the segment following the comma lacks a verb and, therefore, is a sentence fragment. Choice D is not the best answer because the absence of a comma between the words *environment* and *that* creates a restrictive clause that clouds the meaning of the sentence by suggesting that residents of cities will reduce the risk of psychological problems only in those parks and other environments that can reduce stress.

5. **Choice C is the best answer** because it correctly conveys the idea that each subject in the experiment is an individual with one prefrontal cortex.

   Choice A is incorrect because the placement of the apostrophe creates a singular possessive noun in a context where a plural possessive noun is needed. Choice B is wrong because it uses a singular possessive noun where a plural possessive is needed. Using the plural noun *cortexes* introduces the bizarre notion that each person has more than one subgenual prefrontal cortex. Choice D is not the best answer because it creates the ambiguous idea that each subject may have more than one subgenual prefrontal cortex.

6. **Choice C is the best answer** because the use of the impersonal pronoun *one* is consistent with the sentence's other pronouns.

   Choices A and B are incorrect because of a shift from the use of the impersonal pronoun *one* to the second-person pronoun *you*. Choice D is wrong because the plural pronoun *their* does not agree with its singular antecedent *one*.

7. **Choice B is the best answer** because it provides the grammatically standard conjunction *as* to connect the verb *served* and the noun *coolant*.

   Choice A is incorrect because the infinitive form of *to be* creates a grammatically faulty verb construction: *serves to be*. Choices C and D are wrong because in the context they do not conform to standard English usage.

8. **Choice C is the best answer** because it is the only choice that is a grammatically standard and coherent sentence. The phrase *Unlike an occasional glacier* is placed where it properly modifies the block of ice.

Choices A, B, and D are incorrect because the phrase *Unlike an occasional glacier* is misplaced. It modifies *we* in A and an *assumption* in B and D, creating a meaning that the writer could not have intended.

9. **Choice A is the best answer** because in the context it offers the correct form of the verb *cost*.

   Choice B is incorrect because *costed* is not standard English. Choice C is wrong because it shifts the tense of the verbs in the sentence from past to present. Choice D is not the best answer because it inappropriately shifts the verb tense in the sentence from the past to the past perfect.

10. **Choice C is the best answer** because it provides the correct preposition in the context.

    Choices A, B, and D are incorrect because each is a preposition that fails to conform to standard English usage. A person can suffer *through* heat and humidity but not *about*, *from*, or *against* heat and humidity.

11. **Choice D is the best answer** because it contains the relative pronoun and verb that create a coherent sentence in standard English. The relative pronoun *who* refers to the subject *the people*, and the plural verb *try* agrees in number with the plural noun *people*.

    Choices A and B are incorrect because *whom* is a relative pronoun used as an object, and the noun *people* is a subject performing an action (i.e., trying the ice). Furthermore, in both choices, the verbs shift the tense of the passage from the past to the present. Choice C is also wrong because of the shift in verb tense from past to present.

12. **Choice C is the best answer** because it is a syntactically and grammatically correct sentence.

    Choices A and B are incorrect because both of them contain a comma splice. They use a comma to connect two separate, independent sentences. Choice D is not the best answer because a colon is used improperly. Colons may separate two independent clauses when the second clause restates the first in different words, but not when two clauses are otherwise related.

13. **Choice D is the best answer** because the omission of *had* allows the present tense of the verb to be maintained throughout the sentence.

    Choices A, B, and D are incorrect because each contains a verb that is inconsistent with the present tense, in which the sentence is cast.

14. **Choice C is the best answer** because it provides the proper punctuation to create a complete compound sentence that properly links a subordinate clause with an independent clause.

    Choice A is incorrect because *Recently . . . stagefright* is a sentence fragment. Choices B and D are wrong because each contains faulty punctuation. Neither a colon nor a semicolon may be used between the subordinate and the independent clauses of a compound sentence.

15. **Choice A is the best answer** because it pro-vides a transitional phrase that communicates the effects of adrenaline in the body.

    Choices B, C, and D are incorrect because each offers an inappropriate transition from the ideas in the previous sentence.

16. **Choice D is the best answer** because it contains the pronoun *they*, a necessary reference to *such responses* in the previous clause.

    Choices A, B, and C are incorrect because each lacks a necessary subject, such as a noun or a pronoun.

17. **Choice B is the best answer** because it provides the punctuation that clearly places the noun phrase *film actor Daniel Day Lewis*

as an appositive identifying the example being cited by the writer.

    Choices A, C, and D are incorrect because each fails to open and close the uninterrupted appositive noun phrase *film actor Daniel Day Lewis* with commas.

18. **Choice B is the best answer** because it consists of a clear, grammatically accurate statement of the actor's work since he walked out of the theater.

    Choice A is incorrect because it uses a transitional adverb that fails to accurately reflect the relationship between the ideas drawn from the two sentences. Choice C is not the best answer because the pronoun *this* lacks a specific antecedent. Choice D is wrong because the verb *caused* has no discernible subject.

19. **Choice B is the best answer** because the nouns *nausea* and *fever* parallel the other nouns in the series.

    Choices A, C, and D are incorrect because each fails to conform to the parallel structure of the noun series, either by using an adjective or by including an unnecessary subject (*you*) or verb (*feel, feeling*).

20. **Choice A is the best answer** because it uses an appropriate transitional word to introduce a sentence containing an example similar to that described in the previous sentence.

    Choices B and D are incorrect because neither offers a logical transition to the context that precedes or follows the phrase. Choice C is wrong because it uses the word *similar*, an adjective, instead of an adverb to provide a transition between sentences. In addition, the word *similar* is identical to a word used later in the sentence, thereby creating undesirable repetition.

21. **Choice D is the best answer** because the singular verb *was* agrees in number with its singular subject *research*.

Choices A and C are incorrect because both use the plural verb *were,* which fails to agree in number with the singular subject *research.* (The word *for* in Choice A has no bearing on the correct answer.) Choice B is wrong because the present perfect tense of the verb is inconsistent with the past tense, the tense in which the sentence is cast.

22. **Choice C is the best answer** because it provides commas to offset the nonrestrictive clause, *then an affiliate of the U.S. Department of Agriculture.*

    Choices A, B, and D are wrong because none of them contains the punctuation that properly separates the nonrestrictive clause, *then an affiliate of the U.S. Department of Agriculture,* from the clause that begins with *but over half a century . . . .*

23. **Choice D is the best answer** because it provides a verb in the correct tense to create a coherent, grammatical sentence.

Choices A and C are incorrect because both lack a verb to make the sentence complete. Choice B is not the best answer because it uses a present-tense verb instead of a verb in the past tense, the tense in which that section of the passage is written.

24. **Choice C is the best answer** because it is a plural noun that serves as the antecedent of the plural pronoun *they* that is repeated several times later in the sentence.

    Choices A and D are incorrect because both are singular nouns that fail to agree with the plural pronoun *they* to which the nouns are meant to refer. Choice B is not the best answer because the use of the definite article *the* limits the reference to a certain specific group rather than people in general, or literally *everyone,* as stated in the previous sentence.

PRACTICE TEST B

Directions: Carefully read each of the following passages. Each contains underlined and numbered segments that may contain a grammatical usage or mechanical error. To answer each question, choose the alternative that expresses the underlined word or words in standard written English. If you decide that no error exists, choose (A), indicating that NO CHANGE is necessary.

Once you have decided on the answer, fill in the blank space on the answer sheet that corresponds with your choice.

Time limit: 12–15 minutes

ANSWER SHEET

1. Ⓐ Ⓑ Ⓒ Ⓓ
2. Ⓐ Ⓑ Ⓒ Ⓓ
3. Ⓐ Ⓑ Ⓒ Ⓓ
4. Ⓐ Ⓑ Ⓒ Ⓓ
5. Ⓐ Ⓑ Ⓒ Ⓓ
6. Ⓐ Ⓑ Ⓒ Ⓓ

7. Ⓐ Ⓑ Ⓒ Ⓓ
8. Ⓐ Ⓑ Ⓒ Ⓓ
9. Ⓐ Ⓑ Ⓒ Ⓓ
10. Ⓐ Ⓑ Ⓒ Ⓓ
11. Ⓐ Ⓑ Ⓒ Ⓓ
12. Ⓐ Ⓑ Ⓒ Ⓓ

13. Ⓐ Ⓑ Ⓒ Ⓓ
14. Ⓐ Ⓑ Ⓒ Ⓓ
15. Ⓐ Ⓑ Ⓒ Ⓓ
16. Ⓐ Ⓑ Ⓒ Ⓓ
17. Ⓐ Ⓑ Ⓒ Ⓓ
18. Ⓐ Ⓑ Ⓒ Ⓓ

19. Ⓐ Ⓑ Ⓒ Ⓓ
20. Ⓐ Ⓑ Ⓒ Ⓓ
21. Ⓐ Ⓑ Ⓒ Ⓓ
22. Ⓐ Ⓑ Ⓒ Ⓓ
23. Ⓐ Ⓑ Ⓒ Ⓓ
24. Ⓐ Ⓑ Ⓒ Ⓓ

Grammar Tests: SAT

Questions 1–6 are based on the following passage.

Watercolor Painting

In its early years, the art of watercolor was largely associated with landscape painting and was thought to be less important than, say, oil painting or sculpture. Essentially, it was relegated to a lower status where it was practiced by architects, mapmakers, [1] illustrators; and also marginally talented amateurs—mostly young society women in finishing schools.

Starting late in the 1800s, however, technical advancements created many new colors. Paint began to be sold in metal tubes, and watercolor painters started developing innovative and sophisticated techniques: quickening their brush strokes, [2] applied transparent washes instead of thick opaque paint, and preserving the white of the paper to simulate light and reflections.

By the early nineteenth century watercolor had come into its own as one of the art world's essential mediums. In large measure, the direct influence of J.M.W. [3] Turner, a British painter celebrated for executing large-scale, colorful, watercolor works made this happen. Hoping to enjoy and learn from Turner's work, [4] London's National Gallery of London attracted artists from around the world, among them, Winslow Homer, who adapted some of Turner's techniques and arguably would become America's most famous and adored watercolor painter. Also, the renowned John Singer [5] Sargent. He experimented with quick application of paint on paper, enabling him to capture the transparency, light, and movement afforded by the medium.

Public appreciation of water-based paint exploded in the early 20th century as a new generation of younger artists adopted watercolor as their main

1. (A) NO CHANGE
   (B) illustrators: and
   (C) illustrators, and,
   (D) illustrators, and

2. (A) NO CHANGE
   (B) applying
   (C) they applied
   (D) made use of

3. (A) NO CHANGE
   (B) Turner a British painter celebrated for executing large-scale, colorful, watercolor works,
   (C) Turner, a British painter celebrated for executing large-scale, colorful, watercolor works,
   (D) Turner, a British painter, celebrated for executing large-scale, colorful, watercolor, works

4. (A) NO CHANGE
   (B) London's National Gallery became an attraction to artists worldwide,
   (C) attractions at London's National Gallery attracted artists from around the world,
   (D) artists from around the world were attracted to London's National Gallery,

5. (A) NO CHANGE
   (B) Sargent, whose experiments
   (C) Sargent experimented
   (D) Sargent; he tried experimenting

medium. The historic 1913 International Exhibition of Modern Art—also known as the Armory Show—defined modernism for much of the century that followed. The show included watercolor works by artists who are remembered and honored for their distinctive watercolor [6] paintings; Charles Demuth, John Marin, and Charles Burchfield.

6. (A) NO CHANGE
   (B) paintings; and their names were
   (C) paintings:
   (D) paintings: being

Questions 7–12 are based on the following passage.

Home Alone

How do eight-, nine-, and ten-year-olds feel when they come home from school to an empty apartment or house? Do they feel lonely, deserted, resentful, and angry? Or do they feel proud, trusted, responsible, independent, and all grown up? Or doesn't it matter very much one way or the other?

One of the most revealing answers, albeit unscientific, came about as an accidental outcome of a survey of fourth-to-sixth grade children by *Sprint*, a language arts magazine [7] in which they asked readers to respond in writing to this theme: "Think of a situation that is scary to you. How do you handle your fear?" The magazine received an overwhelming response—a total of more than 7,000 [8] letters, altogether the major portion of which dealt with the fear of being home alone after school.

Other studies, more carefully constructed, support the findings suggested by the responses to *Sprint*: [9] Sociologists Long and Long reported that while their parents are working intruders are feared by many children. Some 32 percent of the males and 41 percent of the females reported that they worried when they had to stay home without an adult. Moreover, 20 percent of both boys and girls disclosed [10] to being afraid to go out to play.

7. (A) NO CHANGE
   (B) where they asked
   (C) they asked
   (D) that asked

8. (A) NO CHANGE
   (B) letters. The
   (C) letters, the
   (D) letters, altogether;

9. (A) NO CHANGE
   (B) While their parents are working sociologists Long and Long report that many children fear intruders
   (C) Sociologists Long and Long report that intruders are feared by many children while their parents are working
   (D) Sociologists Long and Long report that while their parents are working intruders are feared by many children

10. (A) NO CHANGE
    (B) about
    (C) that they're
    (D) DELETE the underlined word

Dr. D. McCauley, the head of another research team, along with a panel of three additional child psychologists [11] contends that their studies indicate that the intensity of children's fear of being home alone may be exaggerated. Valid perhaps in the multistory apartment buildings of large [12] cities, conditions differ in homes located in rural areas and the close-knit neighborhoods of small cities and suburbs.

11. (A) NO CHANGE
    (B) contends that his
    (C) contend that its
    (D) contend that their

12. (A) NO CHANGE
    (B) cities, however, conditions
    (C) cities. But conditions
    (D) cities. Conditions

Questions 13–18 are based on the following passage.

Brain Surgery

The prestige of brain surgeons may be [13] higher and more admired than that of all other medical specialists. The professional function of such physicians, who are frequently called neurosurgeons, often [14] require them to remove patients' brain and spine tumors. Almost daily they deal with matters of life and death as well as with issues relating to their patients' need for surgery, chances of complete recovery, and the possibilities of lifelong paralysis and other aftereffects.

The public rarely gets a chance to get inside the head of a brain surgeon, but Dr. Henry Marsh, a London-based [15] physician, he has written a book, *Do No Harm*, in which he discusses his work and the bouts of anxiety he endures while treating patients before, during, and after surgical procedures. Dr. Marsh admits candidly that brain surgery is dangerous in spite of modern technology such as microscopes and a computer navigation system that works like a GPS to guide the surgeon and his instruments as he probes inside his [16] patients' brains. Among his other tools are saws, drills, sponges, and a variety of state-of-the-art instruments he uses with extraordinary finesse

13. (A) NO CHANGE
    (B) high, and more
    (C) higher, and they are
    (D) higher, being more

14. (A) NO CHANGE
    (B) has required
    (C) is requiring them
    (D) requires them

15. (A) NO CHANGE
    (B) physician,
    (C) physician; he
    (D) physician he

16. (A) NO CHANGE
    (B) patients' brains'
    (C) patient's brains
    (D) patient's brain's

and skill. Because he cannot always predict with certainty that a patient will be helped or hurt by surgery, a far more difficult aspect of his work is deciding whether or not to recommend a procedure. Knowing that one false move may do irreparable damage to a patient, he perpetually struggles with such decisions. In addition, he cannot know at the outset what he'll find once probing inside the patient's skull. Success comes only after discovering that the tumor can be totally and safely removed. The inside of human brains consists of a jelly-like substance, some [17] of it may conceal serious problems that no surgeon can discern prior to surgery. Despite their best intentions, surgeons often recognize too late that it may have been a mistake to operate in the first place.

Marsh claims that a degree of luck, both good and bad, plays an ever more important role in his work. [18] Finally, while he cannot speak for all brain surgeons, he faces each operation with both fear and excitement, likening the experience to that of a mountaineer looking up at a great peak he hopes to climb but pondering the odds of whether or not he should even try. Patients ultimately may view their surgeons as heroes or as villains, although Dr. Marsh asserts they are neither heroic nor powerful, despite their public image and reputation.

17. (A) NO CHANGE
    (B) of the substance
    (C) of which
    (D) DELETE the underlined words

18. (A) NO CHANGE
    (B) Consequently,
    (C) Alternatively,
    (D) Nevertheless,

Questions 19–24 are based on the following passage.

The Silent Sea

Until early in the 20th century, the world underneath the surface of the sea was a fearful place: forbidding **[19]** <u>it was dark,</u> and dangerous—a gloomy, lightless graveyard for ships and men, a water-filled wilderness **[20]** <u>inhabited, with</u> menacing sea creatures. As far as anyone knew, **[21]** <u>they were</u> also among the quietest places on the planet.

Less than a century ago, our conception of a silent sea changed dramatically with the wartime invention of hydrophones and other sound-detection devices meant to disclose the presence of enemy submarines hovering near the coasts of the United States and its allies. **[22]** <u>The crew of the research vessel *Atlantis*, while listening for submarines, heard and recorded strange mewing sounds, shrieks, and ghostly moans.</u> To their astonishment, oceanographers discovered that beneath the waves there is a constant uproar of noise produced by fish, porpoises, shrimp, and a huge variety of other creatures. The source of some sounds still **[23]** <u>remain unknown,</u> although some creatures in the deepest zones were captured and put in holding tanks where they had their "voices" recorded for comparison with sounds heard in **[24]** <u>more shallower</u> portions of sea. In many cases satisfactory identification has been made.

19. (A) NO CHANGE
    (B) and it was dark,
    (C) dark
    (D) DELETE the underlined section

20. (A) NO CHANGE
    (B) inhabited with
    (C) inhabited by
    (D) and inhabited by

21. (A) NO CHANGE
    (B) they could also be
    (C) it had been
    (D) it was

22. (A) NO CHANGE
    (B) Strange mewing sounds, shrieks, and ghostly moans, while they listened for submarines, were heard and recorded by the crew of the research vessel *Atlantis*.
    (C) Listening for submarines, strange mewing sounds, shrieks, and ghostly moans were heard and recorded by the crew of the research vessel *Atlantis*.
    (D) The crew of the research vessel *Atlantis* heard and recorded, strange mewing sounds, shrieks, and ghostly moans listening for submarines.

23. (A) NO CHANGE
    (B) remains unknown,
    (C) remains unknown
    (D) remain unknown;

24. (A) NO CHANGE
    (B) the more shallower
    (C) shallower
    (D) the more shallow

ANSWER KEY

1. **D**	4. **D**	7. **D**	10. **D**	13. **A**	16. **A**	19. **D**	22. **A**
2. **B**	5. **C**	8. **C**	11. **B**	14. **D**	17. **C**	20. **C**	23. **B**
3. **C**	6. **C**	9. **C**	12. **A**	15. **B**	18. **B**	21. **D**	24. **C**

Total Correct: _____

SCALE

Correct Answers	Rating
20–24	Superior
15–19	Good
9–14	Fair
0–8	Poor

ANSWER EXPLANATIONS

Note: Although some choices contain multiple errors, only one or two major errors are explained for each incorrect choice.

1. **Choice D is the best answer** because it places commas correctly in order to punctuate a series of nouns.

    Choice A is incorrect because it uses a semicolon instead of a comma, causing the words *and ... schools* to be a sentence fragment. Choice B is wrong because a colon should not be used to introduce a phrase that fails to develop or elaborate on the idea stated just prior to the colon. Choice C is not the best answer because of its use of an improperly placed comma after *and*.

2. **Choice B is the best answer** because its structure parallels that of the other phrases used in the list of the painters' innovative and sophisticated techniques.

    Choices A, C, and D are not good answers because they fail to conform to the parallel structure of other phrases in the series—each beginning with the past tense of a verb and followed by *innovative and sophisticated techniques.*

3. **Choice C is the best answer** because the it uses commas to offset the appositive that identifies *Turner*.

    Choices A, B, and D are incorrect because each fails to provide the correct punctuation needed to separate the appositive from the main clause. In addition, Choice D contains superfluous commas after *colorful* and *watercolors*.

4. **Choice D is the best answer** because it is the only one that conforms to standard English grammar and usage. The clause *artists from . . . Gallery* is the only choice that can be properly modified by the participial *Hoping to enjoy . . . .*

    Choices A, B, and C are incorrect because each results in a dangling modifier which expresses a nonsensical idea saying in effect that *London's National Gallery* (A and B) and *attractions* at the gallery (C) "*hoped to enjoy and learn from Turner's work.*"

5. **Choice C is the best answer** because it is a grammatically complete and coherent sentence.

    Choices A and D are both incorrect because the words *Also . . . Sargent* comprise incomplete sentences. Choice B is wrong because it lacks a verb for the subject *Sargent*, without which it is also a sentence fragment.

6. **Choice C is the best answer** because it is the only choice that properly uses a colon to introduce a list of names.

    Choice A is incorrect because of the improper use of a semicolon, which should be used to separate two complete sentences. The list of names is not a complete sentence. Choice B is stylistically wrong because it is unnecessarily wordy. Choice D is not the best answer because *being* is not needed and creates incoherence since it refers to *paintings* instead of *artists*.

7. **Choice D is the best answer** because it provides the correct relative pronoun *that* to start the subordinate clause that follows.

    Choices A and B are not correct because the pronoun *they* lacks a specific antecedent. Choice C is incorrect because the lack of punctuation between the words *magazine* and *they* creates a run-on sentence.

8. **Choice C is the best answer** because it uses standard English idiom and contains no redundancies.

    Choices A and D are both incorrect because each includes the word *altogether*, which, coming after the word *total*, is redundant. Choice D also results in the construction of a sentence fragment. Similarly, Choice B is wrong because it contains a sentence fragment.

9. **Choice C is the best answer** because it places the clause *while their parents are working* close to *children*, the word it modifies, thereby making the meaning clear.

    Choices A, B, and D are incorrect because each of them contains a misplaced modifier. The clause *while their parents are working* should be placed closer to *children*, the word it modifies.

10. **Choice D is the best answer** because it expresses the idea using standard English idiom.

    Choices A and B are wrong because each contains a combination of words that fails to conform to the idiom of standard English. Choice C contains the contraction for *they are*, thus using a verb in the present tense instead of the past tense—the tense in which the passage is written.

11. **Choice B is the best answer** because its singular verb *contends* agrees with its singular subject *D. McCauley*, and the pronoun *his* agrees with its antecedent *D. McCauley* in number and gender.

    Choice A is not the best answer because the plural pronoun *their* fails to agree with its antecedent *D. McCauley*. Choice C is wrong because its plural verb *contend* fails to agree with its singular subject *D. McCauley*. Choice D is incorrect because the plural pronoun *their* fails to agree with its singular antecedent *D. McCauley*.

12. **Choice A is the best answer** because it is a complete, grammatical, complex sentence beginning with an adjective clause that modifies *cities*, and concluding with an independent clause.

    Choices B, C, and D are wrong because each produces a sentence fragment.

13. **Choice A is the best answer** because by providing the comparative adjective *higher* and the word *more* to make *admired* comparative, the writer has created a phrase in which the adjectives are structured parallel to each other.

    Choices B, C, and D are not correct because none of them includes a phrase in which the adjectives are parallel to each other.

14. **Choice D is the best answer** because the singular verb *requires* agrees in number with the singular subject *function*.

Choice A is not the best answer because the plural verb *require* fails to agree in number with the singular subject *function*. Choice B is wrong because it is a verb in the present perfect tense instead of the present tense. Choice C is incorrect because in the context of the sentence it fails to conform to standard English idiom.

15. **Choice B is the best answer** because it correctly includes the comma at the end of the appositive *a London-based physician*.

    Choice A is incorrect because it creates two independent sentences connected by a comma—i.e., a comma splice. Choice C is not the best answer because the text prior to the semicolon is an incomplete construction—i.e., a sentence fragment. Choice D is not correct because it is a run-on sentence.

16. **Choice A is the best answer** because it properly uses an apostrophe to indicate the plural possessive.

    Choice B includes an unnecessary and misleading apostrophe after the word *brains*. Choice C uses an apostrophe that indicates a singular, instead of plural, possessive. Choice D includes an unnecessary and misleading apostrophe before the final *-s* in the word *brains*.

17. **Choice C is the best answer** because it provides the correct preposition (*of*) and relative pronoun (*which*) that together create a dependent clause following the comma.

    Choices A, B, and D are wrong because each of them creates a comma splice—that is, two sentences joined by a comma.

18. **Choice B is the best answer** because it provides a transitional conjunction that properly relates the relationship between good and bad luck and the thoughts of a mountaineer considering the odds of a successful climb.

    Choices A, C, and D are not reasonable because each is a conjunction that fails to

provide a link between the text that precedes and follows it.

19. **Choice D is the best answer.**

    Choices A and B are incorrect because these clauses are not parallel in structure to the series of single-word adjectives that describe the sea below the surface. Choice C is not the best answer because the word *lightless* in the phrase that follows makes the word *dark* redundant.

20. **Choice C is the best answer** because it provides the correct preposition required in the context.

    Choice A is incorrect because no punctuation is needed in the underlined phrase. Choice B is wrong because the preposition *with* creates a phrase that fails to conform to standard English idiom. Choice C is not the best answer because the conjunction *and* is unnecessary and confusing.

21. **Choice D is the best answer** because it consists of the only possible pronoun and verb required by the context.

    Choice A is incorrect because the pronoun *they* fails to refer to a specific noun or other pronoun. Choice B is wrong because it includes the pronoun *they*, which has no specific antecedent, and inappropriately shifts the verb away from the simple past tense. Choice C is not the best answer because of an inappropriate shift of the verb from the simple past tense to the past perfect.

22. **Choice A is the best answer** because it identifies the *crew*, rather than the *moans*, *listening for submarines*.

    Choice B, C, and D are incorrect because they contain dangling modifiers that suggest impossible actions such as *moans* and *strange mewing sounds* listening for submarines.

23. **Choice B is the best answer** because the singular verb *remains* agrees in number with its antecedent, *source*.

Choice A is incorrect because the plural verb *remain* fails to agree in number with its singular antecedent *source*. Choice C is wrong because a comma is needed between the independent clause at the beginning of the sentence and the dependent clause that follows. Choice D is not correct for the same reason as Choice A, but it also includes a semicolon that, in effect, turns the sentence's dependent clause into a sentence fragment.

24. **Choice C is the best answer** because it properly uses an adjective in the comparative degree.

Choice A is incorrect because of the redundancy in using both *more* and *shallower* in the comparative degree. Choice B is wrong for the same reason as Choice A. Choice D is not the best answer; although grammatically correct, it includes the superfluous word *more*.

PRACTICE TEST C

Directions: Carefully read each of the following passages. Each contains underlined and numbered segments that may contain a grammatical usage or mechanical error. To answer each question choose the alternative that expresses the underlined word or words in standard written English. If you decide that no error exists, choose (A), indicating that NO CHANGE is necessary.

Once you have decided on the answer, fill in the blank space on the answer sheet that corresponds with your choice.

Time limit: 12–15 minutes

ANSWER SHEET

1. Ⓐ Ⓑ Ⓒ Ⓓ
2. Ⓐ Ⓑ Ⓒ Ⓓ
3. Ⓐ Ⓑ Ⓒ Ⓓ
4. Ⓐ Ⓑ Ⓒ Ⓓ
5. Ⓐ Ⓑ Ⓒ Ⓓ
6. Ⓐ Ⓑ Ⓒ Ⓓ

7. Ⓐ Ⓑ Ⓒ Ⓓ
8. Ⓐ Ⓑ Ⓒ Ⓓ
9. Ⓐ Ⓑ Ⓒ Ⓓ
10. Ⓐ Ⓑ Ⓒ Ⓓ
11. Ⓐ Ⓑ Ⓒ Ⓓ
12. Ⓐ Ⓑ Ⓒ Ⓓ

13. Ⓐ Ⓑ Ⓒ Ⓓ
14. Ⓐ Ⓑ Ⓒ Ⓓ
15. Ⓐ Ⓑ Ⓒ Ⓓ
16. Ⓐ Ⓑ Ⓒ Ⓓ
17. Ⓐ Ⓑ Ⓒ Ⓓ
18. Ⓐ Ⓑ Ⓒ Ⓓ

19. Ⓐ Ⓑ Ⓒ Ⓓ
20. Ⓐ Ⓑ Ⓒ Ⓓ
21. Ⓐ Ⓑ Ⓒ Ⓓ
22. Ⓐ Ⓑ Ⓒ Ⓓ
23. Ⓐ Ⓑ Ⓒ Ⓓ
24. Ⓐ Ⓑ Ⓒ Ⓓ

Grammar Tests: SAT

Cut along dotted line.

Questions 1–6 are based on the following passage.

Animal Rescue

Over the centuries, humans have domesticated untold millions of dogs, cats, horses, hamsters, and a variety of other animals that demand our attention, [1] <u>sharing our homes and yards,</u> and win our affection. But most other creatures—those we call "wild"—live in a world separate from our own. Occasionally, we visit them in zoos, or [2] <u>encounter one of them in their habitat</u>. At other times we feed, trap, study, photograph, and hunt them. But rarely do we interact with them physically unless they are in trouble.

Many of their troubles are manmade. Our cars hit deer and [3] <u>raccoons when we cut down trees and destroy birds' nests</u>. We also soak seabirds in spilled oil, knock raptors out of the sky with windmills, pull endangered whales and tunas from the oceans, and destroy habitats on land and sea.

Against this background many humane individuals, on their own or as part of nature-supporting groups, dedicate themselves to helping injured and sick animals get well and return to the wild. One of them is Judith [4] <u>Wakelam, a gentle English woman</u> well-known for her skill with common swifts, those small brown insect-devouring birds known for spending most of their lives in flight. Indeed, they eat and sleep, and even mate on the wing, and continually migrate between Europe and Africa.

Injured swifts are brought to Wakelam from all over eastern England, some from vets, others from citizens who have found them injured. [5] <u>Typically,</u> she has more than two dozen swifts in her care. She tends to their wounds as assiduously as a medical doctor, feeds them crickets and caterpillars coated

1. (A) NO CHANGE
   (B) share homes and yards
   (C) share our homes and yards
   (D) and sharing our homes and yards

2. (A) NO CHANGE
   (B) encounter one in its habitat
   (C) have seen them in their habitats
   (D) encounter one in their habitats

3. (A) NO CHANGE
   (B) raccoons and destroy bird's nests when trees are cut down
   (C) raccoons when cutting down trees, destroying birds' nests
   (D) raccoons. We cut down trees and destroy birds' nests

4. (A) NO CHANGE
   (B) Wakelam, a gentle English woman,
   (C) Wakelam a gentle English woman
   (D) Wakelam, a gentle, English woman,

5. (A) NO CHANGE
   (B) Consequently,
   (C) Regardless,
   (D) Formerly,

with powdered vitamins, and returns them to the wild [6] <u>as quickly as</u> possible. Tending to swifts is more than a sign of Wakelam's humanity and kindness. To her, it feels like an obligation, a means to redress, or even redeem humans for creating an environment that is increasingly hazardous to the wild species of the world. Other animal rescuers and rehabbers echo Wakelam's sentiments. They feel responsible for having contributed to conditions that are harmful to animals.

6. (A) NO CHANGE
    (B) as quickly as it is
    (C) as quick as
    (D) more quicker than

Questions 7–12 are based on the following passage.

George Washington

At some point every school child has been taught that George Washington, the so-called "Father of Our Country," commanded America's revolutionary army and became the United States' first president. Less well-known are facts concerning his family life and his personality, perhaps with one exception. It's the legendary but dubious story about chopping down a cherry tree and [7] <u>he could not</u> tell a lie to his father about what he had done.

At times life was hard for the family. [8] <u>When he was just eleven</u>, George's father died, leaving his survivors short of money and prospects for a bright future. [9] <u>However,</u> George's formal education was limited—just seven or eight years of tutoring, and unlike so many other prominent young men of colonial Virginia—no training in Latin or Greek, or the law. Yet, he learned to write clearly and to express himself forcefully on paper. Experience was his main teacher. Through observation and practice, he mastered the art of behavior in polite society, thus developing perfect manners and polish. Regardless, at sixteen, he decided to leave the social whirl behind and work as a surveyor's

7. (A) NO CHANGE
    (B) refusing to
    (C) with an inability to
    (D) about which he could not

8. (A) NO CHANGE
    (B) When, at eleven
    (C) When the boy was eleven
    (D) At eleven years of age

9. (A) NO CHANGE
    (B) As a matter of fact,
    (C) In consequence,
    (D) In like manner,

apprentice in the wilderness, where he mapped the country beyond Virginia's Blue Ridge Mountains. Later, he was chosen by the governor of the Virginia [10] colony, that wants him to command troops fighting against the French and the Indians in western Pennsylvania, where he established a reputation for fearlessness under fire.

His career lasted but ten years. At age twenty-seven, he returned to Virginia, met and married Martha Dandridge Custis, an attractive and very wealthy widow with two children. Adopting the life of a gentleman plantation owner, he surrounded himself with the trappings of his newfound [11] status; a handsome green coach with brass fittings, fine English clothing, made-to-order leather footwear from London, and a library full of elegantly bound books.

He developed a reputation as an outstanding horseman, riding with the hounds while hunting foxes up to seven hours a day. Stories are told that he was a stronger, [12] taller, and more imposing figure than most of his contemporaries—standing well over six feet at a time in history when most men were far shorter. Another of his hallmarks was utter devotion to Virginia, to Mount Vernon—his now famous home—and to his family. Yet, when called upon to take charge of the colonial army in 1775, he accepted, albeit reluctantly, and served without pay—clear evidence of his commitment to the cause of America's revolt against British rule.

10. (A) NO CHANGE
    (B) colony, who wanted
    (C) colony which wanted
    (D) colony that wants

11. (A) NO CHANGE
    (B) status; and they were
    (C) status: being
    (D) status:

12. (A) NO CHANGE
    (B) tall, and more
    (C) taller, and he was a
    (D) taller, being a more

Questions 13–18 are based on the following passage.

Bierstadt

Mount Bierstadt and Bierstadt Lake in the Colorado Rockies are named after Albert Bierstadt, a nineteenth-century German-American artist known for his sweeping landscapes of the American West. Why he deserved this honor can best be explained by the hundreds of oil paintings that he completed between 1859, when he first traveled from New England to the lands west of the Mississippi River, and his death in 1902.

At first, Bierstadt's paintings were not greatly admired by art critics. Since then, [13] however, his work has earned a niche in major art museums in the United States and abroad. Initially, art lovers are struck by the massive size of Bierstadt's canvases. Bierstadt's works dwarf [14] most other artists and take up a substantial amount of wall space. Most of them depict the American [15] West's imposing mountains, vast plains, and wild rivers swirling through cavernous canyons. In the foreground he often painted diminutive human figures just visible set against the immense grandeur of high peaks, glowing skies, sunbeams, and sunlit clouds that cast shadows on the land. Bierstadt turned cliffs and rocky outcroppings into what has been aptly termed "nature's cathedrals." His panoramas of almost otherworldly beauty inspired comments from numerous [16] contemporaries, such as Mark Twain, who wrote in, his well-known travel memoir, *Roughing It*, that Bierstadt's paintings "swim in a lustrous pearly mist, which is so enchantingly beautiful that I am sorry the Creator hadn't made it instead."

Implied in Twains' remark lies a common reaction to Bierstadt's work. It appears to exaggerate reality. His colors are not always true because he

13. (A) NO CHANGE
    (B) consequently,
    (C) astoundingly,
    (D) conversely,

14. (A) NO CHANGE
    (B) the work of most artists
    (C) the paintings of most other artists
    (D) most other artist's work

15. (A) NO CHANGE
    (B) Western,
    (C) West;
    (D) West

16. (A) NO CHANGE
    (B) contemporaries: such as Mark Twain, who
    (C) contemporaries for example, Mark Twain who
    (D) contemporaries, including, Mark Twain who

painted what he believed was the way things should be, not the way they are. In Bierstadt's vision the sublime scenery of the West is endowed with an almost divine glow, as though it were literally a piece of heaven. Consequently, Bierstadt has been accused of excessive [17] sentimentalism, some people say, his paintings are visual clichés. Nevertheless, countless art lovers everywhere admire his paintings. In recent decades the United States Postal Service, [18] upon tribute to Bierstadt, have twice issued stamps bearing images of his work—in 1998, "The Last of the Buffalo"; and in 2008, "Valley of the Yosemite."

Questions 19–24 are based on the following passage.
Caffeine

The drinking of beverages that contain caffeine has been a controversy debated for centuries. In almost every part of the world where coffee or tea is consumed, religious or government leaders have tried to ban or restrict its use. All such attempts, until the present time, at least, lacked scientific credibility.

Linking caffeine use to problems of the body's central nervous system and to birth defects, [19] caffeine's regulatory status has been reconsidered by scientists and policy makers in the United States. This is a complex task, however, because caffeine is a natural substance in coffee and tea, a food additive in soft drinks, and an added ingredient in many over-the-counter drugs. In 2015, after two otherwise healthy young men died from an overdose of pure caffeine, the Food and Drug Administration (FDA) required producers to put labels on packages of pure caffeine to warn consumers of the [20] dangers using such language

17. (A) NO CHANGE
    (B) sentimentalism. Some people say
    (C) sentimentalism some people say,
    (D) sentimentalism, some people say

18. (A) NO CHANGE
    (B) for
    (C) in
    (D) during

19. (A) NO CHANGE
    (B) caffeine's regulatory status in the United States has been reconsidered by scientists and policy makers
    (C) in the United States, caffeine's regulatory status has been reconsidered by scientists and policy makers
    (D) scientists and policy makers in the United States have reconsidered caffeine's regulatory status

20. (A) NO CHANGE
    (B) dangers of
    (C) dangers, by
    (D) dangers in

as "potentially fatal," [21] "risk of illness," and "harmful to pregnant and lactating women."

A teaspoon of pure caffeine [22] holds approximately the amount of caffeine in 28 cups of coffee, and a tablespoon can kill you. Producers sell about 3.5 ounces of pure caffeine at a time, an amount, depending on how densely the pure caffeine powder has been packed, that is found in roughly 300–400 so-called "tall" cups of Starbucks coffee or more than 3,000 cans of Coca-Cola. The FDA reasoned that because of pure caffeine's potency, safe amounts are extremely difficult to measure. Imprecise [23] instruments like common kitchen measuring spoons are not accurate enough to protect consumers from erratic caffeine-induced heartbeats, seizures, and worse. A super-precise scale is an absolute necessity.

Because pure caffeine is being sold in some tobacco shops and on the Internet, several "watchdog" groups have taken notice. One consumer advocacy group, the Center for Science in the Public [24] Interest petitioned to ban the sale of pure caffeine powder at the FDA in Washington, D.C. In response, the FDA mailed warning letters to several companies about the safety of pure powdered caffeine. At present, it remains unclear whether all the companies would end production or merely sell caffeine powder in much smaller packages.

21. (A) NO CHANGE
    (B) risk for illness
    (C) perilous to health
    (D) may cause illness

22. (A) NO CHANGE
    (B) contains roughly the approximate total also found in
    (C) holds more or less the same sum of caffeine as that found in
    (D) contains more or less the approximate amount as

23. (A) NO CHANGE
    (B) instruments such as common kitchen measuring spoons, are
    (C) instruments like common kitchen measuring spoons being
    (D) instruments, for example, common kitchen measuring spoons, they are

24. (A) NO CHANGE
    (B) Interest, petitioned the FDA in Washington, D.C., to ban the sale of pure caffeine powder.
    (C) Interest petitioned at the FDA in Washington, D.C., the banning of sales of pure caffeine powder.
    (D) Interest, petitioned to ban the sale at the FDA in Washington, D.C., of pure caffeine powder.

ANSWER KEY

1. **C**	4. **A**	7. **B**	10. **B**	13. **A**	16. **A**	19. **D**	22. **A**
2. **B**	5. **A**	8. **C**	11. **D**	14. **C**	17. **B**	20. **C**	23. **A**
3. **D**	6. **A**	9. **C**	12. **A**	15. **A**	18. **C**	21. **C**	24. **B**

Total Correct: _____

SCALE

Correct Answers	Rating
20–24	Superior
15–19	Good
9–14	Fair
0–8	Poor

ANSWER EXPLANATIONS

Note: Although some choices contain multiple errors, only one or two major errors are explained for each incorrect choice.

1. **Choice C is the best answer** because the verb *share* followed by the pronoun *our* parallels the structure of the other items in the series—*demand our* and *win our.*

    Choices A, B, and D are incorrect because they fail to follow the parallel structure of the other phrases in the series. Also Choice D includes a superfluous conjunction (*and*).

2. **Choice B is the best answer** because the present tense of the verb *encounter* is consistent with the tense of the other verbs in the passage. Also the singular possessive pronoun *its* agrees in number with its antecedent *one.*

    Choices A and D are incorrect because both of them use the plural possessive pronoun *their,* which fails to agree with its singular antecedent *one.* Choice C is wrong because the use of the present perfect form of the verb is not consistent with the tense in which the passage is written.

3. **Choice D is the best answer** because it makes use of two sentences, each one containing an example that clearly and logically supports the paragraph's opening sentence.

    Choice A is wrong because faulty modification conveys the nonsensical idea that cars hit deer and raccoons at the time we cut down trees. Choice B is incorrect because an apostrophe is used to create a singular possessive noun where a plural possessive is needed. Choice C is not the best answer because faulty modification conveys the nonsensical idea that cars cut down trees.

4. **Choice A is the best answer** because it uses punctuation in such a way as to make the entire noun phrase *a gentle English woman . . . with common swifts* an appositive identifying the person named in the previous phrase, *Judith Wakelam.*

    Choice B is incorrect because the comma after *woman* causes an erroneous break in the appositive (*a gentle English woman . . . with common swifts*) that identifies *Judith Wakelam.* Choice C is wrong because it lacks a comma between the name *Wakelam* and the appositive that identifies *Judith Wakelam.* Choice D is not the best answer because the comma after *gentle* is superfluous. A second comma causes confusion by interrupting the appositive (*a gentle English woman . . . with common swifts*) that identifies *Judith Wakelam.*

5. **Choice A is the best answer** because it is a transitional adverb that creates a logical link with the previous sentence, which begins a discussion of Wakelam's work with swifts.

Choices B, C, and D are incorrect because none of them offers a coherent link with the preceding sentence.

6. **Choice A is the best answer** because the context calls for an adverb that modifies the verb *returns.*

Choice B is incorrect because it includes the unnecessary phrase *it is.* Choice C is wrong because the context requires an adverb (*quickly*) instead of an adjective (*quick*) to modify the verb *returns.* Choice D is not the best answer because the word *more* preceding an adjective in the comparative degree (*quicker*) is redundant.

7. **Choice B is the best answer** because it parallels the structure of *chopping.* Both *chopping* and *refusing* are objects of the preposition *about.*

Choice A is incorrect because it violates parallel structure by using a clause (*he could not tell a lie*) instead of a noun to complete the prepositional phrase beginning with the word *about.* Choice C is wrong because it uses a preposition (*with*) that is not logically or grammatically related to the previous part of the sentence. Choice D is not the best answer because it contains a relative pronoun (*which*) that lacks a clear cut antecedent.

8. **Choice C is the best answer** because it unambiguously specifies the time of the elder Washington's death.

Choices A, B, and D are incorrect because each of them contains a misplaced clause or phrase saying that George's father died at age eleven—a rather unlikely occurrence. In

addition, Choice B lacks a main verb and, therefore, is a sentence fragment.

9. **Choice C is the best answer** because it is a transitional phrase that communicates the cause-effect relationship between the family's financial limitations and their impact on George's education.

Choices A, B, and D are wrong because none of them provides a logical connection between the family's shortage of funds and George's studies.

10. **Choice B is the best answer** because it includes a relative pronoun (*who*) that correctly refers to the noun *governor.* It also contains the appropriate past-tense verb *wanted* as well as the punctuation needed to create a nonrestrictive clause beginning with the word *who.*

Choice A is incorrect because it lacks an appropriate pronoun to refer to the antecedent *governor.* It also improperly uses a verb in the present instead of the past tense. Choices C and D are not good answers because neither contains an appropriate relative pronoun that refers to the antecedent *governor.* Nor do they include the punctuation needed to help clarify meaning.

11. **Choice D is the best answer** because the colon signals that the list of *trappings* is about to be spelled out.

Choice A is incorrect because semicolons are used to separate two complete sentences, not a sentence and—as in this case—a list of nouns. Choice B is wrong because it contains more words than necessary. Choice C is not the best answer because it leads to the creation of a sentence fragment. (The word *being* may not be used without a helping verb like *is* or *was* as the main verb in a clause or sentence.)

12. **Choice A is the best answer** because it provides a series of comparative adjectives—*stronger, taller, and more imposing*—that are parallel in structure.

Choices B, C, and D are incorrect because none of them contains a list of qualities that are structurally parallel.

13. **Choice A is the best answer** because it offers a transitional adverb, *however*, that communicates the relationship between critics' views and the public acceptance of Bierstadt's work.

    Choices B, C, and D are incorrect because none of them provides a logical transition between the preceding sentence regarding art critics' views and the following sentence about the success of Bierstadt's work.

14. **Choice C is the best answer** because it creates a comparison between like terms: in this case, Bierstadt's *works* and the *paintings* of other artists.

    Choice A is incorrect because it tries to compare unlike terms: Bierstadt's *works* and *most artists*. Choice B is wrong because it is an incomplete comparison. To compare one thing (*works*) to a group of which it is a part, the word *other* is needed, as in *most other artists*. Choice D is not the best answer because the possessive noun *artist's* is improperly punctuated. As a plural possessive, the apostrophe should come after the *-s* (*artists'*).

15. **Choice A is the best answer** because it provides the correct punctuation needed for a singular possessive noun and results in a grammatically complete sentence.

    Choice B is incorrect because it contains an unnecessary comma. Also, the phrase *Western, imposing* is not standard English idiom. Choice C is wrong because it results in a sentence fragment. Choice D is not the best answer because it is followed by several phrases that lack a grammatical relationship with the preceding segment of the sentence.

16. **Choice A is the best answer** because it provides the correct punctuation for introducing the phrase *such as* followed by the relative clause (*who wrote . . .*) that follows.

Choice B is incorrect because of improper punctuation. A comma, not a colon, is required to introduce the phrase *such as* when it is part of a nonrestrictive clause. Choice C is not the best answer because it provides only one of the two commas that should surround the transitional phrase *for example*. Moreover, it lacks the comma needed between *Twain* and the relative clause that follows. Choice D is wrong because of the superfluous comma after *including* and the absence of a comma after *Twain*.

17. **Choice B is the best answer** because it provides the punctuation needed to create two complete sentences.

    Choice A is incorrect because it creates a comma splice by using a comma instead of a period or semicolon to separate two independent sentences. In addition, a superfluous comma appears after the word *say*. Choice C is not the best answer because it is a run-on sentence; that is, it consists of two complete sentences without punctuation between them. Also, a superfluous comma appears after the word *say*. Like Choice A, Choice D is not the best answer because it creates a comma splice.

18. **Choice C is the best answer** because it provides a preposition that in the context conforms to standard English idiom.

    Choices A, B, and D are incorrect because none of them is a preposition that in the context conforms to standard English idiom. One might issue a stamp *in* tribute, but not *upon, for,* or *during* tribute.

19. **Choice D is the best answer.** It is the only choice that provides a grammatically correct and coherent sentence because the participial phrase *Linking caffeine . . . defects* functions as an adjective modifying *scientists and policy makers*.

    Choices A, B, and C all contain a dangling modifier. That is, the phrase *Linking caffeine use . . . defects* cannot grammatically or logically modify *caffeine's regulatory status*.

20. **Choice C is the best answer** because it is the only one that uses the correct preposition to make the meaning of the sentence clear and coherent. In the context producers are required to warn consumers *by* using certain language.

Choices A, B, and C are incorrect because they distort meaning by using prepositions that put the onus of using certain language on *consumers* instead of on *producers*.

21. **Choice C is the best answer** because the structure of the phrase is parallel to the other items in the series, each of which features an adjective (*fatal, harmful*).

Choices A, B, and D are incorrect because they are not structurally parallel to the other items in the series of warnings to the consumer.

22. **Choice A is the best answer** because it results in a concisely expressed standard English sentence.

Choices B and D contain redundancies: *roughly* and *approximate* in B, and *more or less* and *approximate* in D. Choice C is incorrect because in standard English, the word *sum* applies to countable items such as dollars but not to masses or quantities like caffeine.

23. **Choice A is the best answer** because it results in a grammatically complete and accurately punctuated sentence.

Choice B is incorrect because of the unnecessary comma inserted between the subject and the verb. Choice C is wrong because the use of the word *being* creates a sentence fragment. Choice D is not the best answer because the use of *they* creates mixed sentence construction; that is, the first part of the sentence is not grammatically related to the second.

24. **Choice B is the best answer** because it is the only choice that is a grammatically standard and coherent sentence. It also includes punctuation that is correctly placed at the end of the appositive identifying the advocacy group mentioned earlier in the sentence.

Choices A and D are incorrect because they both include a phrase suggesting that the FDA sold caffeine powder in Washington, D.C.—a meaning the writer could not have intended. Choice C is wrong because it is repetitious, awkwardly expressed, and lacking in the punctuation required after *Interest*, the last word of the appositive used to identify the advocacy group mentioned earlier in the sentence.

PRACTICE TEST D

Directions: Carefully read each of the following passages. Each contains underlined and numbered segments that may contain a grammatical usage or mechanical error. To answer each question, choose the alternative that expresses the underlined word or words in standard written English. If you decide that no error exists, choose (A), indicating that NO CHANGE is necessary.

   Once you have decided on the answer, fill in the blank space on the answer sheet that corresponds with your choice.

Time limit: 12–15 minutes

ANSWER SHEET

1. Ⓐ Ⓑ Ⓒ Ⓓ	7. Ⓐ Ⓑ Ⓒ Ⓓ	13. Ⓐ Ⓑ Ⓒ Ⓓ	19. Ⓐ Ⓑ Ⓒ Ⓓ
2. Ⓐ Ⓑ Ⓒ Ⓓ	8. Ⓐ Ⓑ Ⓒ Ⓓ	14. Ⓐ Ⓑ Ⓒ Ⓓ	20. Ⓐ Ⓑ Ⓒ Ⓓ
3. Ⓐ Ⓑ Ⓒ Ⓓ	9. Ⓐ Ⓑ Ⓒ Ⓓ	15. Ⓐ Ⓑ Ⓒ Ⓓ	21. Ⓐ Ⓑ Ⓒ Ⓓ
4. Ⓐ Ⓑ Ⓒ Ⓓ	10. Ⓐ Ⓑ Ⓒ Ⓓ	16. Ⓐ Ⓑ Ⓒ Ⓓ	22. Ⓐ Ⓑ Ⓒ Ⓓ
5. Ⓐ Ⓑ Ⓒ Ⓓ	11. Ⓐ Ⓑ Ⓒ Ⓓ	17. Ⓐ Ⓑ Ⓒ Ⓓ	23. Ⓐ Ⓑ Ⓒ Ⓓ
6. Ⓐ Ⓑ Ⓒ Ⓓ	12. Ⓐ Ⓑ Ⓒ Ⓓ	18. Ⓐ Ⓑ Ⓒ Ⓓ	24. Ⓐ Ⓑ Ⓒ Ⓓ

Grammar Tests: SAT

Cut along dotted line.

Questions 1–6 are based on the following passage.

Edison's Phonograph

Thomas Edison customarily gets credit for inventing the phonograph during the last decades of the 19th century. For all its genius, his phonograph was really just a composite of already well-known [1] <u>technologies, the stylus</u>, the diaphragm, the cylinder, and the feed screw. All had long histories. Indeed, Edison's most critical innovation was just the insight that sound could be recorded at all.

The sound quality of his early phonograph was poor, and repeat playing left much to be desired. The tin-foil cylinders which served as the phonograph's record were ruined after only two or three plays, and irregularity in the speed of cranking created serious distortions of sound.

Crucial for us to realize, however, is the revolutionary nature of such an invention, even if originally imperfect. Here in embryo was a marvelous machine that could actually make a "written" record of sound. Even more striking was the fact that the new device "read" back that record with no human effort, apart from turning a little crank. Onlookers marveled that the contraption talked without lips or [2] <u>tongue, in fact, others</u> were astounded that a metal diaphragm had been made to listen and to speak. Today we take recordings for granted. In Edison's day, listeners considered the phonograph a magical, almost supernatural invention. They claimed that, in effect, this astonishing novelty had the power to raise the dead.

In spite of [3] <u>it's</u> inflated rhetoric, Edison originally had rather modest, mundane goals in mind. He particularly hoped to find a more direct

1. (A) NO CHANGE
   (B) technologies: the stylus
   (C) technologies. The stylus
   (D) technologies; the stylus

2. (A) NO CHANGE
   (B) tongue; in fact, others
   (C) tongue. Others, in fact,
   (D) tongue. Others

3. (A) NO CHANGE
   (B) their
   (C) his
   (D) its

way of archiving and transmitting the human voice as an alternative to written records, mostly for business purposes. Looking back now from this age of MP-3 players and Spotify, [4] <u>we may find it strange that Edison</u> underestimated the significance of his achievement in May 1878, when he stated that the purpose of the phonograph would be [5] <u>concerning</u> taking dictation. The device would also eliminate the "confidential clerk," a fixture in the offices of the time. Edison was already thinking about the kinds of clerical automation we today associate with the personal computer and smart-phone technology—including the storage of voice and images free from human intermediaries in recording, replaying, editing information, ideas, and plans.

Curiously, Edison ranked the recording of music only fourth on his list of applications, after dictation, reading aloud to the [6] <u>blind; and</u> providing lessons in spelling and language. Nevertheless, Edison dreamed that his phonograph might one day capture and replay the actual voice of the newest prima donna and the exquisite melodies of immortal composers like Mozart and Beethoven.

4. (A) NO CHANGE
   (B) Edison strangely
   (C) it was strange that Edison
   (D) we consider it strange, for Edison

5. (A) NO CHANGE
   (B) about
   (C) with
   (D) DELETE the underlined word

6. (A) NO CHANGE
   (B) blind: and
   (C) blind, and
   (D) blind, and,

Questions 7–12 are based on the following passage.

Job Satisfaction

Hello! It won't take long for a young person like you, upon entering the workforce after you earn a diploma from high school or college—or even a graduate degree—to discover that a great many of [7] <u>one's</u> fellow workers would rather be doing something other than the jobs they have. Considering that fully employed people spend about half of their waking hours at work, it is sad

7. (A) NO CHANGE
   (B) their
   (C) your
   (D) you're

that workplaces harbor such large numbers of disaffected employees and that the nature of their work apparently provides them with little or no satisfaction.

On the other hand, maybe the work itself should not be blamed for generating discontent. Rather, working conditions may be partly responsible. In countless offices, factories, and other sites, work may be structured in a way that almost guarantees that worker tension and hostility [8] has been created. If you work in a call center, for instance, every one of your phone calls may be monitored, recorded, and then evaluated based on whether your effort was productive—that is, whether you actually convinced the customer to buy or sign up to receive whatever service or product the employer sells. In effect, the amount in your paycheck will depend on how much you add to the company's earnings.

Many veteran workers say that a job should not be defined by compensation alone, [9] so they'll also complain if they're not earning enough. [10] Employees, typically they prefer work that not only pays a respectable wage but rewards them in other ways too. A job that somehow offers a tangible benefit to society gives workers a sense that their efforts are appreciated. A research study not long ago conducted by Yale professor Amy Wrzesniewski, an organizational behavior [11] specialist. She found that custodians working at a large urban hospital occasionally found themselves performing non-maintenance functions: They distracted patients with stories and jokes while nurses inserted IVs, they comforted families, and they helped visitors find their way around the building. In short, they contributed to the overall sense that the hospital cared sincerely about

8. (A) NO CHANGE
   (B) is the result
   (C) have been created
   (D) will result

9. (A) NO CHANGE
   (B) and
   (C) but
   (D) DELETE the underlined word

10. (A) NO CHANGE
    (B) Typically, employees
    (C) Typical employees they
    (D) Employees being typical when they

11. (A) NO CHANGE
    (B) specialist:
    (C) specialist; she
    (D) specialist,

the welfare of its clientele. For their efforts, the custodians received no extra pay, but that aspect of their work gave them great satisfaction and, as one said, got him "out of bed in the morning."

Similarly, jobs that allow employees to maintain a flexible schedule have become increasingly desirable. An employer, for instance, may subscribe to a work-at-home policy that encourages workers to spend more time with their young family or an ailing parent. Such arrangements, according to [12] those who have them, raise morale and increase productivity.

Questions 13–18 are based on the following passage.

Three Trillion Trees

Based on a recent census of our planet's tree population, conducted at Evergreen State College in Olympia, Washington, Earth is home to slightly more than three trillion trees. This sounds like a large number. Arithmetically, it means that there are over four hundred trees—422 to be [13] exact, for every living man, woman, and child.

That the latest count was eight times higher than expected is good news. "After all," says ecologist Thomas Crowther, who led the survey, "trees provide a wide range of important ecosystem services for humans," including water storage, soil stabilization, and habitats for plants and animals. They also help to maintain our health by absorbing heat-trapping carbon dioxide and generating the oxygen we need to breathe.

Yet, the tree census also revealed some alarming and worrisome statistics. For one thing, Earth, at one time populated by 5.6 trillion trees, has lost about 46 percent of them since human civilizations began to emerge. What's more, every year sees

12. (A) NO CHANGE
    (B) those who have it
    (C) they who have one
    (D) they that have one

13. (A) NO CHANGE
    (B) exact—
    (C) exact;
    (D) exact

the net loss of 10 billion trees. Indeed, humans are destroying trees at an alarming rate, brought about by deforestation to create agricultural land, shortsighted forest-management practices, land-use for industrial purposes, [14] and urban development. Essentially, as the human population grows, [15] so do the net loss of trees worldwide. The redwoods of California, the olive trees of the Mediterranean, the evergreens spread across Canada and Russia—they are all being decimated rapidly, especially in areas where tree-growth is the [16] most dense and vast. As a case in point, [17] the trees of the Amazon River basin, destroyed and thinned almost beyond recognition at an alarming rate. From the tropics, which are home to 43 percent of the world's trees, to the sub-Arctic regions of Russia, Scandinavia, and North America, containing about 24 percent, to the temperate regions, home to about 20 [18] percent. These researchers conclude that the loss of trees has a significant effect on both climate and human health.

14. (A) NO CHANGE
    (B) and urban development has had huge effects
    (C) however, urban development have had huge effects
    (D) but urban development have had huge effects

15. (A) NO CHANGE
    (B) so does
    (C) as do
    (D) it follows that

16. (A) NO CHANGE
    (B) most densest and vastest
    (C) more dense and vast
    (D) densest and vaster

17. (A) NO CHANGE
    (B) having destroyed trees at an alarming rate, the rain forests of the Amazon River basin have been thinned almost beyond recognition
    (C) the rain forests of the Amazon River basin have been thinned almost beyond recognition, its trees destroyed at an alarming rate
    (D) its trees being destroyed at an alarming rate and almost beyond recognition, the thinned rain forests of the Amazon basin

18. (A) NO CHANGE
    (B) percent. Researchers
    (C) percent; these researchers
    (D) percent, researchers

Questions 19–24 are based on the following passage.

Joshua Bell

On a mid-winter morning in Washington, D.C., a man [19] <u>played the violin in a metro station dressed in ragged clothes</u> during the height of the morning rush hour. He looked like a destitute street musician intent on raising money to buy a sandwich or bowl of hot soup.

More than a thousand passers-by ignored the man. A few paused momentarily to listen, [20] <u>and</u> fewer still dropped a dollar or some spare pocket change into a cardboard box at the man's feet. What nobody knew at the time was the man's identity or why he was there.

Later, it was disclosed that the man was Joshua Bell, a world-class performer, probably [21] <u>more better known than any contemporary violinist</u>, playing an 18th century Stradivarius violin worth $3.5 million. He made music in the metro station at the request of *Washington Post* reporter Gene Weingarten, [22] <u>whom, wanting to recruit</u> Bell to conduct an experiment designed to gauge how presentation affects perceptions of quality.

Familiar with the basic marketing principle that consumers will pick one of two identical products based on the attractiveness of [23] <u>their presentation, Weingarten</u> wondered whether this concept also applied to the arts. More specifically, would people recognize the quality of the performance of a world-class virtuoso playing in a commonplace environment and at an unusual hour?

During his time in the metro, performing six classical pieces, twenty donors gave Bell a total of $32. Ironically, just two days earlier he had performed some of the same music at a sold-out

19. (A) NO CHANGE
    (B) playing the violin in a metro station dressed in ragged clothes
    (C) dressed in ragged clothes and playing a violin
    (D) dressed in ragged clothes played the violin in a metro station

20. (A) NO CHANGE
    (B) although
    (C) but
    (D) except

21. (A) NO CHANGE
    (B) more better well-known than any contemporary violinist
    (C) more better known than most any contemporary violinist
    (D) better known than any other contemporary violinist

22. (A) NO CHANGE
    (B) he recruited
    (C) who had recruited
    (D) he had wanted to recruit

23. (A) NO CHANGE
    (B) its presentation; Weingarten
    (C) the presentation: Weingarten
    (D) their presentation, Weingarten,

concert in Boston, where the average ticket price was $100.

Although Weingarten's experiment took less than an hour to complete, he was left grappling for a long time with questions about the [24] peoples' perception, taste, and the priorities of people: Do people usually discern beauty? Do they appreciate it? And perhaps most puzzling of all, if beautiful music and outstanding talent go unrecognized in unexpected contexts, how many of life's other treasures are we missing?

24. (A) NO CHANGE
    (B) peoples' perception, taste, and their priorities.
    (C) people's perception, taste, and priorities:
    (D) people's perceptions, tastes and their priority.

ANSWER KEY

1. B	4. A	7. C	10. B	13. B	16. A	19. D	22. C
2. D	5. D	8. D	11. D	14. A	17. C	20. A	23. A
3. B	6. C	9. C	12. A	15. B	18. D	21. D	24. C

Total Correct: _____

SCALE

Correct Answers	Rating
20–24	Superior
15–19	Good
9–14	Fair
0–8	Poor

ANSWER EXPLANATIONS

Note: Although some choices contain multiple errors, only one or two major errors are explained for each incorrect choice.

1. **Choice B is the best answer** because the colon is properly used to introduce a list of technologies.

   Choice A is incorrect because a comma should not be used to separate a complete independent sentence from a list of items. Choice C is wrong because the text beginning with *The stylus* is a sentence fragment. Choice D is not the best answer because the text beginning with *the stylus* is a sentence fragment.

2. **Choice D is the best answer** because it contains a clear break between two different sentences and eliminates *in fact*, an irrelevant and confusing transitional phrase.

   Choice A is incorrect because it contains a comma splice—two independent sentences separated by a comma. Choices B and C are wrong because they include *in fact*, a transitional phrase used to reinforce or develop a previously stated idea; in this context the phrase is irrelevant because it does not perform that function.

3. **Choice B is the best answer** because the pronoun *their* refers to *They* (listeners), the subject of the previous sentence.

   Choice A is incorrect because the word *it's*, being a contraction that means *it is*, is out of place in the context. Choices C and D are wrong because each is a possessive pronoun that lacks a clear antecedent.

4. **Choice A is the best answer** because it properly identifies *we*, and not *Edison*, as the entity that looks back from the present time to the nineteenth century.

   Choice B is incorrect because it contains a dangling modifier. Edison, long dead, cannot look back from this age of MP-3 players, etc. Choice C is wrong because it contains an improper shift of verb tense from present to past. Choice D is not the best answer because in the context the pronoun *it* lacks a clear, grammatical antecedent.

5. **Choice D is the best answer** because the noun *dictation* most clearly states the phonograph's purpose.

   Choices A, B, and C are incorrect because each is a preposition that creates a phrase that in the context fails to define the purpose of the phonograph.

6. **Choice C is the best answer** because it provides proper punctuation for an item listed in a series, in this case, an application of Edison's invention.

   Choice A is incorrect because a semicolon is used instead of a comma to separate items in a series. Choice B is wrong because a colon instead of a comma is used to separate items in a series. Choice D is not the best

answer because the comma after *and* is both unnecessary and confusing.

7. **Choice C is the best answer** because it is consistent with the second-person pronouns used earlier in the sentence.

   Choice A is incorrect because it shifts the person of pronouns used in the sentence from the second person (*you*) to the impersonal third person (*one*). Choice B is wrong because it is a third-person pronoun inconsistent with the second-person pronouns used in the sentence. Choice D is not the best answer because it is a contraction of *you are*, which makes no sense in the context.

8. **Choice D is the best answer** because it provides a verb in the future tense to complete the thought that a given cause will have a future effect.

   Choices A and B are incorrect because the singular verbs *is* and *has been* fail to agree with the double subject, *tension and hostility*. Choice C is wrong because a verb in the present perfect tense does not fit the context of the sentence.

9. **Choice C is the best answer** because it signals that the ideas in the two clauses of the sentence contrast or conflict in some way.

   Choices A and B are incorrect because neither conjunction indicates a logical relationship between the two clauses of the sentence. Choice D is not the best answer because it results in a comma splice.

10. **Choice B is the best answer** because it correctly provides a comma after the conjunctive adverb *Typically* which introduces the main clause of the sentence.

    Choices A and C both include *they*, a pronoun that is not only redundant with *employees* but introduces a phrase lacking a grammatical relationship with the word that precedes it. Choice D is wrong because it results in a construction that, because it lacks a main verb, is a sentence fragment.

11. **Choice D is the best answer** because it correctly closes the appositive with a comma and also links the subject of the sentence (*study*) to its verb, *found*.

   Choices A and C are incorrect because both the period and the semicolon create sentence fragments. Choice B is wrong because the colon fails to perform its function—to introduce a description or explanation of the phrase *organizational behavior specialist*.

12. **Choice A is the best answer** because it uses *them*, a pronoun that agrees in number with its plural antecedent *arrangements*.

   Choice B is incorrect because the pronoun *it* fails to agree in number with its plural antecedent *arrangements*. Choices C and D are wrong because pronouns that serve as objects of a preposition (*to*) must be in the objective, not the nominative, case. Use *them*, not *they*.

13. **Choice B is the best answer** because it provides the necessary em-dash to close the aside that means *namely* or *in other words* .

   Choices A, C, and D are wrong because they fail to provide the correct closing punctuation for the aside.

14. **Choice A is the best answer** because it grammatically, coherently, and succinctly completes the list of practices that have brought about the destruction of trees.

   Choice B is wrong because it is a complete sentence that lacks coherence as well as structural parallelism with the preceding list of practices that cause tree destruction. Choices C and D are not the best answers because each includes a coordinating conjunction that introduces some sort of contrast to the preceding items, although no contrast is expressed. In addition, Choice C creates a comma splice and contains a plural verb that lacks agreement with a singular subject.

15. **Choice B is the best answer** because it provides a singular verb *does* that agrees with the singular subject *loss*.

   Choice A is incorrect because the plural verb *do* fails to agree with the singular subject *loss*. Choice C is wrong because it consists of words that in the context fail to conform to standard English usage. Choice D is not the best answer because it results in a sentence fragment.

16. **Choice A is the best answer** because it uses the correct adjectives to make a comparison in the superlative degree.

   Choice B is incorrect because the inclusion of *most* is a redundancy when linked to adjectives in the superlative degree. Choice C is wrong because the comparison implied by the use of the word *more* is not provided. Choice D is not the best answer because the context does not allow mixing two adjectives in different degrees of comparison in the same phrase.

17. **Choice C is the best answer** because it is the only choice that provides a grammatically standard, coherent, and complete sentence.

   Choices A and D are incorrect because neither contains a verb needed to turn a fragment into a complete sentence. Choice B is wrong because it contains a dangling modifier. The participial phrase *Having destroyed trees at an overwhelmingly alarming rate* cannot logically refer to *dense rain forests*.

18. **Choice D is the best answer** because it clearly ties the dependent clause to the main clause of the sentence, thereby creating a complete grammatical sentence.

   Choices A, B and C are incorrect because each one fails to properly connect the dependent clause to the main clause, thereby creating an incomplete sentence.

19. **Choice D is the best answer** because it provides an appropriate verb to make a complete sentence and places modifiers close to the phrases they modify.

   Choices A and B are incorrect because the modifier *dressed in ragged clothes* is placed where it seems to modify *station* instead of *man*. Choice C is not the best answer because it uses a verb that results in a sentence fragment.

20. **Choice A is the best answer** because it provides an appropriate coordinating conjunction to connect the ideas in the two clauses of the compound sentence.

    Choices A, B, and D are incorrect because they fail to provide a logical transition between the clauses of the sentence.

21. **Choice D is the best answer** because it is worded in a way that completes a comparison between Bell and all other current violinists.

    Choices A, B, and C are incorrect because they all fail to compare Bell to <u>other</u> contemporary violinists. Rather, they illogically compare him to all concert violinists, including himself. Choices B and C have the additional problem of a redundant double comparison. Use *more* or use *better*, but not both together.

22. **Choice C is the best answer** because it uses a relative pronoun that correctly links the noun *Gene Weingarten* with the appropriate verb *had recruited*.

    Choice A is incorrect because it fails to provide the correct relative pronoun to link the noun *Gene Weingarten* to a suitable verb. The existing verb *wanting* is incorrect because it introduces a participial phrase that creates a sentence fragment. Choice B is wrong because it creates a comma splice—two independent

sentences joined by a comma. Choice D is not the best answer because it introduces a second independent clause, thereby creating a comma splice.

23. **Choice A is the best answer** because it provides the correct punctuation to separate the subordinate and main clauses of the sentence. It also uses *their*, a plural pronoun that agrees in number with its antecedent *products*.

    Choice B is incorrect because the pronoun *its* fails to agree in number with its plural antecedent *products*. It also erroneously uses a semicolon to separate a dependent and an independent clause. Choice C is wrong because it uses a colon to separate clauses where the second clause fails to reiterate or explain the content of the first. Choice D is not the best answer because of the superfluous comma that separates the subject *Weingarten* from the verb *wondered*.

24. **Choice C is the best answer** because it provides the appropriate possessive form, *people's*, and a colon to introduce the list of questions that follows.

    Choices A and B are incorrect because *people*, although the word sounds plural, is a singular noun in this context. Therefore, the apostrophe that indicates possession should precede the *-s*. Choice D is wrong because it is wordy; the inclusion of the pronoun *their* is unnecessary.

Chapter 5
ACT Grammar Questions

The ACT Assessment is made up of four separate tests: English, Math, Reading, and Science. Students applying to some colleges also take an optional ACT Writing Test.

Grammar questions appear only on the ACT English Test, which consists of 75 multiple-choice questions to be answered in 45 minutes. All the questions are presented in the context of five different essays, or passages, each about 300 words long. Portions of each passage are underlined, and your job is to decide whether the underlined segment is correct as it is or whether it needs to be changed.

Each multiple-choice question gives you four choices. The first choice is always NO CHANGE. The choices for odd-numbered questions are labeled A, B, C, and D, and those for even-numbered questions are F, G, H, and J.

TOPICS COVERED ON THE ACT ENGLISH TEST

Each passage includes items in two main categories:

- English grammar and usage, including punctuation and sentence structure (40 questions)
  and
- Rhetoric, including organization, style, and writing strategy (35 questions)

Some passages will contain more questions on grammar than on rhetoric. Others emphasize rhetoric more than grammar. All the questions pertain to matters of everyday grammar, usage, and rhetoric. They won't ask you about obscure rules of grammar, parts of speech, or vocabulary. Nor will you be asked to interpret the meaning of the essay.

The following chart shows the topics covered on the test. Note that the test offers more questions on sentence structure than on any other topic, and that the fewest questions pertain to punctuation. Use this information as you develop a study plan in preparation for the ACT.

Content		Number of Questions
Grammar		12
Sentence structure		18
Punctuation		10
Grammar, usage, and mechanics questions	Total	40
Organization		11
Style		12
Strategy		12
Questions on rhetoric	Total	35

SAMPLE ACT QUESTIONS
Grammar questions

Questions on grammar cover such matters as:

- Agreement between subject and verb
- Pronoun references
- Modification
- Pronoun-antecedent agreement
- Verb forms and tenses
- Pronoun choice
- Making comparisons
- English idiom
- Word choice

What follows is a random sample of ACT questions based on sentences taken from a 200-word passage (not reprinted here). The questions are numbered 3, 10, and 15.

EXAMPLE #1

Saudi Arabia, along with other oil-exporting countries,
<u>are continuing</u> to raise the price of crude oil.
    3

  3. A. NO CHANGE
     B. continue
     C. continuing
     D. is continuing

Explanation: *Saudi Arabia* is the subject of the sentence. It is singular. Because the verb *are continuing* is plural, the subject fails to agree with the verb. The phrase *along with other . . .* that comes between the subject and verb may suggest a plural subject. But this and similar phrases, including *in addition to, as well as,* and *together with,* are not conjunctions and, therefore, do not change singular subjects to plural. In other words, the noun *countries* is not part of the subject. The correct answer, therefore, is D.

Choice B is not a good alternative because *continue,* like *are continuing,* is a plural verb. Choice C turns the entire construction into a sentence fragment because it lacks a verb. Although *continuing* sounds like a verb, the *-ing* form of any verb may not serve as the main verb of a sentence without an additional helping verb, as in *was continuing* or *will be continuing.*

That leaves D as the best answer. Indeed, the singular verb *is* agrees with the singular subject of the sentence, *Saudi Arabia.*

(*For details on subject-verb agreement, turn to page 32.*)

EXAMPLE # 2

At the White House, the President and the Saudi ambassador met to discuss the issue. "Do you remember," <u>he asked</u>, "that we met once

10

before—in 1996 at a conference in Singapore?"

10. **F.** NO CHANGE
  G. he was asked
  H. the President asked
  J. the ambassador was asked by the President

Explanation: The underlined phrase is problematical because pronouns must refer specifically to a noun or another pronoun. In the given sentence, it's anybody's guess who asked the question. Was it the guest or the host? Because neither Choice F nor Choice G identifies the speaker, disregard those answers. Choice J specifies who was speaking, but the construction is written in the passive voice and is wordy. That leaves Choice H as the best answer because it concisely identifies the speaker.

(*For details on pronoun references, turn to page 13.*)

EXAMPLE # 3

Meanwhile, the chairperson of the committee appointed Ms. Dickinson to investigate possible corruption in the oil industry, <u>where she has long worked</u>.

15

15. **A.** NO CHANGE
  B. in which she has long been involved
  C. a business to which she has long been working
  D. in which a long career has been spent

Explanation: The underlined segment raises an issue of modification. That is, each of the choices is meant to modify the noun *industry*. Your job is to decide which one does it most accurately and clearly. Choice B suggests that the chairperson's appointee has been involved in corruption—surely not the intent of the writer. Choice C contains *to which*, a phrase containing an error in English idiom (use *in* instead of *to*). And D, in the passive voice, fails to say whose career has been spent in the industry. Choice A, therefore, is the best and, incidentally, most concise answer.

(*For details on modification, turn to pages 42 and 104.*)

Other grammatical problems found in the ACT are illustrated in the sentences that follow:

- Pronoun-antecedent agreement (*Page 11*)

> **A high school student needs** to be well organized if *they* want to succeed.
> **REVISED: *High school students need*** to be well organized if *they* want to succeed.

- Verb forms and tenses (*Page 22*)

  After the bell had *rang*, the boys rushed to the cafeteria.
  REVISED: After the bell had *rung*, the boys rushed to the cafeteria.

  Tomorrow, when the president *walked* into the hall, everyone should stand.
  REVISED: Tomorrow, when the president *walks* into the hall, everyone should stand.

- Pronoun choice (*Page 6*)

  This is just between you and *I*, but I can't stand Boris.
  REVISED: This is just between you and *me*, but I can't stand Boris.

  Everyone should wear a hat unless you want to freeze.
  REVISED: *You* should wear a hat unless you want to freeze.

- Making comparisons (*Page 37*)

  That star is *more brighter* than the other one.
  REVISED: That star is *brighter* than the other one.

  Mars is closer to Earth than *any planet*.
  REVISED: Mars is closer to Earth than *any other planet*.

- English idiom (*Page 77*)

  Martha intends *on going* to the beach on Saturday.
  REVISED: Martha intends *to go* to the beach on Saturday.

- Word choice (*Page 82*)

  The ghost was seen walking *slow* around the reservoir.
  REVISED: The ghost was seen walking *slowly* around the reservoir.

Sentence structure questions

Questions on the structure of sentences may ask you to recognize and correct:

- Incomplete sentences
- Run-on sentences and comma splices
- Faulty parallelism
- Shifts between the active and passive voice
- Shifts in pronoun person or number
- Shifts in verb tenses
- Faulty coordination and subordination

Grammar Tests: ACT

EXAMPLE # 1

Shopping malls across the country <u>reporting</u> the usual
4

increase during the holiday season and the annual
decline in midsummer.

4. **F.** NO CHANGE
   G. issuing a report of
   H. have reported,
   J. report

Explanation: Here you are being asked to recognize a sentence fragment. The construction has a subject, *malls*, and also what looks like a verb, *reporting*. But the *-ing* form of a verb cannot serve as the main verb of a sentence without an accompanying helping verb, as in *is reporting* or *will be reporting*. Choice G has the same problem—an unusable *-ing* verb. Choice H contains a correct verb, but the addition of a comma between the verb and its object turns a reasonable answer into a wrong one. Only Choice J offers a verb that properly fits the subject and makes the sentence whole.

(*For details on complete sentences, turn to page 64.*)

EXAMPLE # 2

Consumers have grown accustomed to receiving holiday
catalogs <u>by mail they arrive</u> as early as Labor Day each year.
7

7. **A.** NO CHANGE
   B. that arrive by mail
   C. by mail, which arrives
   D. in the mail, many of them arrive

Explanation: The underlined words appear at a turning point in the sentence, the end of the first clause and the start of the second, where a change in the subject and verb occurs. The phrase *Consumers have grown* contains the subject and verb of the first clause. The second clause uses *they* as its subject, and *arrive* as its verb. Because the two clauses have separate subjects and verbs, and because no conjunction or mark of punctuation comes between them, the sentence consists of two independent clauses that have improperly been run together. Therefore, eliminate Choice A as a possible answer. Choice C contains *which*, a relative pronoun meant to refer to *catalogs*, but instead it appears to refer to *mail* because the verb *arrives*, like the noun *mail*, is singular. This ambiguity disqualifies C as a good choice. Choice D is similar to A except that the two sentences are erroneously joined by a comma. That leaves Choice B as the correct answer because it turns the second clause into a dependent clause beginning with *that*.

(*For details on run-on sentences and comma splices, turn to pages 66 and 67.*)

EXAMPLE # 3

The holiday season causes anxiety and depression
in many people who can't cope with crowded stores,
endless advertisements, <u>and less than cheerful feelings</u>.
8

8. **F.** NO CHANGE
   G. and they don't feel cheerful
   H. and less feeling of cheerfulness
   J. and their feelings of cheer are less

Explanation: This question tests your understanding of parallel structure. The sentence lists three problems that many people face during the holiday season. Each problem is stated in the same grammatical form—as the object of the preposition *with*. Each object—*stores, advertisements,* and *feelings*—is preceded and modified by an adjective. Because Choices G, H, and J fail to maintain this pattern, they are incorrect. Choice F is the best answer.

(*For details on parallel structure, turn to page 68.*)

Additional issues of sentence structure are illustrated in the following pairs of sentences:

- Shifts between the active and passive voice (*Page 72*)

  In the early spring colleges tell applicants whether they have been admitted, and decisions about which college to attend are made by students.
  REVISED: In the early spring colleges tell applicants whether they have been admitted, and students decide which college to attend.

- Shifts in pronoun person or number (*Page 6*)

  In our cooking class, you were graded on how well you seasoned the pea soup.
  REVISED: In our cooking class, we were graded on how well we seasoned the pea soup.

  An owl hoots at night, but they are silent during the day.
  REVISED: An owl hoots at night, but it is silent during the day.

- Faulty coordination and subordination (*Pages 48 and 49*)

  The canoe turned over in the rapids and a rock hit it.
  REVISED: The canoe hit a rock and turned over in the rapids.

  Ellie lost her sneakers because she found them again.
  REVISED: Ellie lost her sneakers, but she found them again.

Punctuation questions

Questions ask you to apply rules governing the use of:

- Commas (*page 85*)
- Semicolons, colons, and dashes (*pages 87 and 88*)
- Question marks and exclamation points (*page 89*)

EXAMPLE

For untold ages the game of life played according to
certain <u>rules</u>; meant that some of us won and others lost.
      7

7. A. NO CHANGE
  B. rules
  C. rules:
  D. rules,

Explanation: This is a punctuation question, pure and simple, because the choices differ from each other only in the mark of punctuation that follows *rules*. Read the whole sentence from start to finish before analyzing its parts. If you read only the first few words it may seem that the subject of the sentence is *game* and that its verb is *played*. A complete reading, however, reveals that *played* is really part of a clause, *played according to certain rules*, which modifies *game*.

Choice A is not a good choice because the material before the semicolon is a sentence fragment, and since semicolons may not be used to separate incomplete sentences, the punctuation is faulty. Choice C is equally poor because colons are used to introduce independent clauses that explain or illustrate previously stated ideas, or to introduce lists of items.

If you are drawn to Choice D, you may be thinking that commas sometimes come before and after a subordinate clause to set it apart from the rest of the sentence. That's true, but here, because no comma precedes the clause, no comma is needed to follow it. Moreover, commas don't normally separate subjects and predicates. In other words, D is incorrect because no comma is needed. Choice B, then, is the best answer.

During the timed ACT, a lengthy, time-consuming analysis such as this isn't necessary, or even possible. Most students would probably land on the right answer after a few seconds of checking which punctuation mark best fits the context.

The ACT almost never asks punctuation questions *per se*. That is, no question is devoted exclusively to the use of semicolons, commas, dashes, and so on. Rather, you'll encounter punctuation problems in the context of compound and complex sentences, appositives, sentence fragments, run-on sentences, comma splices, conjunction usage—all matters discussed earlier in this book.

Questions on Rhetoric

Questions relate to:

* Organization, including sequence of ideas, coherence, paragraphing, introductions, and conclusions
* Style, including word choice, wordiness, tone, use of language
* Strategy, including overall purpose, use of appropriate details, relevance to audience

To answer questions on rhetoric, it helps to be aware of the point and purpose of a given passage and each of its paragraphs. Understanding the passage and the role of each paragraph will help you decide whether the author has used an appropriate style, organized the material sensibly, and fully developed ideas in a clear, coherent manner.

EXAMPLE # 1

Divorce is a concept that many American children have come to
understand by bitter experience. <u>Indeed, it has obligated</u> suffering
5

on countless young people.

   5. A. NO CHANGE
      B. Though, it has caused
      C. In fact, it has imposed
      D. However, it has compelled

Before choosing an answer, examine the relationship between the two sentences by asking questions like these:

- Are the tone and style of the two sentences consistent with each other and with the whole passage?
- What is the function of the second sentence? Does it follow logically from the first? Does it develop an idea stated in the first? Does it offer an alternative point of view? Does it contradict the validity of the first sentence?

In other words, when a question consists of two or more sentences, it's important to consider how they relate to each other and to the passage as a whole.

Let's look at the choices for Example #1: Choice A contains the conjunctive adverb *indeed*, a word that links the two sentences and indicates that the second sentence is intended to support or develop the idea stated by the first. So far, so good. But the use of the word *obligated* in the second sentence presents a problem. Because *obligated*, which means *required* or *demanded*, makes little sense in the context, discard Choice A as the best answer.

Choice B begins with *Though*, a word that ordinarily introduces a contrasting thought or idea. But the second sentence, instead of departing from the idea of the first, seems to support it. Therefore, eliminate B as a possible answer.

Choice D is similar to B because the word *However* also implies the introduction of a contrasting idea. Yet, no contrast is stated in the second sentence. Also, the use of *compelled* is not appropriate in the context. For those reasons, D cannot be correct.

Choice C is the best and only answer. The phrase *In fact* clearly and logically links the two sentences. In addition, the verb *imposed* expresses just what the writer intended.

EXAMPLE # 2

The attorney's official report concluded that the root of the district's
problem is that the school administration customarily hires teachers who
<u>are incompetent toward</u> the subject they teach.

   10. F. NO CHANGE
      G. are inadequately trained in
      H. haven't a clue about
      J. are complete ditzes in

This sentence describes a serious problem in an unnamed school district. Your job is to decide which choice is error-free.

Choice F states the reason for trouble in the school district, but the phrase *incompetent toward* is not standard English usage. Instead, *incompetent in* should be used.

Choices H and J are expressed in strong, colorful words that are not likely to appear in an attorney's official report on a school district's educational program. Because the language is not consistent with the serious purpose of the report, eliminate H and J.

That leaves Choice G, a grammatical and appropriately worded description of the problem. G is the best answer.

ACT PRACTICE TEST A
ANSWER SHEET

Passage 1 The Good Old Days

1. Ⓐ Ⓑ Ⓒ Ⓓ
2. Ⓕ Ⓖ Ⓗ Ⓙ
3. Ⓐ Ⓑ Ⓒ Ⓓ
4. Ⓕ Ⓖ Ⓗ Ⓙ
5. Ⓐ Ⓑ Ⓒ Ⓓ

6. Ⓕ Ⓖ Ⓗ Ⓙ
7. Ⓐ Ⓑ Ⓒ Ⓓ
8. Ⓕ Ⓖ Ⓗ Ⓙ
9. Ⓐ Ⓑ Ⓒ Ⓓ
10. Ⓕ Ⓖ Ⓗ Ⓙ

11. Ⓐ Ⓑ Ⓒ Ⓓ
12. Ⓕ Ⓖ Ⓗ Ⓙ
13. Ⓐ Ⓑ Ⓒ Ⓓ
14. Ⓕ Ⓖ Ⓗ Ⓙ
15. Ⓐ Ⓑ Ⓒ Ⓓ

Passage 2 Policeman on Patrol

16. Ⓕ Ⓖ Ⓗ Ⓙ
17. Ⓐ Ⓑ Ⓒ Ⓓ
18. Ⓕ Ⓖ Ⓗ Ⓙ
19. Ⓐ Ⓑ Ⓒ Ⓓ
20. Ⓕ Ⓖ Ⓗ Ⓙ

21. Ⓐ Ⓑ Ⓒ Ⓓ
22. Ⓕ Ⓖ Ⓗ Ⓙ
23. Ⓐ Ⓑ Ⓒ Ⓓ
24. Ⓕ Ⓖ Ⓗ Ⓙ
25. Ⓐ Ⓑ Ⓒ Ⓓ

26. Ⓕ Ⓖ Ⓗ Ⓙ
27. Ⓐ Ⓑ Ⓒ Ⓓ
28. Ⓕ Ⓖ Ⓗ Ⓙ
29. Ⓐ Ⓑ Ⓒ Ⓓ
30. Ⓕ Ⓖ Ⓗ Ⓙ

Passage 3 Romping in the Pumpkin Patch

31. Ⓐ Ⓑ Ⓒ Ⓓ
32. Ⓕ Ⓖ Ⓗ Ⓙ
33. Ⓐ Ⓑ Ⓒ Ⓓ
34. Ⓕ Ⓖ Ⓗ Ⓙ
35. Ⓐ Ⓑ Ⓒ Ⓓ

36. Ⓕ Ⓖ Ⓗ Ⓙ
37. Ⓐ Ⓑ Ⓒ Ⓓ
38. Ⓕ Ⓖ Ⓗ Ⓙ
39. Ⓐ Ⓑ Ⓒ Ⓓ
40. Ⓕ Ⓖ Ⓗ Ⓙ

41. Ⓐ Ⓑ Ⓒ Ⓓ
42. Ⓕ Ⓖ Ⓗ Ⓙ
43. Ⓐ Ⓑ Ⓒ Ⓓ
44. Ⓕ Ⓖ Ⓗ Ⓙ
45. Ⓐ Ⓑ Ⓒ Ⓓ

Cut along dotted line.

Grammar Tests: ACT

Passage 4 Preparing for Success

46. Ⓕ Ⓖ Ⓗ Ⓙ   51. Ⓐ Ⓑ Ⓒ Ⓓ   56. Ⓕ Ⓖ Ⓗ Ⓙ
47. Ⓐ Ⓑ Ⓒ Ⓓ   52. Ⓕ Ⓖ Ⓗ Ⓙ   57. Ⓐ Ⓑ Ⓒ Ⓓ
48. Ⓕ Ⓖ Ⓗ Ⓙ   53. Ⓐ Ⓑ Ⓒ Ⓓ   58. Ⓕ Ⓖ Ⓗ Ⓙ
49. Ⓐ Ⓑ Ⓒ Ⓓ   54. Ⓕ Ⓖ Ⓗ Ⓙ   59. Ⓐ Ⓑ Ⓒ Ⓓ
50. Ⓕ Ⓖ Ⓗ Ⓙ   55. Ⓐ Ⓑ Ⓒ Ⓓ

Passage 5 Getting Along with the Amish

60. Ⓕ Ⓖ Ⓗ Ⓙ   66. Ⓕ Ⓖ Ⓗ Ⓙ   72. Ⓕ Ⓖ Ⓗ Ⓙ
61. Ⓐ Ⓑ Ⓒ Ⓓ   67. Ⓐ Ⓑ Ⓒ Ⓓ   73. Ⓐ Ⓑ Ⓒ Ⓓ
62. Ⓕ Ⓖ Ⓗ Ⓙ   68. Ⓕ Ⓖ Ⓗ Ⓙ   74. Ⓕ Ⓖ Ⓗ Ⓙ
63. Ⓐ Ⓑ Ⓒ Ⓓ   69. Ⓐ Ⓑ Ⓒ Ⓓ   75. Ⓐ Ⓑ Ⓒ Ⓓ
64. Ⓕ Ⓖ Ⓗ Ⓙ   70. Ⓕ Ⓖ Ⓗ Ⓙ
65. Ⓐ Ⓑ Ⓒ Ⓓ   71. Ⓐ Ⓑ Ⓒ Ⓓ

Directions: In each of the five passages printed on the left you will find sentences with segments underlined and numbered. A multiple-choice question about each underlined segment appears on the right. To answer the question, choose the alternative that best expresses the underlined word or phrase in standard written English or is most consistent with the style or tone of the passage. If you decide that the original is best, choose either A or F, indicating that NO CHANGE is needed.

Some questions will direct your attention to specific words or phrases, others to a broader section of the passage or to the passage as a whole. These questions are indicated with a number inside brackets or inside a box.

Once you have decided on an answer, fill in the blank space on the answer sheet. You are advised to read each passage completely before answering the questions. Also be mindful that to answer some questions you may need to read one or more sentences that precede or follow the sentence containing a question.

Passage 1

The Good Old Days

America's consumers spend forty to sixty dollars to
<u>1</u>
fill up their gasoline tanks with fuel costing

between three and four dollars a gallon, many yearn

for the good old days. Older drivers recall the

<u>decades when gasoline</u> cost thirty cents a gallon
<u>2</u>
and price wars among competing service stations

sometimes <u>have sent</u> the cost of a gallon
<u>3</u>
plummeting into the teens. <u>Imagine; Only nineteen</u>
<u>4</u>
<u>cents a gallon!</u> <u>The bottled water so popular today</u>
<u>4</u>   <u>5</u>
<u>costs more than that.</u>
<u>5</u>

1. **A.** NO CHANGE
   B. American consumers
   C. Because Americans
   D. Americas' consumers

2. **F.** NO CHANGE
   G. decades of time when gasoline
   H. decades, in which gasoline
   J. decades, when gasoline

3. **A.** NO CHANGE
   B. sended
   C. sent
   D. sending

4. **F.** NO CHANGE
   G. Imagine! only nineteen cents a gallon.
   H. Imagine nineteen cents a gallon.
   J. Imagine—only nineteen cents a gallon!

5. **A.** NO CHANGE
   B. A fill-up would cost less than two dollars.
   C. Automobiles had smaller gas tanks in those days, however.
   D. For five dollars you could buy a fill-up and then take your sweetheart out to dinner.

Yes, it's tempting sometimes to think back to old times and wish that life today were as easy, not to mention as cheap, <u>as the past</u>. If you go back <u>half a century, fifty years ago,</u> it seems that people lived in a consumer's paradise. <u>Because few people had credit cards, prices were low and people paid for goods in cash.</u>
> **6**　　　　　　　　　　**7**
> **7**
> **8**
> **8**
> **8**

In the early 1960's, food staples for a family of five might cost forty dollars a week. Milk was almost as cheap as gasoline, and a loaf of bread cost a quarter. Eggs sold for a nickel apiece. Butter, sugar, cheese, potatoes, beef—all were available at a fraction of today's cost. <u>Returning</u> to the mid-nineteenth century, the cost of living would be <u>lesser than</u> one-twentieth of what it is today. The price for a quart of milk in 1849, for example, was ten cents <u>a quart</u>. To buy a hundred pounds of flour would set you back two dollars. A pound of potatoes cost a penny and a half. In some places, especially rural areas, the market value of both food and nonfood items <u>was</u> immaterial. For a bushel of rice, a pair of shoes, or an iron kettle, a housewife had <u>to barter, she paying,</u> not in dollars but in sacks of homegrown
> **9**
> **10**
> **11**
> **12**
> **13**
> **13**

6. **F.** NO CHANGE
   G. as it was in the past
   H. as the past was
   J. like in the past

7. **A.** NO CHANGE
   B. half a century
   C. half a century,
   D. fifty years ago,

8. **F.** NO CHANGE
   G. Prices were low, and people could not spend their money recklessly.
   H. Although people paid for low-priced goods in cash.
   J. Prices were low and people paid for goods in cash.

9. **A.** NO CHANGE
   B. By going back
   C. If you went back
   D. To return

10. **F.** NO CHANGE
    G. less than
    H. still lesser than
    J. fewer than

11. **A.** NO CHANGE
    B. for a quart
    C. per quart
    D. OMIT the underlined words.

12. **F.** NO CHANGE
    G. were
    H. had been
    J. had to have been

13. **A.** NO CHANGE
    B. bartered, her paying
    C. to barter. She paid
    D. bartered, and paid,

potatoes, a blanket, or outgrown children's clothing.

Considering today's prices, you might think that our ancestors had it easy. But look at the facts and figures: Wages and the cost of living <u>having grown</u> [14] in virtually equal proportions through the generations. A minimum-wage worker in 1850, spending forty hours on the job each week, brought home about fifteen dollars. For an equivalent work week today, the wages would be three-hundred dollars or more. [15]

14. **F.** NO CHANGE
  G. have grown
  H. growing
  J. grows

15. Which of the following factual statements, if inserted at the end of the passage, would serve as the conclusion most consistent with the purpose and tone of the passage?
  A. The numbers differ significantly, of course, but in real dollars, or more important, in buying power, the amount is virtually the same.
  B. In "the good old days," people suffered from poorer health, lower life expectancy, greater lawlessness, and fewer recreational opportunities.
  C. The U.S. GNP (Gross National Product) in the 21st century exceeds the country's mid-19th century GNP by over 5,000 percent.
  D. Today we still spend roughly 40 percent of our income on food, clothing, and other essentials.

Passage 2

Policeman on Patrol

[1] Dan Lewis is an <u>officer, in his seventh year,</u> [16] with the Washington, D.C., police force. [2] Dan's beat <u>was</u> the northeast quadrant of the <u>city; one</u> of [17]   [18] the more dangerous sections of town. [3] On patrol, he wears a bulletproof vest and carries a nightstick, a gun, extra ammunition, two pairs of

16. **F.** NO CHANGE
  G. officer, in his seventh year
  H. officer in his seventh, year
  J. officer in his seventh year

17. **A.** NO CHANGE
  B. is
  C. was located
  D. being

18. **F.** NO CHANGE
  G. city one
  H. city, one
  J. city one,

handcuffs, pepper spray, <u>and his two-way radio is</u>
<u>portable</u>. [4] Whatever comes up he investigates.

[5] For most of his years on the force he's been doing "midnights," the only shift that starts on one date and ends on the next. [6] Between 11 PM and 7 AM Dan listens to his police radio and responds to the situations that crackle over the airwaves—a collision at New York Avenue near P Street, reports of broken glass or a stolen car, a bunch of guys shouting obscenities in the street. [20]

Sometimes Dan's nights are manic—moments of intense activity followed by endless lulls. On a quiet night, Dan might pick up a couple of domestic disputes or <u>assist</u> in an emergency medical evacuation. [22]

One wintry night last December, responding to a "man-with-a-gun" call, Dan shot someone to death, a man gone berserk on PCP. <u>Recalling the incident,</u> the man <u>had barged into the backseat</u> of a passing car stopped at a red light. As Dan ran toward the car, a late-model BMW with vanity plates, he yelled to the motorist that the man had a

19. **A.** NO CHANGE
    B. and a two-way radio that is portable
    C. and a two-way radio
    D. and a portable, two-way radio

20. The logic and coherence of the passage are best served by placing sentence 4:
    F. where it is now
    G. before sentence 2
    H. after sentence 2
    J. after sentence 6

21. **A.** NO CHANGE
    B. he is assisting
    C. would assist
    D. had assisted

22. The writer of the passage now wants to develop the idea of "intense activity" introduced earlier in the paragraph. Which of the following sentences would best accomplish this?
    F. A policeman must be prepared to handle an emergency at any time.
    G. On most nights Dan takes a coffee break, but sometimes he can't.
    H. Then there are nights when the city explodes, and Dan repeatedly puts his health and safety—even his life—on the line.
    J. His shift lasts eight hours, and during every one he is busy as a little beaver.

23. **A.** NO CHANGE
    B. Dan explained what happened
    C. Reviewing what happened,
    D. As Dan recalls the incident,

24. **F.** NO CHANGE
    G. had barged in the backseat
    H. barged in the rear seat
    J. into the rear seat had barged

gun. 25 Immediately, the driver and front seat passenger leaped out. Approaching the car, Dan ordered the man to raise both of his hands to the roof. The man looked at Dan <u>through vacantly eyes</u> [26] and said, "Shoot me." Then his body turned toward Dan, who sensed that the man was about to bring the muzzle of his pistol around to fire at him through the window. But Dan fired first. Yet the man kept turning toward Dan. It took three more rounds before the man was still.

Immediately Dan was put on administrative leave, a standard procedure following a shooting. An investigation <u>took place and five months later</u> [27] Dan was exonerated and returned to active duty. During his first night back, another <u>incident that has changed the course</u> of Dan's life: Responding to [28] another "man-with-a-gun" call, Dan went to the address <u>he'd been given, it turned</u> out to be a bad [29] call. That is, <u>neither a gun nor a suspect was</u> found. [30] Ever since, Dan has been worrying whether he has it in him to shoot again. He's grown tense on the job. He is short-tempered and brusque with his fellow officers. Anxious about doing the right thing, he's tempted to find a less dangerous way to earn a living.

25. The writer of the passage is thinking about deleting the phrase *a late-model BMW with vanity plates* from the previous sentence. By doing so, the main effect on the passage would be:
   A. NO CHANGE
   B. the removal of irrelevant material
   C. a loss of suspense in the account of the shooting incident
   D. a heightening of reality

26. F. NO CHANGE
   G. through eyes which are vacant
   H. with vacant eyes
   J. with vacancy

27. A. NO CHANGE
   B. took place, and five months later
   C. took place and in five months later
   D. took place, and, five months later

28. F. NO CHANGE
   G. incident, changing the course
   H. incident, that has changed the course
   J. incident occurred that has changed the course

29. A. NO CHANGE
   B. address he received, but it turned
   C. address that he'd been given, it turned
   D. address, it turned

30. F. NO CHANGE
   G. neither a gun or a suspect was
   H. neither a gun nor a suspect were
   J. a gun and a suspect was not

Passage 3

Romping in the Pumpkin Patch

Labor Day <u>commences</u> the start of pumpkin
₃₁
season. Piled on supermarket shelves, stacked on

roadside veggie stands, and displayed on countless

<u>front porches from</u> Maine to California, <u>an</u>
₃₂   ₃₃
<u>epidemic of pumpkins sweeps</u> across the land
₃₃
<u>between September to Halloween</u>. America buys
₃₄
most of <u>their</u> pumpkins in grocery stores, but
₃₅
<u>increasing amounts of consumers</u> make their way
₃₆
to the <u>countryside, in an effort</u> to be closer to
₃₇

31. A. NO CHANGE
    B. marks
    C. will symbolize
    D. has commenced

32. F. NO CHANGE
    G. front, porches from
    H. front porches; from
    J. front, porches, from

33. A. NO CHANGE
    B. an epidemic of pumpkins sweep
    C. millions of pumpkins sweep
    D. pumpkins in the million sweeps

34. F. NO CHANGE
    G. in between September to Halloween
    H. from September to Halloween
    J. from September and Halloween

35. A. NO CHANGE
    B. they're
    C. its
    D. it's

36. F. NO CHANGE
    G. consumers in larger amounts
    H. increasing numbers of consumers
    J. numbers of consumers in increasing
       amounts

37. A. NO CHANGE
    B. countryside in an effort
    C. countryside, trying
    D. countryside. In an effort

nature they pick pumpkins right off the ground. 38

Alas, harvesting a fresh pumpkin may not thrill every member of the family. 39 For an additional fee pumpkin sellers will drive you around on a hay wagon, serve you cider and pie, <u>let one feed the</u>
<u>goats</u>, and promise you a hair-raising trip
40
<u>through man-made artificial caves, where</u> witches
41
will shriek at you, wolves will howl, and spooks will try to scare you out of your wits. Such attractions

38. The writer wants to add a concluding sentence to the first paragraph. Which of the following would provide the most effective ending?
F. Around every bend in the road, they look for signs bearing such come-ons as "Find perfect pumpkins at Pete's U-Pik-It Pumpkin Patch" or "Polly's Pumpkin Farm. Free Doughnuts. Since 1975."
G. According to the U.S. Department of Agriculture, pumpkin farming has grown over 60 percent during the last decade.
H. Pumpkin meat has found its way into such food specialties as pumpkin pie, pumpkin jam, pumpkin fritters, pumpkin bread, and the ever-popular french fried pumpkin.
J. The increased commercialization of Halloween has helped pumpkin farmers make huge profits.

39. The writer is thinking of revising this paragraph by inserting a sentence between the first and second sentences. Which of the following would be LEAST appropriate?
A. To leave the passage as it is.
B. To add this sentence: "To keep their customers happy, growers have turned their farms into mini-amusement parks."
C. To add this sentence: "So, enterprising pumpkin growers have added glitzy diversions to the picking ritual."
D. To add this sentence: "Knowing this, growers have tried to broaden the appeal of the pumpkin-picking experience."

40. F. NO CHANGE
G. feed the goats
H. let you feed the goats
J. have the goats be fed

41. A. NO CHANGE
B. through man-made, artificial caves in which
C. through artificial caves throughout which
D. through man-made caves, where

have taken on a name: agri-tainment. What <u>it has</u>
₄₂
to do with picking pumpkins is anyone's guess, <u>but</u>
₄₃
amusement park distractions have become as
fundamental to pumpkin-picking as jack-o'-
lanterns are to Halloween.

Few pickers realize that the annual rite is largely
a ruse foisted on unwary consumers. It's true that
some pumpkins are picked right where they grew
from seeds, but the major portion of pumpkins
dragged home from the patch have been grown
somewhere else and placed strategically in an open
field. In effect, the pumpkins have become stage
props <u>prettily arranged</u> to entice unwitting
₄₄
shoppers. Farmers claim that cutting pumpkins off
the vine ahead of time makes the picking process
<u>cleaner, easier, and more safer</u>: no knives, no
₄₅
pruning shears, no dirt to wash off.

42. F. NO CHANGE
   G. it is having
   H. they have
   J. these have had

43. A. NO CHANGE
   B. nevertheless
   C. but nevertheless
   D. but, nevertheless

44. F. NO CHANGE
   G. whose pretty arrangement are for
   H. arranged careful and pretty
   J. carefully, and prettily, arranged

45. A. NO CHANGE
   B. cleaner, easier, and safer
   C. more cleaner, more easier, and safer
   D. more clean, easier, and more safer

Passage 4

Preparing for Success

Success means different things to different people, but everyone wants it. <u>To have wealth is also something that people want.</u> A desire to be
46
successful <u>which seems to be</u> built into the human
47
nervous system. It's an instinct, like self-preservation, and <u>as natural to do as breathing.</u>
48
<u>Unlike breathing however success</u> doesn't come
49
naturally for most people. It must be worked for.

Most ordinary success stories <u>begin in childhood,</u>
50
frequently with parents or other adults
taking a special interest in <u>his or her</u> development
51
and helping the youngster to acquire habits that
typically lead to success. Some children are taught
a work ethic early on and respond favorably to discipline and high expectations. Others thrive under
<u>the freedom that is guaranteed by the Constitution,</u>
52
youthful self-expression, and an abundance of
positive reinforcement. Some child-development
experts comment, <u>though,</u> that overabundant
53
praise can be damaging. Children accustomed to
effusive praise for everything they do may develop
a good self-image, but when reality sets in, they
often discover that the real world is relatively indif-

46. F. NO CHANGE
    G. Everyone also wants wealth.
    H. (Only wealth is something that people want more.)
    J. OMIT the underlined section.

47. A. NO CHANGE
    B. which seems to have been
    C. seems to have been
    D. would seem to be

48. F. NO CHANGE
    G. as natural as breathing
    H. as natural as doing breathing
    J. as natural like breathing

49. A. NO CHANGE
    B. Unlike breathing, however,
    C. Different than breathing, however,
    D. Different from, breathing however

50. F. NO CHANGE
    G. begin with childhood
    H. are introduced at the time of childhood
    J. start by the time of the elementary grades

51. A. NO CHANGE
    B. their
    C. children's
    D. a child's

52. F. NO CHANGE
    G. freedom,
    H. freedom, which is a guarantee of the Constitution,
    J. freedom, which, under the Constitution, is our right,

53. Which of the following alternatives to the underlined word would be the LEAST desirable?
    A. therefore
    B. however
    C. nevertheless
    D. while

ferent to the behaviors <u>that, once</u> won generous
                              54
approval.

<u>Growing up in a highly regimented and tightly</u>
                        55
<u>disciplined atmosphere, on the other hand, can</u>
                        55
<u>teach children to value high achievement through</u>
                        55
<u>hard work</u>. Many successful people attribute
   55
their <u>becoming successful people</u> not only to the
         56
discipline that had been imposed on them, <u>but on</u>
                                              57
the example set by their parents who dedicated
themselves for hours every day, <u>sometimes</u>
                                    58
<u>patiently sometimes in frustration</u> teaching them to
                58
use their time and talent constructively. They may
not have appreciated their parents' attentiveness at
the time, but in the end they think it paid off.

Observers note that some children raised in
<u>unceasing</u> strict and demanding circumstances
   59
grow up inhibited and feeling shortchanged about
having missed a real childhood. A sheltered
upbringing has kept these children from seeing the
world as it really is. Later in life they may rebel,
especially when they are let go, say, during their

54. **F.** NO CHANGE
    G. that once
    H. that, once,
    J. that once,

55. Which choice would be the most effective sentence for leading the reader from the previous paragraph to this one?
    A. NO CHANGE
    B. Theories about how children should be raised have changed over the years and often go through cycles.
    C. Standards of good behavior are difficult to enforce, as any parent will tell you.
    D. Teachers, for example, must often decide whether to reward students for trying hard even when the work is mediocre.

56. **F.** NO CHANGE
    G. fame
    H. success
    J. OMIT the underlined words.

57. **A.** NO CHANGE
    B. but also on
    C. but to
    D. but also to

58. **F.** NO CHANGE
    G. sometimes patiently, sometimes in frustration,
    H. sometimes patiently; sometimes not
    J. sometimes with patience, and, sometimes not

59. **A.** NO CHANGE
    B. unceasingly
    C. unending
    D. nonstop

freshman year in college. Feeling insecure, they may withdraw socially, and in the worst cases, become self-destructive. 60

60. This question deals with the entire passage. If the writer had intended to write an essay showing that success is more regularly achieved by people who had been brought up in strict, demanding circumstances, would this essay fulfill the writer's intention?
   F. Yes, because the essay contains more evidence to support the position that strict discipline is a prerequisite for success.
   G. Yes, because the writer implies that adults who lacked freedom as children learn to make choices regardless of their upbringing.
   H. No, because the writer doesn't say that one type of upbringing is better than another.
   J. No, because the writer suggests that child development experts cannot make up their minds about which kind of upbringing works best.

Passage 5

Getting Along with the Amish

[1]

The Amish are a Christian group with roots going back to sixteenth-century Europe. It has distinguished themselves in America by their plain clothing, simple living, and rejection of everyday conveniences such as electricity, telephones, and cars. In short, they favor traditional customs that, go back hundreds of years.

61. **A.** NO CHANGE
   B. It's distinguished
   C. Distinguishing themselves
   D. They have distinguished themselves

62. **F.** NO CHANGE
   G. customs that go back
   H. customs, that, go back
   J. customs, going back,

[2]

Most Amish in the United States live in: rural Pennsylvania, Ohio, and Indiana. More than 10,000 also live in Wisconsin, some of them near the little

63. **A.** NO CHANGE
   B. in: rural Pennsylvania, Ohio, and Indiana
   C. in rural Pennsylvania, Ohio, and Indiana
   D. in rural Pennsylvania; Ohio; and Indiana

town of Loyal. Although the Amish <u>live independ-</u>
⁶⁴
<u>ently separate lives</u> from "the English," as they call
⁶⁴
non-Amish people, they have a history of <u>getting</u>
⁶⁵
<u>along peaceful with</u> the citizens of Loyal.
⁶⁵
<u>Nevertheless,</u> a rift has grown <u>between</u> them in
⁶⁶   ⁶⁷
recent years. At the root of the problem is the

Amish use of horses and buggies. Whenever Amish

farmers <u>drives to</u> town for shopping or banking,
⁶⁸
they go by horse and buggy.

[3]

69 The citizens of Loyal have wearied of the

stench left by Amish horses and have grown tired

of stepping with care whenever they walk around

64. **F.** NO CHANGE
   G. live apart from
   H. live separately and independent lives
   J. live lives that are separate and independent

65. **A.** NO CHANGE
   B. peacefulness to
   C. peaceful getting along with
   D. getting along peacefully with

66. Which of the following would be the LEAST effective transition between this and the previous sentence?
   F. NO CHANGE
   G. However,
   H. By all means,
   J. Yet,

67. **A.** NO CHANGE
   B. among
   C. amongst
   D. up in between

68. **F.** NO CHANGE
   G. drives into
   H. drive to
   J. are driving into

69. The writer is thinking of adding a new sentence to introduce paragraph 3. Which of the following would be the most effective addition?
   A. Conversation at the town's post office and in coffee shops is usually about keeping the streets clean.
   B. The Amish tend to their horses and buggies as avidly as teenagers care for their first cars.
   C. Buggies present no problem, but horses, being horses, have a habit of dropping manure wherever they go.
   D. "The issue is that those people are different from us, and that's unfortunate," says Martha Peterson, a lifelong resident of Loyal.

town. <u>Besides</u>, they resent paying for crews to clean
70
their streets almost every day.

[4]

<u>Several years ago the Amish and the townspeople</u>
71
<u>tried to negotiate an agreement:</u> The Amish would
71
drive their horses only on certain streets and would

pay a fine if they neglected to clean up the areas

where they hitched their horses. In return, the town

would drop its insistence that the Amish put a

manure-catching device—a kind of diaper—on

their horses. But negotiations got nasty, causing the

Amish to withdraw their money from the local

banks and to boycott Loyal's stores and other busi-

nesses for a year. Since then, the town council has

discussed the matter repeatedly, but a solution has

yet to be found.

[5]

In the meantime, some members of the non-

Amish community harbor ill feelings about the

strangers who live so close by <u>but remain aloof.</u>
72
<u>Others welcome</u> the Amish, not for their sociability
72
but for their trade. For example, the owner of the

70. What is the best location for the underlined
word?
  F. Where it is now
  G. After the word *resent*
  H. After the word *paying*
  J. After the word *day*

71. **A.** NO CHANGE
  B. An agreement was attempted to be negoti-
ated several years ago by the Amish and the
townspeople.
  C. At attempt at negotiations for an agreement several years ago by the Amish and
the townspeople.
  D. OMIT the underlined sentence.

72. **F.** NO CHANGE
  G. and remain aloof, others welcome
  H. remaining aloof. Others welcome
  J. and are aloof and others welcome

town's hardware store, Tom Zettler, <u>asserts,</u> he
                                      73
makes 25 percent of his sales to the Amish.

73. **A.** NO CHANGE
    B. asserts
    C. asserts, that
    D. asserts, that,

74. Having reread the passage, the writer decides to add a sentence containing information that had been left out. The sentence is:

The head of the Amish community claimed that it was unsafe for buggies to be stopped in the middle of the street every time a horse relieved itself.

The most logical and effective place to insert this sentence is paragraph
    F. 2
    G. 3
    H. 4
    J. 5

75. Suppose the writer had planned to compose an essay comparing and contrasting the Amish way of life with that of other Loyal residents. Would this essay successfully achieve the writer's purpose?
    A. No, because the essay has a limited purpose—to describe one source of disagreement between the Amish and the townspeople.
    B. No, because the essay focuses on secret deals made between the Amish and the town administration.
    C. Yes, because the essay shows that diverse religious beliefs have led to longstanding hostility between the Amish and the townspeople.
    D. Yes, because the essay points out that the Amish use horses and buggies, whereas the residents of Loyal prefer cars.

ANSWER KEY

1. C	11. D	21. A	31. B	41. D	51. D	61. D	71. A
2. F	12. F	22. H	32. F	42. H	52. G	62. G	72. F
3. C	13. C	23. D	33. C	43. A	53. D	63. C	73. B
4. J	14. G	24. F	34. H	44. F	54. G	64. G	74. H
5. B	15. A	25. B	35. C	45. B	55. A	65. D	75. A
6. G	16. J	26. H	36. H	46. J	56. H	66. H	
7. C	17. B	27. B	37. D	47. C	57. D	67. A	
8. J	18. H	28. J	38. F	48. G	58. G	68. H	
9. C	19. C	29. B	39. A	49. B	59. B	69. C	
10. G	20. J	30. F	40. H	50. F	60. H	70. F	

ANSWER EXPLANATIONS

Passage 1

1. **C** Leaving the original version intact makes *consumers* the subject of the sentence and leads to a comma splice after the word *gallon*. Choice B has the same problem as Choice A. By maintaining *consumers* as the subject, you are left with a comma splice following the word *gallon*. Choice D is similar to A and B, with the additional problem of an apostrophe after the *-s* in *Americas*, suggesting that America is plural. The use of *because* in Choice C turns the construction into a dependent clause, thereby eliminating the comma splice.

2. **F** Choice G contains a redundancy: *decades* and *time*. Use one or the other but not both words. Choices H and J both include a misplaced and unnecessary comma.

3. **C** Choice A contains faulty verb tense. Because the sentence is cast in the past tense, *have sent*, a verb in the present perfect tense, is not appropriate. Choice B is wrong because *sended* is not standard English. Choice C is correct because the past tense of the verb *to send* is *sent*. Choice D attempts to use *sending* as the main verb of the clause beginning with *price wars*. The problem is that the *-ing* form of a verb may not serve as the main verb without a helping verb, as in *is sending* or *were sending*.

4. **J** Choice F misuses a semicolon to separate a word from a phrase. Choice G places the exclamation point in the wrong place—after the interjection *Imagine* instead of after the exclamation itself. The meaning expressed by Choice H is unrelated to the point of the passage. The use of the dash in Choice J creates an effective pause between *Imagine* and the rest of the sentence.

5. **B** Although interesting, the information given by the underlined statement wanders from the point of the paragraph. Choice B succinctly highlights the difference in gasoline prices between then and now. It is the best answer. Choices C and D include irrelevancies that weaken the coherence of the passage.

6. **G** The original version tries to compare *life* and *the past*, two things that cannot logically be compared. Choice H is the same as G. Choice J uses nonstandard English idiom. A properly worded comparison may use an *as . . . as*

construction: "*as* wild *as* a tiger," but never an *as . . . like* construction.

7. **C** The underlined portion of the sentence should be changed because the phrases *half a century* and *fifty years ago* are redundant. Choice B leaves out a necessary comma after the "*If*" clause. Choice D contains an error in standard English expression because one does not go back *fifty years ago* but one goes back *fifty years*. Delete *ago*.

8. **J** The transitional sentence needed here should provide a link between a paragraph discussing an idealized image of a long-ago consumer's paradise and the actual prices of everyday products. The original sentence (Choice A) attempts to attribute low prices to the scant use of credit cards, an inappropriate and essentially wrong-headed idea. Choice G introduces an idea about reckless spending that is not relevant to the passage. Choice H relates to the content of the passage but is a sentence fragment. Choice J is the best answer because it reiterates the idea that prices were low and introduces a discussion of a family's expenditures.

9. **C** Choice A contains a dangling participle. *Returning* modifies *cost* instead of a performer of the action such as *you* or some other pronoun or a noun. Choice B is similar to A. It fails to say who is "going back." D suggests that the writer is about to discuss the 19th century again, but the passage previously made no mention of the 19th century. C is the best answer: It uses an "if clause" followed by the conditional verb, *would be*.

10. **G** Choice F is incorrect because the comparative form of *less* is not *lesser* but *less*. Choice H is the same as F. Choice J uses

fewer, a word reserved for comparing things that are countable, such as marbles and cars. G is the best answer.

11. **D** Choices A, B, and C are all grammatically correct, but are also redundant because *quart* was used earlier in the sentence.

12. **F** Choice G contains disagreement between the singular subject (*value*) and the plural verb (*were*). Choices H and J improperly shift the verb away from the simple past tense.

13. **C** The underlined segment contains a pronoun, *she*, that serves as the subject of the second clause. The verb *paying*, however, is incorrect because an *-ing* verb requires a helping verb (as in *was paying* and *has been paying*) to serve as the main verb in a clause or sentence. Choice B is the same as A, but is an even poorer choice because *her* is an objective pronoun ineligible to be used as a subject. Choice D includes two superfluous commas.

14. **G** The underlined verb causes the construction to be a sentence fragment because a verb in the past progressive form may not act as the main verb of a sentence. H is a sentence fragment because the construction lacks a verb. The *-ing* form of a verb may not be the main verb without a helping verb as in *is growing* or *had been growing*. J is a singular verb that disagrees with its plural subject—*wages* and *cost*.

15. **A** The passage, which compares the cost of living then and now, makes the point that, although prices seemed lower in the past, in terms of purchasing power and wages they were not much different. Choices B, C, and D state ideas that are only marginally related to the point of the passage.

Passage 2

16. **J** The underlined words require no punctuation.

17. **B** Because the passage is in the present tense, the use of *was*, a verb in the past tense, is incorrect. Choice C also uses a verb in the past tense. Choice D improperly uses an *-ing* verb as the main verb of the sentence, causing the construction to be a sentence fragment.

18. **H** Choice F is incorrect because semicolons may not be used to separate a clause and a phrase. Choice G fails to include a comma to indicate that the phrase beginning with the word *one* is an appositive that defines the *northeast quadrant of the city*. Choice J includes a misplaced and unnecessary comma.

19. **C** The underlined phrase is not grammatically parallel to the other items on Dan's equipment list. Choice B is parallel to the other items but contains the word *portable*, a redundancy, because anything that is carried is portable by definition. Choice D includes an unnecessary comma and has the same redundancy as B.

20. **J** Because of its meaning, the sentence fits best after the list of problems Dan encounters on patrol.

21. **A** The verb *assist* is structurally parallel to the verb *pick up*. Choices B, C, and D lack the necessary parallelism.

22. **H** Choice F is unrelated to the idea of intense activity. Choice G does no more than weakly suggest nights of intense activity. Choice J supports the idea of intense activity, but the tone of "busy as a little beaver" is inconsistent with the rest of the passage. Only Choice H fulfills the writer's purpose.

23. **D** Choice A is a dangling modifier because the phrase *Recalling the incident* modifies *man* instead of *Dan*. Choice B is an independent clause that lacks punctuation, thereby forming a run-on sentence. Choice C has a modification problem similar to that of Choice A.

24. **F** Choice G contains a faulty word choice. The word *in* means "within," not "into," which refers to the motion of going from outside to inside. Choice H is the same as G with the addition of the incorrect use of the past tense of the verb. The past perfect *had barged* is called for because the action described took place before another past action, namely Dan's shooting of the man. Choice J uses inverted word order in an inappropriate context.

25. **B** Because the description of the car is unimportant, especially at a moment of tension in Dan's story, the passage is improved by the deletion.

26. **H** The underlined words include an adverb where an adjective is needed to modify the noun *eyes*. Choice G is wordy and shifts the verb tense from past to present. Choice J is awkwardly expressed.

27. **B** Choice A lacks a comma that is needed to separate the clauses of a compound sentence. In Choice C the phrase *in five months later* is a nonstandard English idiom. Choice D includes an unnecessary comma after *and*.

28. **J** Choices F, G, and H are sentence fragments. Each clause has a subject but lacks a viable verb.

29. **B** Choices A, C, and D contain a comma splice. Only Choice B recognizes the construction as a compound sentence requiring the use of a comma and a conjunction (*but*) between clauses.

30. **F** Choice G incorrectly pairs *or* and *neither*. Choice H uses a plural verb (*were*) with a singular subject. Choice J uses a singular verb (*was*) with the plural subject *gun* and *suspect*.

Passage 3

31. **B** Choice A, which contains *commences* and *start*, is redundant. Choice C uses the future tense instead of the present tense of the verb. Choice D contains a redundancy similar to that in A.

32. **F** Choice G includes a misplaced comma between the adjective *front* and *porches*, the noun it modifies. The semicolon in Choice H is an error because semicolons should function like periods, separating independent clauses. Choice J contains two superfluous commas.

33. **C** Both Choices A and B suffer from a problem in modification. The phrases beginning with *piled*, *stacked*, and *displayed* should modify *pumpkins*, not *epidemic*. Choice D contains a lack of agreement between the plural subject *pumpkins* and the singular verb *sweeps*.

34. **H** Choices F, G, and J contain nonstandard English idiom.

35. **C** The plural pronoun *their* lacks agreement with *America*, its singular antecedent. Choice B uses a contraction meaning *they are*. Choice D is a contraction meaning *it is*.

36. **H** The word *amounts* refers to uncountable quantities. *Numbers* refers to things that can be counted. Because consumers can be counted, *numbers* is the word to use in this context.

37. **D** Choices A and C are incorrect because each consists of two sentences separated by a comma instead of an end mark of punctuation. Choice B is a run-on sentence.

38. **F** Only Choice F continues to add details about the phenomenon of picking your own pumpkin. The other choices pertain to other aspects of the pumpkin industry.

39. **A** Choices B, C, and D contain sentences that improve the coherence of the paragraph by providing a link between the first and second sentences. Choice A leaves a gap.

40. **H** In Choice F the pronoun person shifts from second to third person. Choices G and J are not grammatically parallel to the other phrases in the list of activities at the pumpkin patch.

41. **D** Choices A and B contain redundancies because *man-made* and *artificial* mean essentially the same thing. Choice C is wordy and awkwardly expressed.

42. **H** Choices F and G contains the singular pronoun *it*, which lacks agreement in number with its plural antecedent *attractions*. Choice J shifts the sentence from the present to the past perfect tense.

43. **A** The use of *nevertheless* in Choice B creates a comma splice between two independent clauses. Both Choices C and D contain redundancies. Use *but* or *nevertheless*, not both.

44. **F** Choice G is wordy and awkward. It also lacks noun-verb agreement. Choice H uses adjectives instead of adverbs to modify the verb *arranged*. Choice J includes superfluous, inappropriate punctuation.

45. **B** Choices A, C, and D are incorrect because comparisons using *more* may not be made with adjectives in the comparative degree.

Passage 4

46. **J** The sentences in Choices F, G, and H digress from the main idea of the paragraph and detract from the paragraph's unity.

47. **C** Choices A and B are sentence fragments because each lacks a main verb. Choice D uses *would seem,* a weak conditional phrase.

48. **G** Choice A contains the awkward, nonstandard construction *to do breathing.* Similarly, Choice H uses *doing breathing.* In Choice J, *like* may not be used in place of *as.*

49. **B** Because *however* functions like a conjunction in Choice A, it must be set off by commas. Choice C contains *different than,* a nonstandard phrase. Choice D uses the standard phrase *different from*, but includes an unnecessary comma after *from* and fails to provide commas before and after *however.*

50. **F** In Choice G, the use of *with* instead of *in* is nonstandard English idiom. Choice H, a construction in the passive voice, suggests that most success stories are told to children—surely not the intent of the writer. Choice J makes little sense in the context of the passage.

51. **D** The pronouns in Choices A and B fail to refer to a specific noun or other pronoun. Choice C uses the plural *children* when the discussion is about a single *youngster.*

52. **G** References to the Constitution are irrelevant. The passage discusses freedom in a more personal sense—that is, parents giving children opportunities to make choices for themselves.

53. **D** Choices A, B, and C provide an appropriate link between contrasting ideas in the passage.

54. **G** In this context, no commas are needed.

55. **A** The underscored sentence introduces a paragraph on the effects of strict discipline. The other choices wander from this purpose.

56. **H** Choice F is wordy and needlessly repetitive. Choice G improperly narrows the focus of the passage, which discusses success in general, not *fame.* Choice J leaves the sentence without a coherent meaning.

57. **D** Choices A and B lack grammatical parallelism to the phrase *to the discipline.* Choice C lacks the word *also,* needed to complete the paired expression *not only . . . but also.*

58. **G** Choice F needs commas to separate the phrases inserted almost parenthetically into the structure of the sentence. Choice H misuses a semicolon, which should function like a period, separating two independent clauses. Choice J contains two superfluous commas.

59. **B** Choices A, C, and D are adjectives, but an adverb is needed to modify the adjectives *strict* and *demanding.*

60. **H** Choice H accurately describes the essay, which presents the pros and cons of each point of view.

Passage 5

61. **D** Choice A uses the singular pronoun *It* to refer to *The Amish*, a plural noun. In Choice B, the use of the contraction meaning *it is* turns the rest of the sentence into nonstandard English. Choice C is a sentence fragment because it lacks a main verb.

62. **G** Choices F, H, and J include improperly placed and unnecessary commas.

63. **C** Choices A and B are incorrect because colons should not be used to introduce a list or series when the list or series grammatically completes the introductory statement. Choice D is incorrect because semicolons should be used in lists only when items in the list contain commas, as in *Boston, Massachusetts; Bangor, Maine*, etc.

64. **G** Eliminate Choice F because *independently* and *separate* express essentially the same meaning, and *live . . . lives* is repetitive. Choices H and J are similar to Choice F.

65. **D** Choice A is incorrect because it uses the adjective *peaceful* instead of an adverb to modify the verb *getting along*. The use of *to* instead of *with* in Choice B is nonstandard English idiom. Choice C is the same as A.

66. **H** Choices F, G, and J are words that are used to introduce ideas that contrast with those stated previously. Choice H fails to do that.

67. **A** Choice B is incorrect because *among* refers to division of more than two. Choice C is a word that means *surrounded by*. Choice D uses the prepositions *up* and *in*, both unnecessary.

68. **H** In Choice F the singular verb *drives* fails to agree with the plural subject *farmers*. Choice G is the same as F. Choice J improperly shifts the verb to a different tense.

69. **C** Choice C, which alludes to the problem mentioned in the previous paragraph, deals with the substance of paragraph 3 and provides a bridge between the paragraphs. None of the other choices work as effectively.

70. **F** To move the underlined word to the places specified by Choices G, H, and J would do nothing but make the language awkward and unidiomatic.

71. **A** Choice B uses awkward passive construction. Choice C is a sentence fragment because it lacks a verb. Choice D would deprive the paragraph of a topic sentence.

72. **F** Choice G contains faulty punctuation because a period or semicolon (instead of a comma) must be used to separate sentences. Choice H contains faulty parallelism. The phrase *remaining aloof* is not grammatically parallel to *live so close by*. Choice J suffers from a stylistic flaw: Because it is a compound sentence meant to contrast opposing attitudes toward the Amish, the conjunction *and* is a weak choice of words. *But* would be better. In addition, the clauses of a compound sentence should be separated by a comma.

73. **B** Choices A and C include an unnecessary comma between the verb and the indirect quotation. Choice D contains two superfluous commas, the first between the verb and the indirect quotation, the other between *that* and the clause it introduces.

74. **H** Paragraph 4 discusses the details of the agreement between the town and the Amish. The sentence in question adds a new dimension to the discussion.

75. **A** Choice A accurately describes the purpose of the passage.

ACT PRACTICE TEST B
ANSWER SHEET

Passage 1 Runners Beware!

1. Ⓐ Ⓑ Ⓒ Ⓓ   6. Ⓕ Ⓖ Ⓗ Ⓙ   11. Ⓐ Ⓑ Ⓒ Ⓓ
2. Ⓕ Ⓖ Ⓗ Ⓙ   7. Ⓐ Ⓑ Ⓒ Ⓓ   12. Ⓕ Ⓖ Ⓗ Ⓙ
3. Ⓐ Ⓑ Ⓒ Ⓓ   8. Ⓕ Ⓖ Ⓗ Ⓙ   13. Ⓐ Ⓑ Ⓒ Ⓓ
4. Ⓕ Ⓖ Ⓗ Ⓙ   9. Ⓐ Ⓑ Ⓒ Ⓓ   14. Ⓕ Ⓖ Ⓗ Ⓙ
5. Ⓐ Ⓑ Ⓒ Ⓓ   10. Ⓕ Ⓖ Ⓗ Ⓙ   15. Ⓐ Ⓑ Ⓒ Ⓓ

Passage 2 The World's Worst Nuclear Accident

16. Ⓕ Ⓖ Ⓗ Ⓙ   21. Ⓐ Ⓑ Ⓒ Ⓓ   26. Ⓕ Ⓖ Ⓗ Ⓙ
17. Ⓐ Ⓑ Ⓒ Ⓓ   22. Ⓕ Ⓖ Ⓗ Ⓙ   27. Ⓐ Ⓑ Ⓒ Ⓓ
18. Ⓕ Ⓖ Ⓗ Ⓙ   23. Ⓐ Ⓑ Ⓒ Ⓓ   28. Ⓕ Ⓖ Ⓗ Ⓙ
19. Ⓐ Ⓑ Ⓒ Ⓓ   24. Ⓕ Ⓖ Ⓗ Ⓙ   29. Ⓐ Ⓑ Ⓒ Ⓓ
20. Ⓕ Ⓖ Ⓗ Ⓙ   25. Ⓐ Ⓑ Ⓒ Ⓓ   30. Ⓕ Ⓖ Ⓗ Ⓙ

Passage 3 Ghosts in the House

31. Ⓐ Ⓑ Ⓒ Ⓓ   36. Ⓕ Ⓖ Ⓗ Ⓙ   41. Ⓐ Ⓑ Ⓒ Ⓓ
32. Ⓕ Ⓖ Ⓗ Ⓙ   37. Ⓐ Ⓑ Ⓒ Ⓓ   42. Ⓕ Ⓖ Ⓗ Ⓙ
33. Ⓐ Ⓑ Ⓒ Ⓓ   38. Ⓕ Ⓖ Ⓗ Ⓙ   43. Ⓐ Ⓑ Ⓒ Ⓓ
34. Ⓕ Ⓖ Ⓗ Ⓙ   39. Ⓐ Ⓑ Ⓒ Ⓓ   44. Ⓕ Ⓖ Ⓗ Ⓙ
35. Ⓐ Ⓑ Ⓒ Ⓓ   40. Ⓕ Ⓖ Ⓗ Ⓙ   45. Ⓐ Ⓑ Ⓒ Ⓓ

Cut along dotted line.

Grammar Tests: ACT

Passage 4 Pros and Cons of Child Care

46. Ⓕ Ⓖ Ⓗ Ⓙ   51. Ⓐ Ⓑ Ⓒ Ⓓ   56. Ⓕ Ⓖ Ⓗ Ⓙ

47. Ⓐ Ⓑ Ⓒ Ⓓ   52. Ⓕ Ⓖ Ⓗ Ⓙ   57. Ⓐ Ⓑ Ⓒ Ⓓ

48. Ⓕ Ⓖ Ⓗ Ⓙ   53. Ⓐ Ⓑ Ⓒ Ⓓ   58. Ⓕ Ⓖ Ⓗ Ⓙ

49. Ⓐ Ⓑ Ⓒ Ⓓ   54. Ⓕ Ⓖ Ⓗ Ⓙ   59. Ⓐ Ⓑ Ⓒ Ⓓ

50. Ⓕ Ⓖ Ⓗ Ⓙ   55. Ⓐ Ⓑ Ⓒ Ⓓ   60. Ⓕ Ⓖ Ⓗ Ⓙ

Passage 5 Cinderella: A Rags to Riches Story

61. Ⓐ Ⓑ Ⓒ Ⓓ   66. Ⓕ Ⓖ Ⓗ Ⓙ   71. Ⓐ Ⓑ Ⓒ Ⓓ

62. Ⓕ Ⓖ Ⓗ Ⓙ   67. Ⓐ Ⓑ Ⓒ Ⓓ   72. Ⓕ Ⓖ Ⓗ Ⓙ

63. Ⓐ Ⓑ Ⓒ Ⓓ   68. Ⓕ Ⓖ Ⓗ Ⓙ   73. Ⓐ Ⓑ Ⓒ Ⓓ

64. Ⓕ Ⓖ Ⓗ Ⓙ   69. Ⓐ Ⓑ Ⓒ Ⓓ   74. Ⓕ Ⓖ Ⓗ Ⓙ

65. Ⓐ Ⓑ Ⓒ Ⓓ   70. Ⓕ Ⓖ Ⓗ Ⓙ   75. Ⓐ Ⓑ Ⓒ Ⓓ

Directions: In each of the five passages printed on the left you will find sentence segments that are underlined and numbered. A multiple-choice question about each underlined segment appears on the right. To answer the question, choose the alternative that best expresses the underlined word or phrase in standard written English, or the one that is most consistent with the style or tone of the passage. If you decide that the original is best, choose either A or F, indicating that NO CHANGE is needed.

Some questions will direct your attention to specific words or phrases, others to a broader section of the passage or to the passage as a whole. These questions are indicated with a number inside brackets or inside a box.

Once you have decided on an answer, fill in the blank space on the answer sheet. You are advised to read each passage completely before answering the questions. Also be mindful that to answer some questions you may need to read one or more sentences that precede or follow the sentence containing a question.

Passage 1

Runners Beware!

<u>Whether or not knowing it</u>, marathoners and
                    1
other long-distance runners face a host of common

perils. A little-known one <u>that surprise</u> most
                                    2
<u>runners however,</u> is one of the most <u>dangerous. Its</u>
       3   **4**
<u>the threat</u> that comes from drinking too much
   4
water.

To stave off dehydration, <u>runners, as well as</u>
                                        5
<u>athletes, in virtually every sport,</u> tend to drink
       5

1. **A.** NO CHANGE
   B. They have the knowledge or not
   C. Wanting to be informed,
   D. OMIT the underlined portion

2. **F.** NO CHANGE
   G. that surprises
   H. had been surpising
   J. surprised

3. **A.** NO CHANGE
   B. runners, however
   C. runners, however,
   D. runners however

4. **F.** NO CHANGE
   G. dangerous, it is the threat
   H. dangerous—the threat
   J. dangerous threats

5. **A.** NO CHANGE
   B. runners, as well as athletes in virtually every other sport,
   C. including runners and athletes, in virtually every sport
   D. runners as well as athletes,

plenty of water, especially in hot weather. <u>Before a</u>
₆
<u>race, runners cast off extra clothing they may</u>
₆
<u>have brought to the starting gate.</u> Because a
₆
marathon takes hours to complete, most partici-
pants drink still more during the race itself in order
to replenish the liquids they've lost through perspiration. Unaware of the dangers of drinking too
much, their health and well-being are <u>put to risk.</u>
₇
An excessive amount of water <u>dilutes your</u>
₈
blood. Water seeps into cells throughout the
body, including the brain. Swollen brain cells then
press against the inside of the skull, resulting in
hyponatremia—a condition that <u>completes the</u>
₉
<u>score.</u>
₉

    <u>Marathon authorities have lately spread the word</u>
₁₀
that runners should <u>limit and restrict their water</u>
₁₁
<u>intake</u> to no more than eight ounces of water every
₁₁
twenty minutes. They want to avoid situations such
as <u>that having occurred</u> during the New York City
₁₂

6. Given that all the choices are true, which one
develops the paragraph most logically and
effectively?
  F. NO CHANGE
  G. Sponsors provide bottled water and
Gatorade free of charge.
  H. Before the race they often guzzle water or
popular sports drinks such as Gatorade.
  J. Some runners carry plastic bottles filled
with water or a sports drink.

7. **A.** NO CHANGE
  B. in risk
  C. risky
  D. put at risk

8. **F.** NO CHANGE
  G. dilutes the
  H. diluted
  J. has diluted your

9. **A.** NO CHANGE
  B. has its limits
  C. can be fatal
  D. is without exception

10. **F.** NO CHANGE
  G. The word spread by marathon authorities
have lately been
  H. Spreading the word, which marathon
authorities say lately
  J. To spread the word, marathon authorities,
say

11. **A.** NO CHANGE
  B. restrict the amount of water they drink
  C. limit the amount and restrict the quantity
of their water intake
  D. limit their water drinking by restricting the
amount

12. **F.** NO CHANGE
  G. those occurring
  H. them which had occurred
  J. those which occurred

Marathon <u>in 2004, when more than</u> 350 runners
₁₃
were hospitalized with hyponatremia. Because the

symptoms of hyponatremia—leg cramps, dizzi-

ness, nausea—<u>are similar with those of</u> dehy-
₁₄
dration, or too little water, doctors treated some

patients by giving them intravenous fluids, <u>making</u>
₁₅
<u>medical malpractice lawsuits more widespread</u>.
₁₅

13. **A.** NO CHANGE
    B. in 2004, when more then
    C. in 2004 as over
    D. in 2004; when, over

14. **F.** NO CHANGE
    G. are similar to that of
    H. resemble those of
    J. is like

15. **A.** NO CHANGE
    B. opening them up to charges of malpractice
    C. giving patients grounds for suing the doctors
    D. OMIT the underlined portion.

Passage 2

The World's Worst Nuclear Accident

On April 26, 1986, Nuclear Reactor #4 at

Chernobyl in the former USSR (now Ukraine)

<u>overheated excessively and suddenly exploded</u>. The
₁₆
explosion, history's <u>most worse</u> nuclear
₁₇
accident, created a fireball that spewed tons of

radioactive material into the atmosphere. Winds

spread the radioactivity across Earth's

Northern Hemisphere. Thirty people died in the

<u>explosion; many more were to die later</u> in Ukraine,
₁₈
neighboring Belarus, and Russia. More than

135,000 people had to be evacuated from their

homes and farms. To this day, many <u>thousands, had</u>
₁₉
<u>not returned yet</u>.
₁₉

16. **F.** NO CHANGE
    G. overheated and exploded
    H. overheated excessively, and afterward exploded suddenly
    J. suddenly, exploded after overheating excessively

17. **A.** NO CHANGE
    B. most worst
    C. worst
    D. terrible

18. **F.** NO CHANGE
    G. explosion, many more were to die later
    H. explosion. Many more had died later
    J. explosion; much more died later

19. **A.** NO CHANGE
    B. thousands have not returned
    C. thousands, haven't yet returned
    D. thousands are still not returned

The Ukraine Radiological Institute reported that radiation poisoning <u>might have caused</u> more than
20
2,500 deaths within a few months of the accident.

<u>Their studies also find that</u> the incidence of
21
<u>cancer, especially thyroid cancer</u> increased by 64
22
percent among people who lived within a 20-mile radius of the reactor as well as among the "liquida-tors" (that is, the men and women <u>who helped</u>
23
<u>clean up after</u> the accident). Masses of people
23
suffered long-term psychological disorders from the trauma and stress of the experience. They became depressed and overcome with feelings of extreme hopelessness, leading to social withdrawal and iso-lation. [24]

Now, a generation later, the accident's aftereffects are still being felt. Belarus contains some of the most contaminated places on the globe. Much of the land is still <u>radioactive, in fact,</u> in <u>only a 1 percent</u>
25   **26**
<u>fraction</u> of the region's farmland has contami-
26

20. F. NO CHANGE
    G. might of caused
    H. could of caused
    J. could cause

21. A. NO CHANGE
    B. Their studies also found that
    C. It's studies also found that
    D. It also found

22. F. NO CHANGE
    G. cancer—especially thyroid cancer—
    H. cancer; especially thyroid cancer,
    J. cancer, cancer of the thyroid,

23. A. NO CHANGE
    B. which helped clean up after
    C. that have helped afterward to clean up
    D. who helped clean from

24. Which of the following true statements, if added here, would provide the best evidence to support the assertion that residents close to the accident suffered from psychological problems?
    F. The suicide rate increased by 30 percent during each of the five years after the accident.
    G. In Ukraine, clinics and hospitals were built rapidly to treat victims of the blast.
    H. Many more students in medical colleges throughout the country began to specialize in the treatment of mental diseases.
    J. Alcohol consumption remained higher than ever, and the life expectancy of men fell from 62 to 58 years.

25. A. NO CHANGE
    B. radioactive, that
    C. radioactive; in fact,
    D. so radioactive that in fact

26. F. NO CHANGE
    G. just that 1 percent
    H. a 1 percent fraction
    J. only a fraction

nation <u>cooled off sufficient to let</u> farmers to plant
₂₇
and grow rye, barley, and other crops. Although
horse breeding has begun, and cattle are being
raised for beef, dairy farming hasn't returned
because of <u>people's fear toward</u> radiated milk.
₂₈
Health authorities still warn people not to eat wild
game, mushrooms, or berries, which absorb high
levels of radiation. <u>Fish caught</u> in lakes and streams
₂₉
are toxic, and the honey produced by local bees is
unsafe.

   [1] Chernobyl's legacy is bound to continue for a
long time. [2] Ever so slowly the people of the area
are trying to reclaim lands and enjoy the lifestyle of
pre-Chernobyl days. [3] Complete normalcy, however, isn't likely to return until the 22nd century, if
ever. 30

27. **A.** NO CHANGE
    B. cooled off sufficient for
    C. cooled down sufficiently so as to let
    D. cooled sufficiently for

28. **F.** NO CHANGE
    G. people's fear of
    H. the peoples' fear to
    J. people's fear with respect of

29. **A.** NO CHANGE
    B. Fishing
    C. Catching fish
    D. The fish catched

30. The writer is considering the addition of the following true sentence to the last paragraph:

    Radioactive materials such as censium-137 take decades to lose their potency.

    Should the sentence be added to the paragraph, and if so, where should it be placed?
    F. Yes, before sentence 1.
    G. Yes, after sentence 2.
    H. Yes, after sentence 3.
    J. The sentence should NOT be added.

Passage 3

Ghosts in the House

The majority of Americans don't believe in
UFOs, in Elvis sightings, making contact with dead
ancestors, and most other supernatural phenomena. Yet, a large percentage—over a third of the
adults interviewed during a recent Gallup Poll—
admitted believing that ghosts reside among us and
haunting many of our houses.

[1] A case in point is the Zamora family of
Cypress, Texas. [2] The day ten years ago that
Harry and Lesli Zamora moved into their home on
a dead-end street, they have been tormented by
mysterious visions, unusual flashes of light, a door
that locks itself, and appliances that ran when
nobody is home. [3] The Zamoras claim to keep
losing things. [4] They leave their car keys on the
kitchen counter, but later they show up in a
bedroom. 36

Mrs. Zamora says that she has felt hands brushing

31. At this point in the essay the writer wants to show that Americans are not a terribly super-stitious people. Given that all of the choices are true, which one best conveys that idea?
A. NO CHANGE
B. For years, reports of UFOs, ESP, Elvis sightings, and making contact with dead relatives have made headlines in newspapers and other media.
C. Because people are fascinated by super-natural phenomena, publishers have made a great deal of money selling books that describe mysterious happenings.
D. A vast number of otherwise rational people get excited by made-up stories of UFOs, ESP, Elvis sightings, and otherworldly occurrences.

32. F. NO CHANGE
G. among us and haunt
H. in, and haunt
J. among us, and haunting

33. A. NO CHANGE
B. On the day ten years ago
C. From the day ten years ago
D. Beginning in the day ten years ago

34. F. NO CHANGE
G. running
H. having been run
J. that run

35. A. NO CHANGE
B. the keys show up
C. it shows up
D. they appear

36. For the sake of clarity, the writer is considering a change in the ending of sentence 4. Which of the following would best clarify the meaning of the sentence?
F. NO CHANGE
G. . . . bedroom; where they were taken by a ghost.
H. . . . bedroom; after the keys are moved there.
J. . . . bedroom; ghosts presumably relocated it.

her as she moves around the house. <u>An ominous</u>
<u>black-clad figure behind her husband when he was</u>
<u>emerging from the shower was once seen by her.</u>
She also recounts an episode in early 2010. While she chatted on the phone with a friend, a strange white dog with a pink collar darted through the room. Explaining what occurred, <u>the previous</u>
<u>occupant, who died</u> in the house, owned a dog that had left deposits of white hair all over the premises. <u>The Zamoras' since then</u> have bought a dog of their <u>own; but he or she avoids</u> certain areas of the backyard where police cadaver dogs have detected human remains buried <u>in what once has been</u> the cemetery for the plantation <u>standing on the</u>
<u>property long ago in the nineteenth century.</u>

37. **A.** NO CHANGE
    B. She once saw an ominous black-clad figure behind her husband when he was emerging from the shower.
    C. Emerging from the shower, her husband once had an ominous black-clad figure behind him, and Mrs. Zamora had seen it.
    D. Once, as he emerged from the shower, an ominous black-clad figure seen by Mrs. Zamora.

38. **F.** NO CHANGE
    G. the former owner had died
    H. she recalls that the previous occupant, who had died
    J. Mrs. Zamora makes clear that the former owner died

39. **A.** NO CHANGE
    B. The Zamora's since then
    C. Since then, the Zamoras
    D. Since, the Zamoras'

40. **F.** NO CHANGE
    G. own, he or she avoids
    H. own it avoids
    J. own, but it avoids

41. **A.** NO CHANGE
    B. in formerly what had been
    C. in what once had been
    D. in what previously in former times was

42. **F.** NO CHANGE
    G. standing on the property long ago in the nineteenth century
    H. that they had on the site long ago
    J. that stood on the site in the nineteenth century

Irrespective of the years, science has been
<u>unable to explain</u> the events occurring in the
43
Zamoras' home. The Zamoras are not a wacky,
delusional couple out to perpetuate a hoax.

<u>A toughly minded realist</u> Harry Zamora is a well-
44
respected Houston police officer. But a researcher
from a group that studies the paranormal says,
"Once an idea that a place is haunted takes hold
with susceptible people, things are no longer accidental." <u>Consequently, "she is confident that the</u>
<u>Zamoras are on the level."</u>
45

43. Given that all the choices are true, which of the following provides the most effective opening for the last paragraph of the passage?
   A. NO CHANGE
   B. For some people, they might say that science is unable to account for
   C. Starting in 2010, then, no one is smart enough to fully explain
   D. Science can't explain

44. F. NO CHANGE
   G. Tough and realistic
   H. As a toughly minded realist
   J. Realistically and toughly minded

45. A. NO CHANGE
   B. With confidence, therefore, the researcher says that the Zamoras are "on the level."
   C. "Consequently," the researcher says, "she is confident that the Zamoras are on the level."
   D. Therefore, she believes "that the Zamoras are on the level," she says confidently.

Passage 4

Pros and Cons of Child Care

[1] <u>Being a worrisome issue</u> for many working
46
parents, both single dads and moms as well as
couples, is how to care for their young children, age
two to four, on days when they can't be at home.
[2] Parents deal with this problem in many different
ways, one of the most <u>common, is</u> public child care
47
programs. [3] Whether children thrive <u>by</u> such
48

46. F. NO CHANGE
   G. A worrisome issue
   H. Worrying an issue
   J. Worry about the issue

47. A. NO CHANGE
   B. common, is
   C. common: are
   D. common being

48. F. NO CHANGE
   G. on
   H. in
   J. for

programs <u>is long been</u> an unanswered question.
49

[4] Recent studies, however, have found mixed results that are both comforting and alarming at the same time. ⬚50

The most hopeful data show that group child care ultimately leads to higher skills in math and <u>reading, the greatest gains are being recorded</u> by
51
children from poor families. <u>Unlike poor children,</u>
52
<u>the</u> gains by children from middle-class homes are
52
more modest, and <u>an affluent child from the most</u>
53
<u>well-to-do families standing</u> to gain the least from
53
group child care, probably because their home environments <u>had already given</u> them a head start
54
in early language and mathematical learning.

Studying the long-term effects of group child care, a research team from the National Institute of Child Health and Human Development <u>have</u>
55
<u>followed</u> the progress of thousands of children
55
from preschool through the primary years. <u>It was</u>
56
<u>found</u> that youngsters who spend 30 or more
56

49. **A.** NO CHANGE
B. is long
C. has long been
D. has been long

50. For the sake of logic and coherence in the first paragraph, where should Sentence 4 be located?
F. NO CHANGE
G. After Sentence 1
H. After Sentence 2
J. DELETE it from the passage.

51. **A.** NO CHANGE
B. reading, and the greatest gains are being recorded
C. reading, with the greatest gains recorded
D. reading the greatest gains recorded

52. **F.** NO CHANGE
G. In contrast with
H. Different from
J. DELETE the underlined words (begin the sentence with *Gains by…*).

53. **A.** NO CHANGE
B. an affluent child stands
C. children from well-to-do families stand
D. an affluent child from a well-to-do home stands

54. **F.** NO CHANGE
G. have given
H. already gives
J. already gave

55. **A.** NO CHANGE
B. followed
C. following
D. in order to follow

56. Which of the following alternatives to the underlined words is NOT acceptable?
F. They found
G. The findings reveal
H. The study provides evidence
J. An analysis of the research confirms

hours a week in group child care <u>scored more</u>
<u>higher</u> academically than those cared for in other
ways. After third grade, however, the differences
between the groups diminish, and other factors,
such as <u>some had greater natural ability, family</u>
<u>income, and the educational level</u> of parents, seem
to have a greater bearing on in-school performance.

On the downside, children in early child care
programs experience slower social development
than peers who are cared for at home or in other
settings. Their behavior is more aggressive and
negative, especially among the offspring of the
wealthiest parents. But by third grade, these differences by and large disappear.

These findings suggest a need for changes that
<u>will encourage greater public support for early</u>
<u>child care programs, regardless of the income</u>
<u>level</u>. The caregivers in the programs may also
need more advanced training in group <u>management</u>
<u>because of modifying</u> the behavior of socially
challenged youngsters while giving all children a
chance to grow and excel.

57. A. NO CHANGE
    B. scored more highly
    C. score higher
    D. have scored high

58. F. NO CHANGE
    G. some have greater natural ability, or family income or educational level
    H. natural ability, family income, and the educational level
    J. greater natural ability; higher family income; and more advanced education

59. Given that all the choices are valid, which one contains ideas that are most crucial to the development of the essay as a whole?
    A. NO CHANGE
    B. leave no child behind, including those in private and parochial schools
    C. provide nicer experiences for all young children, rich and poor alike
    D. make early child care programs beneficial to all young children regardless of their income level

60. F. NO CHANGE
    G. management in order to modify
    H. management, for modification of
    J. management. This modifies

Passage 5

Cinderella: A Rags to Riches Story

If you <u>drop by a toy store, recently, as I did,</u> to buy
₆₁
a gift for my kid sister, you will probably see
Cinderella in every nook and corner. <u>Nevertheless,</u>
₆₂
she's not the Cinderella I remember from my
childhood, <u>the one that once was a TV musical.</u>
₆₃
Only the intervention of a fairy godmother gave
her <u>a temporary and short-lived moment of relief</u>
₆₄
from a life of drudgery and abuse. Her transformation into a beautiful debutante wearing eye-
catching <u>clothes last only</u> a few hours. At midnight,
₆₅
back in <u>rags, she sits</u> humbly in the dust.
₆₆

As everyone knows, her story doesn't end there.
The Prince, smitten by the anonymous beauty he
danced with at the ball, sends out his aides to locate
the one foot in all the land that will fit into the
glass slipper she left behind. The foot belongs to
<u>Cinderella, of course, all ends happily</u> ever after.
₆₇

61. **A.** NO CHANGE
 B. recently drop by a toy store, as I did,
 C. drop by recently, as I did, a toy store,
 D. drop by a toy store, as I did recently,

62. **F.** NO CHANGE
 G. Furthermore,
 H. As a consequence,
 J. OMIT the underlined word.

63. Given that all the following choices are valid, in the context of the passage which one best defines the character that the narrator remembers from childhood?
 A. NO CHANGE
 B. the poor, soot-covered young waif, cowering in fear of her wicked stepmother and tyrannical stepsisters
 C. a symbol of social and economic deprivation
 D. the one that my mother said brought back sad memories of her own girlhood

64. **F.** NO CHANGE
 G. moment of relief
 H. temporary moment of relieved
 J. temporarily, a short-lived moment of relief

65. **A.** NO CHANGE
 B. clothes that last only
 C. clothing that only lasts
 D. clothes lasts only

66. **F.** NO CHANGE
 G. rags, sitting
 H. rags and she sits
 J. rags she is sitting

67. **A.** NO CHANGE
 B. Cinderella, of course, and all ends happily
 C. Cinderella, of course all ends happily
 D. Cinderella of course, and all ends happy

As I've already said, I was on a shopping expedition
                                                68
to a toy store. Knowing that two- to six-year-old
    68
girls would be unable to resist a line of Cinderella

products, the Disney company has evidently turned

Cinderella into a commercial bonanza. Naturally,
                                                69
Cinderella dolls for sale and a Cinderella app for
        69   70
running on their pink and blue Cinderella smart
    70
phones and iPads. You can buy Cinderella costumes

complete with sparkly tiaras and glass slippers.

The shelves are packed with Cinderella games,

puzzles, tea sets, toy coaches, coats for dogs, even

a waffle iron that can stamp an image of a smiling

Cinderella right into the batter. ⟨71⟩

    Using this approach, amid all the Cinderella
                    72
glitter, hardly a trace of the wonderful old fairy tale

can be found. The original Cinderella, a patient,

68. Given that all the choices are valid, which one
    would serve most effectively as the introduc-
    tory sentence of the paragraph?
    F. NO CHANGE
    G. My sister usually likes the presents I give
       her.
    H. In the store, I found Cinderellas by the
       hundreds.
    J. When I was growing up, Barbie was the
       doll of choice among little girls.

69. A. NO CHANGE
    B. Selling Cinderella dolls naturally,
    C. Naturally, that sale of Cinderella dolls
    D. Cinderella dolls are for sale, naturally,

70. F. NO CHANGE
    G. app to be run on
    H. app for running by
    J. app for the running on

71. The writer is considering the addition of the
    following true statement:

    **For $70 you can take home Magical Talking
    Vanity, among a multitude of other products.**

    Should the writer make the addition here?
    A. Yes, because it is important for readers to
       know the cost of toys.
    B. Yes, because it helps the reader develop a
       deeper understanding of what the narrator
       observed in the toy store.
    C. No, because it's unclear that a Magical
       Talking Vanity has anything to do with
       Cinderella.
    D. No, because it is anticlimactic; the writer
       has already proved that a multitude of
       Cinderella products is available.

72. F. NO CHANGE
    G. Explicitly
    H. Hopefully
    J. Sad to say

modest, good-hearted lass who <u>has befriended</u>
                                    73
mice and scrubbed floors until she dropped,

possessed virtues that little girls might have emu-

lated. Now, however, she's been transformed into

an elegant socialite, <u>whom</u> promotes only crass
                         74
materialism among the legions of her fans and

admirers. ⁊5̄

73. **A.** NO CHANGE
    B. has made friends with
    C. befriended
    D. befriending

74. **F.** NO CHANGE
    G. who
    H. which
    J. DELETE the underlined word.

75. Given that all the choices are valid or true,
    which one would provide the most fitting
    conclusion to the essay as a whole?
    A. Stunned by the makeover, I bought my
       sister the biggest Cinderella doll I could
       find.
    B. Depressed, I left the store empty-handed.
    C. As a girl, I don't remember many such
       opportunities coming along.
    D. The array of Cinderella products will no
       doubt inspire many shoppers like me to
       re-read the story.

ANSWER KEY

1. D	11. B	21. D	31. A	41. C	51. C	61. D	71. D
2. G	12. J	22. G	32. G	42. J	52. J	62. J	72. J
3. C	13. A	23. A	33. C	43. D	53. C	63. B	73. C
4. H	14. H	24. F	34. J	44. G	54. G	64. G	74. G
5. B	15. D	25. C	35. B	45. B	55. B	65. D	75. B
6. H	16. G	26. J	36. F	46. G	56. F	66. F	
7. D	17. C	27. D	37. B	47. D	57. C	67. B	
8. G	18. F	28. G	38. H	48. H	58. H	68. H	
9. C	19. B	29. A	39. C	49. C	59. D	69. D	
10. F	20. F	30. J	40. J	50. F	60. G	70. G	

ANSWER EXPLANATIONS

Passage 1

1. **D** Because the perils of running are described as *common*, the underlined words, which are awkwardly expressed and confusing, are unnecessary. Choice B is a complete sentence that creates a comma splice and is neither grammatically nor logically related to the sentence that comes next in the passage. Choice C is a participle phrase that has no logical connection with the sentence it modifies.

2. **G** In Choice F the plural verb *surprise* disagrees in number with the singular pronoun, *one*. Choices H and J incorrectly shift the verb tense away from the present, the tense in which the passage is written.

3. **C** The word *however*, when used as a transitional word between two contrasting ideas, must be set off by commas.

4. **H** Choice F uses *Its*, the possessive pronoun, instead of *It's*, the contraction meaning *it is*. Choice G contains a comma splice. Choice J lacks punctuation between *dangerous* and *threats*, where a comma is needed.

5. **B** Choices A and C contain commas that unnecessarily separate the noun *athletes* from the phrase *in virtually every sport*. The meaning of Choice D suggests that runners are different from athletes, an idea that the writer certainly didn't intend.

6. **H** Because the topic being discussed is the amount that marathoners drink while racing, Choice H contributes most to the paragraph's coherence.

7. **D** The use of *to* in Choice A is nonstandard, unidiomatic English. Likewise, Choice B misuses the preposition *in*. Choice C misstates the writer's intent by describing health and well-being as *risky*.

8. **G** Choice F improperly shifts the text, written in third person, to second person. Choice H shifts the text from present to the past tense. Choice J changes both the verb tense from present to present perfect and the use of pronouns from third person to second person.

9. **C** Only Choice C uses understandable language that accurately conveys meaning.

10. **F** In Choice G the singular subject *word* fails to agree in number with the plural verb *have been*. Choice H is an incomplete sentence because the construction lacks a main verb. Choice J includes an improperly placed comma between the subject *authorities* and the verb *say*.

11. **B** Choice A contains a redundancy because *limit* and *restrict* have essentially the same meaning. Choices C and D contain similar redundancies.

12. **J** Choice F uses the singular *that* to refer to the plural *situations*. Choice G improperly uses a verb in the present progressive tense instead of a verb in the past tense. Choice H uses the objective case pronoun *them* instead of the subject pronoun *those*.

13. **A** Choice B uses *then* instead of *than*. Choice C leaves out the comma needed to separate the clauses of the sentence. Choice D improperly uses a semicolon instead of a comma to separate the independent and dependent clauses of the sentence.

14. **H** Choice F contains *similar with*, an unidiomatic, nonstandard phrase. In Choice G, the singular *that* refers to the plural *symptoms*. In Choice J the singular verb *is* lacks agreement in number with its subject *symptoms*.

15. **D** Choices A, B, and C contain ideas only marginally related to the subject of the passage.

Passage 2

16. **G** Note that *overheated* and *excessively* are redundant, as is *suddenly exploded* because explosions are always sudden; they never

happen gradually. Choices F, H, and J contain these redundancies. Choices H and J also include superfluous commas.

17. **C** The problem with Choice A lies in the use of *most* with an adjective in the comparative instead of the positive degree. Choice B contains the same error as A, except that an adjective in the superlative degree has been used. Choice D makes little sense in the context because the adjective *terrible* implies that history has seen but one terrible nuclear accident—implying that other accidents were not terrible.

18. **F** Choice G contains a comma splice. Choice H improperly shifts the verb tense from the past tense to the past perfect. Choice J contains an error in word choice. The phrase *much more* applies to mass quantities—quantities that cannot be counted, such as water and wheat. Because deaths can be counted, the proper phrase is *many more*.

19. **B** Because the situation being described still exists, the present perfect tense should be used, and Choice A improperly uses the past perfect tense. Choice C contains an unnecessary comma between the subject and verb. It also contains a redundancy: The word *yet* is virtually identical in meaning to the phrase *to this day*. Choice D, which substitutes *still* for *yet*, contains a redundancy similar to that in Choice C.

20. **F** The word *of* in Choices G and H is nonstandard English usage. Choice J inappropriately shifts the verb tense from the past perfect to the future, as if to say that someday the deaths may occur.

21. **D** Choice A contains the plural pronoun *Their*, which lacks agreement with its singular antecedent, *Institute*. It also shifts the

verb tense of the passage from past to present. Choice B contains the same problem in pronoun-antecedent agreement as A. Choice C uses the contraction meaning *it is* instead of the possessive pronoun *its*.

22. **G**   *Especially thyroid cancer* is an explanatory phrase that must be set off by equivalent marks of punctuation. In Choice G the second comma has been omitted. Choice H uses two different punctuation marks to set off the phrase. Choice J uses the proper punctuation, but the repetition of *cancer* is a stylistic flaw.

23. **A**   In Choice B, the relative pronoun *which* may not be used to refer to people. (Instead, use *who* or *that*.) Choice C improperly shifts the verb tense from the past to the present perfect. Choice D includes the phrase *clean from*, a substandard, unidiomatic construction.

24. **F**   Choice F provides the most relevant evidence to support the idea that many people felt hopeless and isolated.

25. **C**   Choice A contains a comma splice between *radioactive* and the phrase *in fact*. Choice B is a mixed construction in which the clause beginning with *that* has no grammatical relationship with the previous part of the sentence. Choice D lacks the necessary commas to set off the phrase *in fact*, and it also contains a clause (beginning with *that*) whose meaning is not logically related to the previous part of the sentence.

26. **J**   Choice F is redundant because *fraction* and *1 percent* express essentially the same meaning, even though *fraction* is a less precise word. Choice G contains the pronoun *that*, which fails to refer to a specific noun or other pronoun. Choice H contains the same redundancy as F.

27. **D**   Choice A incorrectly uses an adjective, *sufficient*, instead of an adverb to modify the verb *cooled*. Choice B is the same as A. Choice C is wordy. Because the word *sufficiently* and the phrase *so as* are somewhat redundant, one or the other—preferably the phrase—should be deleted.

28. **G**   Choice F contains an error in diction. In this context, *toward* is an unidiomatic choice. The apostrophe in Choice H is misplaced; put it before the *-s*. Also, the word *to* is not idiomatic in this context. Choice J contains an error in diction. Correct usage calls for *with respect to* instead of *with respect of*.

29. **A**   In Choice B, the subject *Fishing* is not logically or grammatically related to the remainder of the sentence. In addition, the singular subject fails to agree with the plural verb *are*. Choice C contains the same problems as B. Choice D includes an incorrect form of the verb: *Caught* is the past tense of *to catch*.

30. **J**   Because Choice F changes the paragraph's topic sentence, it is a poor choice. The paragraph relates generally to the long-term influence of Chernobyl, not to the properties of radioactive materials. Choice G would cause the proposed sentence to intrude on the discussion of the effort to restore life as it once was. Choice H would turn the sentence into an irrelevant afterthought. If the sentence were to be located between sentences 1 and 2, it would not be out of place, but since that is not an option, the sentence shouldn't be included at all.

Passage 3

31. **A**   In one way or other, Choices B, C, and D support the idea that people in large

numbers accept the validity of supernatual phenomena. Because the paragraph's second sentence begins with *Yet,* a word that introduces a contrasting idea, none of these choices is appropriate.

32. **G** Choice F contains an error in parallel structure. Because coordinate sentence parts should be in the same grammatical form, *haunting* should be *haunt*—that is, parallel to *reside.* Choice H includes a misplaced and unnecessary comma. Choice J, like F, contains an error in parallel structure, and, like H, contains a superfluous comma.

33. **C** Choice A introduces a construction that lacks a grammatical relationship with the second clause of the sentence. Choice B limits the scope of the Zamoras' experience to one day, although the rest of the sentence indicates an ongoing problem. Choice D contains unidiomatic usage; the correct phrase is *Beginning on.*

34. **J** Choices F, G, and H improperly shift the verb tense away from the present. In F, the tense changes to the past, in G to the present progressive, and in H to the present perfect.

35. **B** The pronoun *they* in Choice A refers ambiguously to either the keys or to the Zamoras. In Choice C the pronoun *it* lacks agreement in number with its antecedent, *keys.* Choice C is the same as A.

36. **F** Considering the alternatives, the writer should leave the sentence as it is. Choice G can be interpreted in two ways: that the ghost carried the keys to the bedroom or that the bedroom is where the ghost picked up the keys. Choice H muddies the meaning still further by implying that the keys were moved either by a ghost or by

a Zamora. The clarity of Choice J is questionable because it says that the ghosts relocated the bedroom—a meaning that the writer could not have intended. All these choices also misuse a semicolon, which, when used correctly, separates independent clauses.

37. **B** Choice A is written in the passive voice, a stylistic flaw that dilutes the impact of what must have been a chilling experience. Choice C is a compound sentence in which the coordinate clauses are not equivalent. The fact that Mrs. Zamora had seen the figure would be more effectively expressed in a subordinate clause or even in a phrase embedded in the main clause. Choice D is a sentence fragment because it lacks a main verb.

38. **H** Choice F contains a dangling modifier. The phrase *Explaining what happened* should modify or refer to a person doing the explaining—i.e., Mrs. Zamora—not *previous occupant.* In Choice G, the phrase *Explaining what happened* incorrectly modifies *former owner* instead of *Mrs. Zamora* or *she.* Choice J is a construction that causes a subsequent mismatch of sentence parts.

39. **C** The apostrophe in Choice A improperly turns *Zamoras'* into a plural possessive noun. Choice B is a possessive noun in a context where there is no need for one. Choice D includes both a superfluous comma and an unnecessary apostrophe.

40. **J** Choice F contains the awkward usage *he or she,* a phrase often used when the gender of human beings is uncertain. For a dog the usage is inappropriate. Choice G contains a comma splice. Lacking punctuation to separate two independent clauses, Choice H is a run-on sentence.

41. **C** Choice A improperly shifts the verb tense from the past to the present perfect. Choice B is redundant because the verb *had been* implies a former condition, making the adverb *formerly* unnecessary. Choice D, which includes both the adverb *previously* and the phrase *in former times*, is redundant in the extreme.

42. **J** Choice F improperly shifts the verb tense from the past to the present progressive. Choice G contains a redundancy; in this context *nineteenth century*, almost by definition, implies *long ago*. Choice H uses *they*, a pronoun without an antecedent.

43. **D** Choice A includes *Irrespective of the years*, a phrase that in this context makes no sense. Choice B begins with a vague and meaningless phrase that is not grammatically related to the remainder of the sentence. Choice C is confusing because the word *then* suggests a relationship with a previous idea that does not exist.

44. **G** Choices F and H use an adverb (*toughly minded*) instead of an adjective (*tough-minded*) to modify the noun *realist*. Choice J uses adverbs instead of adjectives to modify the pronoun *he*.

45. **B** Choices A and C improperly put quotation marks around an indirect quote. Choice D places the quotation marks properly but contains the redundant phrase, *she believes* and *she says*. One or the other, but not both, may be used.

Passage 4

46. **G** Choice F creates a sentence fragment because the construction lacks a grammatical subject to go with the verb *is*. Choice H contains a grammatical mismatch of sentence parts that garbles

meaning. Choice J is unclear and confusing. It refers to *the issue*, when no issue has been mentioned.

47. **D** Choice A is a comma splice. Choices B and C include superfluous commas. Also, the colon in Choice C is improperly used.

48. **H** Choices F, G, and J include a preposition that violates standard English idiom.

49. **C** Choice A incorrectly uses *is* instead of *has*. Choice B contains a present tense verb in a context that calls for a verb in the past perfect. Choice D is not idiomatic English.

50. **F** To move the sentence from its present location makes little sense because, if the order of sentences was changed, the transitional word *however* would become meaningless. Therefore, G and H are poor alternatives. Choice J is not acceptable because Sentence 4 is needed to introduce the main subject of the essay—that studies of child care programs have been conducted.

51. **C** Choice A is a construction containing a comma splice. Choice B is grammatically correct, but stylistically weak because the two coordinate clauses of the compound sentence lack equivalence. The sentence would be strengthened by subordinating one of the clauses to the other. Choice D lacks the required comma between *reading* and *the greatest*.

52. **J** In Choice F *children* are being compared with *gains*, an illogical and meaningless comparison. Choice G is essentially the same as F and, in addition, contains nonstandard, unidiomatic construction; use *to* instead of *with*. Choice H leads to a construction that contains mismatched grammatical parts, resulting in a totally confusing message.

53. C Choice A contains an incorrect form of a verb. In context, the simple present tense of the verb *to stand* is called for. Choice B is grammatically correct but uses a singular noun, *child*, that fails to agree in number with the pronoun *their* that follows. Choice D contains a redundancy: *affluent* and *well-to-do* have essentially the same meaning.

54. G Choice F improperly shifts the verb tense from the present to the past perfect. Choice H uses a singular verb, *gives*, that lacks agreement with the plural subject, *environments*. Choice J incorrectly shifts the verb tense from the present to the past.

55. B In Choice A the plural verb *have followed* fails to agree in number with *team*, the singular subject of the sentence. Choice C is a sentence fragment because it lacks a verb. The word *following*, as a participle, may not function as the main verb. Choice D is a sentence fragment because it lacks a main verb. *To follow* is an infinitive and may not serve as the main verb in a sentence.

56. F Choices G, H, and J are grammatically correct and appropriate phrases to use in the context. Choice F is not correct because the pronoun *they* does not agree in number with its antecedent, *team*.

57. C Choice A is an incorrectly worded comparison. The word *more* (or *less*) is not needed when the adjective in the positive degree is a one-syllable word, such as *high*. Choice B uses an adverb, *highly*, in a phrase that calls for an adjective (*scored higher*). Choice D does not fit the context because it fails to make a comparison.

58. H Choice F contains a problem in parallel structure. The clause *some had greater nat-ural ability* is not grammatically parallel to the phrases *family income* and *educational level*. Choice G contains a problem in parallel structure (see F). Choice J misuses semicolons, which should not be used in a series of phrases unless the phrases contain commas, as in *Seattle, Washington; Las Vegas, Nevada; and Roanoke, Virginia.*

59. D Choice A raises an issue—public support for child care programs—that is not discussed in the passage. Choices B and C bring up matters that are unrelated to the content of the essay.

60. G Choice F creates an illogical cause-and-effect relationship. *Group management* is meant to modify *behavior*, not *because of modifying the behavior*. Choice H comes close to a valid answer, but the phrase *for modification of* is vaguely worded. Choice J contains the pronoun *This*, which has no clear antecedent. It also uses the present tense of the verb where the context calls for a verb in the future (*will modify*) or future conditional (*would modify*) tense.

Passage 5

61. D Choice A contains confusing and unidiomatic English because *recently* refers to past action, whereas *drop by* refers to present or future action. Choice B is an illogical statement: *If you recently drop by a toy store* takes liberties with time sequence that make no sense. Choice C is similar to B. *If you drop by recently* conveys a garbled message.

62. J In this context, Choices F, G, and H are *non sequiturs*. That is, they fail to create a meaningful transition between sentences. Therefore, it would be best to delete them altogether.

63. **B** Choices A, C, and D may be interesting, but they digress from the purpose of the paragraph, which is to describe the character rather than to add a piece of miscellaneous information about the tale of Cinderella.

64. **G** Choice F is full of redundancies. *Temporary* and *short-lived* mean essentially the same thing, and a *moment*, by definition, is a brief period of time. Choices H and J, being variations of F, are equally redundant.

65. **D** In Choice A the plural verb *last* fails to agree in number with the singular subject *transformation*. Choices B and C are sentence fragments because the subject *transformation* lacks a verb.

66. **F** Lacking a verb, Choice G is an incomplete sentence. Choice H contains mismatched sentence parts. The conjunction *and* introduces a clause that is grammatically unrelated to the previous part of the sentence. Choice J lacks the comma after *rags* that is needed to separate the phrase *back in rags* from the main clause of the sentence.

67. **B** Choice A contains a comma splice between *course* and *all*. The structure of Choice C confuses the reader because it is unclear whether the phrase *of course* ends the first clause or starts the second. Either way, however, the construction contains an error. It is a run-on sentence if you assume that the phrase comes at the end of the first clause, and it contains a comma splice if you put *of course* at the beginning of the second. Choice D lacks a comma between *Cinderella* and *of*.

68. **H** Choice F needlessly repeats information given earlier in the passage. Choice G has only a remote connection to the ideas expressed in the rest of the paragraph. Choice J raises a new topic that is not related to the substance of the paragraph that follows.

69. **D** Because a verb is missing from Choice A, it is a sentence fragment. Choice B is a participle without a noun to modify. In addition, using the adverb *naturally* to modify *Selling* is a puzzle. What is the meaning of "selling naturally"? Choice C is a problem not only because the construction lacks a verb, but also because it refers to *that sale*, an event that hadn't been mentioned earlier in the passage.

70. **G** Choice F includes a pronoun, *their*, that has no antecedent. Choice H contains an error in word choice: In standard English usage, apps are not run *by* smart phones and iPads but *on* smart phones and iPads. Choice J is an example of an unidiomatic, awkward expression.

71. **D** It would be hard to justify Choice A because the price of toys is irrelevant to the point of the passage. Choice B may be a tempting answer, but the writer has already discussed the abundance of Cinderella products available. Choice C is not valid because the writer has already listed at least one product—the coats for dogs, for example—that seems unrelated to Cinderella.

72. **J** Choice F is meaningless in this context and should be cast aside quickly. Choice G seems like a possibility, but the remainder of the sentence is hardly explicit; indeed, it is a rather general observation concerning the erosion of the original story of Cinderella. Choice H contradicts the writer's feelings, which are far from hopeful.

73. **C** In Choices A and B the verb tense has inappropriately shifted from the past to the present perfect. Choice D contains an error in parallel structure. The verb *befriending* should be in the past tense—in the same grammatical form as the verb *scrubbed*.

74. **G** Choice F uses a pronoun in the objective case when the context calls for a pronoun in the nominative case: Use *who* instead of *whom*. Choice H uses the pronoun *which* that is meant to refer to things rather than to people. Choice J leaves the sentence with two grammatical segments unrelated to each other.

75. **B** Discard A as a choice because the writer was stunned negatively, not in a way to inspire the purchase of a big doll. Choice C raises a matter unrelated to the passage. Choice D makes an assumption that cannot be supported by anything in the essay. If anything, the writer seems to have been repelled by the mass of Cinderella products, justifying Choice B as the best answer.

Part III

Essay Writing on the SAT and ACT

Chapter 6
Writing a Grammatical Essay

Hey, wait a minute! What is a chapter on essay writing doing in an SAT and ACT grammar book?

A fair question, and one with a fairly simple answer: Both the SAT and the ACT offer an optional essay to be written once you've completed answering all the multiple-choice questions in math, reading, and other subjects. In the essay, unlike the other sections of the exam, you're given a chance to show college admissions personnel that you can organize ideas and present them clearly and coherently in standard grammatical English.

In a word, correct grammar counts. It isn't everything, but it adds considerably to the overall quality of an essay, along with your ideas and the manner in which they are expressed and developed.

As you may know, the SAT and the ACT essays are optional. But they are not optional for students applying to the increasing number of colleges that require the essay for admission. You may also have heard that a great many colleges "recommend" that applicants write the essay. Opinions vary on how important it is to accept such a recommendation. Here's a way to think about it: If you are really serious about getting into a particular college, it makes a good deal of sense to show your interest and demonstrate initiative by writing an essay. Besides, it takes less than an hour to complete.

> Although the SAT and ACT essays are "optional," they are required for admission to certain colleges.

THE SAT ESSAY

ON SAT TEST DAY

After you've finished taking the three-hour SAT, you'll have a short break before receiving the essay assignment, which will tell you to write an essay that analyzes a nonfiction prose passage known as a "source text." Every source text chosen for the SAT is written by an author who has taken a position on an issue and presents an argument on its behalf. Your job is not to comment on the validity of the author's position but rather to analyze what the author has done to build a persuasive argument.

221

In other words, the topic of your essay is *rhetoric*—the techniques used by the author of the source text to build an argument meant to convince readers to accept or even embrace a point of view on a particular subject. Or, to put it another way, your job is to identify and explain the rhetorical strategies or devices used by the author.

To do that, you might discuss the author's use of facts, statistics, or examples that back up a particular claim. Or you may describe how the author uses logic to build a persuasive case. You might also identify individual words, phrases, or ideas that the author uses to arouse and influence readers' emotions.

The passage you'll be writing about will most likely be a sober, high quality, rational piece of writing in which the author has used a variety of persuasive, or rhetorical, strategies to support a particular position. You've probably written persuasive prose yourself—perhaps as a class assignment or in a text to a friend. Whatever your purpose, you probably stated your opinion and then mustered facts, reasons, and details—all carefully chosen to convince a reader to agree with you.

A source text used for the SAT Essay can be on virtually any subject: the arts, science, politics, social issues, or any other topic of interest and concern to a reasonably literate audience.

> In your essay, don't accept or reject the author's opinions—or even comment on them. Instead, **analyze** them!

Whatever the topic, your essay should not be about *what* the writer says but rather about *how* the writer says it. To write a successful essay you must, of course, understand what the passage says. But your primary goal is to explain the elements of language and thought that contribute most effectively to the persuasiveness of the author's argument. In short, you must **analyze** the writing in the passage.

The Prompt

A "prompt" provides the essay assignment. It tells you what to do and suggests ways to do it. According to the SAT's essay prompt, during the test you should expect to do at least three things:

1. Read the source text.
2. Analyze how the writer uses rhetoric (evidence, reasoning, stylistic features) to support his or her point of view on the subject.
3. Present your ideas in a well-organized, interesting, and correctly written essay.

Part 1 of the prompt reiterates these instructions, but uses words such as these:

> As you read the source text, observe how the author
>
> - supports and develops claims using evidence such as facts and examples.
> - uses reasoning such as logical thinking to connect claims and evidence.
> - incorporates persuasive elements, such as emotional language and effectively expressed ideas.

Every time the SAT is given, a different passage is used, but these instructions for writing the essay never change. After the passage, you'll find Part 2 of the prompt. In a sense, its placement is a gift, because it literally spells out the author's main idea and tells you exactly what to focus on as you write your essay.

Write an essay that explains what (name of author) has done to build an argument meant to persuade an audience that etc., etc., etc.

No, it won't actually say "etc., etc., etc." Instead, the prompt will tell you in a few words (*highlighted in italics below*) exactly what the unifying idea of your essay should be—the point to keep in mind and return to again and again as you write.

Your essay should explain how *Anthony Kahn* builds an argument meant to persuade readers that *students should be paid a small salary as an encouragement to attend school*. Be sure to analyze rhetorical features that strengthen the logic and persuasiveness of his argument. You may use features of your own choice as well as those listed in the box above.
    Don't discuss whether you agree or disagree with *Kahn's* opinions. Instead, concentrate on his rhetorical techniques and strategies.

Other prompts will be about passages meant to persuade readers that "*noise pollution is out of control,*" or "*hospitals can be hazardous to one's health,*" or "*grade inflation in high schools erodes the work ethic of students who experience it,*" or any one of thousands of other issues that the College Board might select.

How the Essay is Scored

Your essay will be evaluated according to three criteria—**1. Reading, 2. Analysis,** and **3. Writing**—and scored on a scale of 1 to 4 for each one. A total essay score of **4/4/4** is top of the line. It means you did splendidly in all three domains. A score of **1/1/1** means … well, the exact opposite. An essay rated, say, **3/2/4** shows that your reading of the passage was rated "3" out of "4"—good but not exceptional. The "2" for analysis signifies that you did a mediocre job in analyzing the passage, and the "4" says that you've got what it takes to write first-rate prose.

Be confident that your scores will also reflect how well you followed the instructions given by the prompt and whether your essay contains evidence that you've 1. read the source text with understanding, 2. analyzed the persuasive rhetoric used by the author of the source text, and 3. written an organized essay with a well developed main idea, varied sentence structures, precise words, and an appropriate writing style. Your score will be helped, too, if you follow all the conventions of standard English—in other words, ***if you know your grammar!***

As SAT essay raters read your essay, they'll weigh your performance in each of the three categories considering such questions as these:

1. **Reading**
   Does your essay show that you read the source text with understanding and insight?
   Does your essay show that you recognized the source text's main idea and how details in the text relate to it?
   Does your essay include specific and appropriate use of quotations from the text, as well as accurate paraphrases or brief summaries of important ideas?

2. **Analyzing claims and evidence**
   Does your essay analyze the text rather than merely summarize it?
   Does your essay correctly identify the author's claims and the evidence, reasoning, stylistic techniques, or other persuasive features used to support them?

Does your essay focus on the most significant rhetorical features?

Does your essay explain how the rhetorical features contribute to the overall meaning and effect of the author's argument?

Does your essay comment specifically on the purpose and effectiveness of each feature?

3. **Writing effectively**

Does your essay include a precise main idea that consistently serves as the focus of your essay? Are the ideas sensibly organized?

Did you vary your sentences to create interest and to emphasize important ideas? Did you choose precise, appropriate, and interesting words?

Did you use an appropriate and readable writing style?

Did you avoid errors in standard written English?

Actually, SAT Essay readers don't use such checklists to see whether you've done everything well. Instead, they'll read your essay *holistically*, meaning that they'll read it quickly for an overall impression of your writing and then assign it a grade. Yet, the effective use of a quotation or two from the text is likely to register in the reader's mind, as will a few particularly well-chosen words or an unusually astute comment or observation. With training and practice, essay readers develop the knack of scoring essays fairly and uniformly. In fact, two experienced readers reviewing an essay separately will give it the same score 95 percent of the time.

HOW TO EARN A HIGH SCORE
Reading

Read the source text at least twice—the first time mainly to see what it's about. During a second reading, either jot down or highlight in some way the author's major claims* and the evidence used to support them. How you read the source text is up to you, of course, but to get the most out of your effort during the exam, it pays to choose beforehand a reading technique that produces the best results for you. Try different methods as you prepare to take the test:

Option A. *Read the source text carefully from start to finish.* Note where the writer makes claims and provides some kind of evidence that supports the claims. Remain on the lookout for secondary claims meant to support major ones.

Option B. *Skim the source text.* Read faster than you normally would. Stay alert for specific instances of rhetorical strategies—statistics, quotations, examples, appeals to emotion, and so forth. Then go back and locate the claims that each piece of evidence is meant to support.

Option C. *Skim the source text for a general impression of the writer's argument.* Then go back and read it more carefully. During the second reading, concentrate on details the writer uses to make claims and how the claims are supported by evidence.

* What is a *claim*?

Basically, it's another word for an assertion, allegation, pronouncement, premise, presumption, supposition, or conclusion. It's a statement that may have the ring of truth, but it's not unquestionably true. A claim may seem valid, but its validity ultimately depends on the type, quality, and amount of evidence the author has gathered to back it up.

Give each of these options a chance to work for you. Over time, you'll discover a default method, the one that increases comprehension and helps you remember what you've read. Once you've nailed down your method, stick with it. Use it deliberately every time you read, or until it becomes second nature and you don't have to think about it any more.

To prove to the evaluators that your essay deserves a high reading score, be sure to make specific references to the source text in your essay. Use quotes, paraphrases, and brief summaries of key points; but don't mention these things without somehow tying them to the main idea of the passage. Mentioned in isolation they may show that, yes, you read the passage, but explaining how they bolster the author's argument demonstrates that you've understood not only the passage itself but why the author included these elements.

Analysis

Earn a top score in analysis by dealing specifically and fully with the following three features of the author's presentation:

1. Although the author's main point is spelled out in the prompt, be sure to look for some version of it within the passage itself. It may appear at the outset, but not necessarily. Wherever it is, be sure in your essay to quote or clearly paraphrase it. (Although you won't win any points for originality, you could just copy the words from the prompt.) Writers occasionally choose not to state their main idea all at once but to scatter segments of it strategically throughout the passage, leaving you, the reader, to piece it together. If possible, cite reasons that explain the format and placement of the main idea. Also discuss at least one of the author's secondary claims. Two might be better, but three or more may be risky because time won't allow you to fully develop a discussion of each. Some secondary claims may themselves require support, but again, dwell only on crucial ones. Don't drown the reader in a sea of minor details.

2. Describe the evidence that the writer uses to support both the main claim and secondary claims. Keep in mind that supporting evidence may not necessarily appear in the same paragraph, or even in the same neighborhood where a claim is made. Some evidence may appear early in the passage, so early that you won't yet recognize it as evidence. Then, after the claim is made, the writer may provide additional evidence or perhaps allude to the evidence stated earlier. What that means for you, the reader (and analyzer) of the passage, is that your search for evidence must be comprehensive—far-reaching enough to include the entire passage and not limited to the proximity of each claim.

3. Don't be content to simply summarize the writer's claims and list pieces of evidence used to support them. Take your analysis one step further: Once you've identified a piece of evidence, discuss the effect of that evidence on the reader. That is, explain what you think the writer achieved by using it. Is the evidence persuasive because it has been well reasoned or logically thought out? Do quotations, if any, come from well-informed, reputable sources? Is the evidence convincing because it contains specific data from a prestigious source, such as a university or reputable research organization? Does the evidence depend on emotional or technical language for its persuasiveness? Answers to such questions can give your essay a real lift.

TIP: A first-rate analysis explains how and why evidence affects readers.

Writing

Many criteria are used to determine your essay score. Naturally, an essay that's mostly correct will make a better impression than one that's full of mistakes. Like other readers, evaluators enjoy good writing and delight in thoughtful, neatly phrased ideas. They abhor empty platitudes and know in an instant when a writer is throwing the bull. Almost instantly readers will notice whether you've grasped the purpose of the assignment and whether ideas are coherently organized, clearly expressed, and fully developed. Along the way they'll observe your choice of words, sentence structure, and ability to locate and describe the rhetorical features used by the author of the source text.

> Essay readers are prepared to reward you for what you've done well.

Evaluators will approach your essay with a positive mindset, prepared to reward you for what you've done well. They'll compare it to other essays written about the same source at the same time. Your essay, in other words, won't be competing against some ideal essay by a professional writer.

FINDING AND ANALYZING EVIDENCE

The author of a source text may use several different kinds of evidence to support both the primary and secondary claims. Study the short passages below. Each contains a claim and a certain amount of evidence meant to support its validity.

- **Examples and facts, including statistics**

  [Claim]: Water scarcity is among the main problems to be faced by many societies and the world in the 21st century.

  [Evidence]: Around 1.2 billion people, or almost one-fifth of the world's population, live in areas of physical scarcity, and 500 million people are approaching this situation. Another 1.6 billion people, or almost one quarter of the world's population, face economic water shortage (where countries lack the necessary infrastructure to take water from rivers and aquifers).

- **Findings and conclusions drawn from research studies**

  [Claim]: Excessive noise pollution in working areas such as offices, construction sites, and even in our homes has long influenced psychological health.

  [Evidence]: Studies conducted by the National Institutes of Health show that the occurrence of aggressive behavior, disturbance of sleep, constant stress, fatigue, and hypertension can be linked to excessive noise levels. These in turn can cause more severe and chronic health issues later in life.

- **Quotations from informed/qualified authorities**

  [Claim]: There is no better way to teach future military officers at America's service academies the grit needed for combat than to require freshmen of both sexes to take boxing lessons.

[Evidence]: "We want to expose them [freshmen] to fear and stress and teach them confidence to respond," said Lieutenant Colonel Nicholas Gist, the director of physical education at West Point. "We'd rather teach that at the academy than in Iraq or Afghanistan."

- **Reasoning such as logical thinking to connect evidence and claims**

  [Claim]: The perpetual use of smart phones and other electronic means of communication causes a decline in human empathy.

  [Evidence]: Masses of people engage in conversation with one person while simultaneously typing messages to someone else. Logic dictates that dividing attention necessarily dilutes open-ended, spontaneous conversation that includes vital eye-contact and awareness of others' posture, tone, feelings, and vulnerabilities.

- **Stylistic or persuasive elements, such as emotional language and effectively expressed ideas**

  [Claim]: There is a kind of madness at work in the plight of refugees from the Middle East and Africa.

  [Evidence]: Recently, a group of refugees, many from war-ravaged Syria, broke out of what amounted to a holding pen, where the Hungarian authorities had kept them for days in increasingly desperate conditions. When the police tried to bring them back, they started to run. As a lean, bedraggled man carrying an infant raced away, a bystander tripped him, and he and the child tumbled to the ground. Blood gushed from his forehead, but he scrambled to his feet, and still tightly gripping the baby, limped away in a cloud of dust.

- **Also, consider rhetorical elements not on the provided list**

  Because no list can include every technique that authors might use to bolster their arguments, remain on the lookout for additional rhetorical devices. For example, if you notice the author's use of figures of speech—metaphors, similes, hyperbole, and so forth—feel free to discuss their impact on the persuasiveness of the passage. Be cautious, however. Don't pick out figures of speech just to show off your ability to identify them. Mention them only if you can show how the use of such devices adds to the rhetorical impact of the author's argument.

SAMPLE ANALYSIS OF A SOURCE TEXT

Here is a sample essay assignment. It consists of a prompt, the text of a source, and a student-written essay, followed by an SAT essay reader's comments and scores for reading, analysis, and writing.

As you read the following source text, observe how the author

- supports and develops claims using evidence such as facts and examples.
- uses reasoning such as logical thinking to connect evidence and claims.
- incorporates persuasive elements, such as emotional language and effectively expressed ideas.

Adapted from "Do Animals Feel Pain?" by Peter Singer. Originally published in *Animal Liberation*, 2nd edition, Avon Books, 1990.

1   Do animals other than humans feel pain? How do we know? Well, how do we know if anyone, human or nonhuman, feels pain? We know that we ourselves can feel pain. We know this from direct experience of pain when, for instance, we stumble and fall to the ground, scraping an elbow or knee. But how do we know that anyone else feels pain? We cannot directly experience someone else's pain, whether that "anyone" is our best friend or a stray cat. Pain is a state of consciousness, a "mental event," and as such it can never be observed. Behavior like writhing, crying, or even bellowing in agony is not pain itself; nor are the recordings a neurologist might make of an activity within the brain observations of pain itself. Pain is something we feel, and we can only infer that others are feeling it from various indications . . .

2   If it is justifiable to assume that other humans feel pain as we ourselves do, is there any reason why similar inferences should not be justifiable in the case of other animals? Nearly all external signs that lead us to infer pain in other humans can be seen in other species, especially those most closely related to us—species of mammals and birds. The behavioral signs include facial contortions, moaning, yelping or other forms of calling, attempts to avoid the source of the pain, appearance of fear at the prospect of its repetition, and so on. In addition, we know that these animals have nervous systems very like ours, which respond physiologically like ours do when the animal is in circumstances in which we would feel pain: an initial rise of blood pressure, dilated pupils, perspiration, an increased pulse rate, and, if the stimulus continues, a fall in blood pressure. Although human beings have a more developed cerebral cortex than other animals, this part of the brain is concerned with thinking functions rather than with basic impulses, emotions, and feelings. These impulses, emotions, and feelings are located in the diencephalon, which is well developed in many other species of animals, especially mammals and birds.

3   We also know that the nervous systems of other animals were not artificially constructed—as a robot might be constructed—to mimic the pain behavior of humans. The nervous systems of animals evolved as our own did, and in fact the evolutionary history of human beings and other animals, especially mammals, did not diverge until the central features of our nervous systems were already in existence. The capacity to feel pain obviously enhances a species' prospects for survival, since it causes members of the species to avoid sources of injury. It is surely unreasonable to suppose that nervous systems that are virtually identical physiologically, have a common origin and a common evolutionary function, and result in similar forms of behavior in similar circumstances should actually operate in an entirely different manner on the level of subjective feelings.

4   The overwhelming majority of scientists who have addressed themselves to this question agree. Lord Brain, one of the most eminent neurologists of our time, has said: "I personally can see no reason for conceding mind to my fellow men and denying it to animals … I at least cannot doubt that the interests and activities of animals are correlated with awareness and feeling in the same way as my own, and which may be, for aught I know, just as vivid."

5   A hazy line of thought deriving from the influential philosopher, Ludwig Wittgenstein, maintains that we cannot meaningfully attribute states of consciousness to beings without language. This position seems very implausible. States of pain have nothing to do with language. After all, human infants and very young children are unable to use language. Are we to deny that a year-old child can suffer? If not, language cannot be crucial.

6   So to conclude: there are no good reasons, scientific or philosophical, for denying that animals feel pain. If we do not doubt that humans feel pain, we should not doubt that other animals do so too.

> Your essay should explain how *Peter Singer* builds an argument meant to persuade readers that *animals feel pain just as humans do.* Be sure to analyze rhetorical features that strengthen the logic and persuasiveness of his argument. You may use features of your own choice as well as those listed in the box above.
>
> Don't discuss whether you agree or disagree with Singer's opinions. Instead, concentrate on his rhetorical techniques and strategies.

SAT Essay by Monica P., A High School Senior
(Printed just as it was written)

Peter Singer is trying to answer a question that has probably puzzled mankind since ancient days—like in Egypt and maybe even in the Bible. His major claim is that animals definitely feel pain. This opinion is supported mostly by using logical reasoning based on several similarities between humans and animals. He admits that it may be impossible to know 100% that all humans can feel pain, however, its a safe assumption that they do due to the fact that they usually react to pain by acting in certain ways, such as "writhing, crying, or even bellowing in agony," while animals show signs of pain by "moaning, yelping or other forms of calling."

Using these and other similarities as evidence, Singer concludes that animals must feel pain. He presents his arguement in a way to sway readers to his position by asking an almost rhetorical question: "If it is justifiable to assume that other human beings feel pain, is there any reason why similar inferences should not be justifiable in the case of other animals?" He answers his own question in a convincing way by giving details about the external behavior of animals when they are in painful circumstances coming to the conclusion that like humans, they show signs of pain, especially mammals and birds.

To strenghten his arguement, Singer describes the physical symptoms of both human's and animal's experience in painful situations. There is cited a good number of examples like "rise in blood pressure, dilated pupils, perspiration, and increased pulse rate." Possibly expecting some readers not to accept the idea about a resemblance between humans and animals, Singer adds that humans, even though they resemble animals in some ways, they are more intelligent, and have a "more developed cerebral cortex than other animals, which gave them the power to think better than any creatures in the animal kingdom. Emphasizing that point and also to appeal to his audience Singer makes several referrals to "our" (meaning human) "intelligence." He repeatedly uses first-person pronouns such as <u>we, our, ours, ourselves, us</u>—all to the purpose of stressing a distinction between we humans and "them," meaning those lower creatures known as animals who don't even come close to intelligence like ours.

Through almost all of the passage, Singer uses the scientific evidence to make his arguement persuasive. Just the word itself, "SCIENCE" has a certain power, because we generally have great confidence in truth of something determined by "science." His arguement is boosted still more by using the phrase "overwhelming majority of scientists" who agree that animals and humans have similar responses to pain. Singer obviously chose the word "overwhelming" on purpose in order to emphasize that the idea is widely accepted. Then, to top it off, he adds a quotation from a scientist with a perfect name, Lord <u>Brain</u>, who authoritatively confirms Singer's claim.

Just in case the reader might still hold doubt regarding the scientific evidence that animals feel pain, Singer concludes his discussion of the issue by approaching the question through philosophy. The philosopher Wittginstein said that states of consciousness (being aware of pain is obviously the example that Singer has in mind) depends on having command of language however, Singer dismisses that by using human infants. He says that the youngest children don't use language, yet having no trouble crying or making other sounds and gestures in order to tell a parent or other care giver that they're uncomfortable or in pain.

At the end, Singer summarized the point of his entire arguement with a succinct tag line stated as a fact so that there can't be the slightest doubts about the validity of his claim: "Animals can feel pain."

Comments to Monica from an SAT Essay Reader:

Reading. This response demonstrates your thorough comprehension of the text. You provide appropriate and abundant textual evidence (paraphrases and quotations) to capture the main ideas of the passage (*If it is justifiable to assume that other human beings feel pain, is there any reason why similar inferences should not be justifiable in the case of other animals?*) and important specific details (*rise in blood pressure, dilated pupils, perspiration, and increased pulse rate … overwhelming majority of scientists*) and others. Your essay makes no significant errors or misinterpretations of the text. Basically, you have demonstrated a complete understanding of Fisher's argument, especially in discussing the similarities between humans' and animals' responses to pain. You also show an understanding of the writer's rejection of a philosophical approach to the main issue. On the whole, then, your response shows highly proficient reading comprehension.
Score: 4

Analysis. Your response offers an effective and insightful analysis of the source text, demonstrating a proficient grasp of the purpose of the essay assignment. In your third paragraph, for instance, you effectively analyze Singer's sensitivity to readers who may be skeptical of his claims regarding animals' pain: *expecting some readers not to accept the idea about a resemblance between humans and animals, Singer adds that humans, even though they resemble animals in some ways, they are more intelligent and have a "more developed cerebral cortex than other animals."* Your subsequent discussion of Fisher's use of first-person pronouns as a persuasive device is especially astute and reveals a perceptive understanding of the analytical task. This effective analysis continues in the next paragraph with the discussion of Singer's use of *science* as a means to enhance the validity of his argument (*His arguement* [sic] *is boosted still more by using the phrase "overwhelming majority of scientists" who agree that animals and humans have similar responses to pain. Singer obviously chose the word "overwhelming" on purpose—in order to emphasize that the idea is widely accepted.*) Your observation that the scientist Lord Brain, has a "perfect name" is witty to be sure, but more than that testifies to your understanding that every word of the text is subject to analysis. On the whole, then, your response demonstrates high analytic proficiency.

Score: 4

Writing. Your response demonstrates you have the ability to organize ideas efficiently. You focus consistently on the author's central claim (*. . . Singer concludes that animals must feel pain . . . coming to the conclusion that like humans, they show signs of pain, especially mammals and birds . . . Animals can feel pain*), cite specific references to the text, and maintain unity by following the basic structure of the source text. Each paragraph of your essay remains on topic and contains a clear progression of ideas. Sentences by and large vary in length and structure, although some are worded ungracefully or incorrectly (*. . . since ancient days—like in Egypt and even maybe in the Bible . . . There is cited a good number of examples . . . Singer makes several referrals to "our" (meaning human) "intelligence . . . Singer dismisses that by using human infants*). Unfortunately, some potentially strong ideas lose their potency because of errors in sentence structure. Almost every paragraph contains a sentence error, a misspelling, or incorrect punctuation. Cumulatively, these mistakes cause confusion, which weakens the overall impression of what might otherwise be a first-class essay. For these reasons, your essay represents only partially successful writing.

Score: 2

ACT WRITING TEST

The optional ACT Writing Test follows the four multiple-choice sections of the ACT and consists of one essay to be written in 40 minutes.

The test is optional because not all colleges require it. Whether or not to take it depends on the colleges where you plan to apply. Some require it, some recommend it, and others don't care. Check the ACT website for a list of colleges that require it. If you expect to take the writing test, sign up when you register for the ACT examination.

If you're not yet sure where you'll be applying, it makes sense to take the test. That way you'll avoid the trouble and expense of later taking a make-up test consisting of the English multiple-choice section of the ACT and the essay question.

Your Writing Test score adds an important dimension to your college admissions profile. It tells admissions officials how well you write, especially under the pressure of time. More

Essay Writing

specifically, your performance provides colleges with important information about 1. the depth of your analytical thinking, 2. your ability to organize and develop ideas, 3. the way you express yourself, and 4. your mastery of standard written English—including grammar!

1. The *depth of your analytical thinking* is demonstrated by writing about the issue specified in a prompt. Your essay shows how well you can formulate and support a position on an issue that you may not have even thought about before.

   The ACT essay assignment includes a unique twist. It won't be enough to make a simple statement of your opinion and back it up with a few supporting details. No, you must also discuss three different perspectives on the issue, each one briefly articulated by the prompt.

   > The ACT essay obliges you to write about an issue you may not have thought about before.

   If the position you advocate coincides even partially with one of the perspectives, your essay should develop an argument supporting that point of view. In addition, though, you'll have to explain the shortcomings of the perspectives you've rejected. If you happen to disagree completely with all three perspectives, you must say why and then develop an argument that supports your own distinctive point of view.

2. You show your ability to *organize ideas* by arranging material purposefully—in a way that makes the most persuasive argument on behalf of your point of view. The organization that is sure to fail is the aimless one, the one in which ideas are presented solely according to when they happen to have popped into your head. To prevent such aimlessness, list your ideas and then rank them in order of their importance to your argument. Then work toward your best point, not away from it. If your argument contains three good supporting ideas, save the most potent one for last. Launch your discussion with your second best, and sandwich your least favorite between the other two. Try to end your essay with something memorable: a thought that essay readers will have fresh in their minds when they score your essay.

3. You reveal your ability to *express yourself* by accurately and succinctly conveying your thoughts to the reader. A plain, natural style is best. An English teacher may once have told you never to use the first-person pronoun "I" in a formal essay. That's sensible advice in many contexts, but not necessarily on the ACT. After all, the prompt asks you to explain your opinion on an issue, and to avoid "I" while doing so may cause you to write awkward, stilted prose. Moreover, it may keep you from using the plain, natural style that best gives expression to your voice.

   Incidentally, the ACT essay is not the place to show off your vocabulary. Use a complex word only when it's the only one that says exactly what you mean and will add something to the essay's tone or meaning that would otherwise be lost. Elegant words have their place, of course, but to use them merely to sound elegant is pretentious and, if the meaning is not exactly right, sort of foolish.

4. You demonstrate your use of *correct English* by writing an essay that follows those conventions of standard usage and grammar that you studied in the earlier chapters of this book—no doubt with great pleasure, fervor, and excitement. Well, even if that overstates the degree of your enthusiasm, the fact is that, whether it's fair or not, essay scores will rise and fall based in part on the presence or absence of grammar and usage errors.

EVALUATING THE ESSAY

Your essay will be scored on a scale of 6 (best) to 1 (worst). The ACT readers, mostly high-school and college teachers with plenty of experience reading students' essays, are trained to read the essays quickly, or *holistically*. That is, they won't hunt down every little error but rather base their evaluation on an overall impression of your writing. Recognizing that ACT essays have been written in 40 minutes, they won't hold minor mistakes against you and won't deduct a certain amount for every error. If an essay is overrun with flaws, however, it will leave a less favorable impression than one that is mostly correct. Like other readers, the evaluators enjoy good writing and delight in lively, neatly phrased ideas. They also take great pleasure in awarding high scores to deserving essays.

> Readers base evaluations on an overall impression of your writing.

Evaluating Your Essay

Each essay is scored in four categories, called "domains." Because your essay will be read by two different evaluators, the range of scores for each domain will be reported on a scale of 2 to 12.

> **Domains**
> Ideas and Analysis   2–12
> Development and Support   2–12
> Organization   2–12
> Language Use and Conventions   2–12

Your essay score will also play a part in determining a composite English/Writing Score and an ELA (English Language Arts) score—the average of the ACT English, reading, and essay tests.

If the two readers' assessments differ by more than one point, the essay will be read by a third evaluator. No list of criteria can include everything that may impress a reader, but the descriptions below highlight many of the standards that ACT essay readers take into account.

Every effort is made to be objective, but being human, ACT readers must ultimately exercise their judgment. Consequently, an essay that receives a low 5 may not be appreciably better than an essay that earns a high 4. The rating difference is likely to be based on intangibles that cause readers to assign the grade that in their view is most appropriate.

Score: 6 Outstanding An *outstanding* essay is a well-conceived, orderly, and insightful treatment of the analytical task. The writer has generated a convincing thesis amply supported by appropriate and specific details regarding the multiple perspectives on the issue. Its point of view, syntax, imagery, and diction demonstrate the writer's ability to control a wide range of elements of composition. Errors in standard written English, if any, are inconsequential. Overall, the work is a model of clarity and sophistication.

Score: 5 Very Good A *very good* essay contains a sound thesis and demonstrates the writer's grasp of the rhetorical task. It develops the main idea with purpose and conviction but may be somewhat less persuasive and insightful than an essay rated "outstanding." It also may fall just short of the mastery, sophistication, and organization exemplified by essays earning a 6.

Nevertheless, its organization is logical, its language and usage appropriate, and it is largely free of errors.

Score 4: Good A *good* essay deals competently with the analytical task. It uses conventional and essentially appropriate language and sentence structure and makes appropriate references to the three perspectives provided by the prompt. It gives evidence of the writer's acquaintance with essay organization, coherence, and paragraph development. Some errors in word choice and awkward expression may exist, but no error in standard written English seriously interferes with meaning.

Score 3: Fair A *fair* essay suggests mediocrity in writing. It may adequately respond to the prompt but gives evidence of an inconsistent control of the elements of composition. Although the essay has a recognizable structure, the organization may be confusing or not fully realized. Inaccuracies or lapses in logic may weaken the essay's overall effect. Occasional errors in grammar may detract from the essay's clarity but don't necessarily obliterate meaning.

Score 2: Poor A *poor* essay demonstrates a marginal understanding of the prompt. The essay's development is meager and its treatment of the subject imprecise and unconvincing. The point of the essay may be perceptible, but the presentation of ideas may be characterized by faulty diction, weak syntax, and a hard-to-follow, incoherent organization.

Score 1: Very Poor A *very poor* essay reveals the writer's inability to deal with the analytical task. It may discuss an irrelevant topic or misinterpret the purpose of the assignment. It may also be unacceptably brief or undeveloped. The prose may lack organization, coherence, and meaning. The writer shows little evidence of control of English syntax or the conventions of standard usage and grammar.

In general, essays scored 4, 5, and 6 are considered average or above and attest to a level of proficiency in writing suitable for first-year college students. Essays rated 1, 2, or 3 are below average and may suggest the writer's need for remediation.

What You Will Write About

The topic of your essay will be provided by the "prompt," which introduces and explains broadly an issue to think and write about. It also includes instructions for what to include in your response. In essence, your job is to choose a perspective on a given issue and develop a convincing argument supporting your position.

You can support your argument with evidence drawn from almost any relevant source—your studies, reading, culture, current events, personal experience. The topics pertain to real-life situations and conditions that affect significant numbers of people. They relate in various degrees to matters of interest and concern to individuals as well as segments of society and the world around us.

The prompt concludes with the so-called "Essay Task," a set of precise instructions telling you what to do as you plan and write your essay.

SAMPLE PROMPT

> ## Trigger Warnings
>
> At colleges and some high schools, students have requested "trigger warnings"—notifications that material they've been assigned to see or read may be upsetting in some way and may trigger grievous emotional reactions.
>
> Considerable controversy has developed about trigger warnings both on campuses and in the media. Those who defend them claim that students should not be assigned material that unsettles or distresses them. Victims of rape or child abuse, for example, should not be forced to read about such matters in literary works. Opponents, on the other hand, argue that trigger warnings are a dangerous form of censorship and an affront to academic freedom.

Perspective 1	Perspective 2	Perspective 3
Studying the humanities involves a vast array of things of a disturbing nature. That's what "getting an education" means—especially a college education. It's also learning about real life.	Demands for trigger warnings indicate that many current students are pampered, sheltered, and immature. Coddling them like babies is harmful and demeaning.	Grim topics such as war, torture, and suicide can dredge up memories of traumatic experiences and cause students to feel unsafe and unable to cope.

> ## Essay Task
>
> Write a well-organized essay that assesses the three perspectives on the use of trigger warnings in educational settings. Be sure that your essay
>
> - analyzes and evaluates the three perspectives.
> - explains and supports your own perspective on the issue.
> - discusses the similarities and/or differences between your perspective and those stated above.

An Essay-Writing Strategy

An essay completed in 40 minutes is bound to be shorter than most essays required in high-school or college courses. Yet, 40 minutes gives you plenty of time to prove that you have what it takes to write a substantial essay. No doubt you've done it before in English, social studies, and other classes. The big difference here, of course, is that you can't study ahead of time. Because you don't know the topic, you must quickly process your thoughts and get them onto paper. Although the prompt can't be predicted, you can depend on the consistency of the Essay Task. Study it, memorize it, if necessary, so you won't waste precious time re-reading it on test day.

You'll find a page in the ACT test booklet called "Planning Your Essay." It's mostly blank, but as its name suggests, it is meant to serve as a place for you to collect and organize ideas before writing your essay. Whatever you put down on this page will be for your eyes only. It

Essay Writing

won't be read or evaluated by essay readers. On this page you'll find suggestions for planning your essay:

Use the space below and on the back cover to generate ideas and plan your essay. You may wish to consider the following as you think critically about the task:

Strengths and weaknesses of the three given perspectives

- What insights do they offer, and what do they fail to consider?
- Why might they be persuasive to others, or why might they fail to persuade?

Your own knowledge, experience, and values

- What is your perspective on this issue, and what are its strengths and weaknesses?
- How will you support your perspective in your essay?

If you think about it, the ACT people have done you a favor by telling you exactly what to think about as you prepare to write, and by extension, what sorts of ideas to include in your essay. In a sense, too, they have suggested a workable outline for essay organization: Begin with an assessment of the "strengths and weaknesses of the three perspectives" by discussing what insights the perspectives do and don't offer. Next, analyze the persuasiveness of each perspective . . . and so on.

Once you have decided on your own unique perspective, present your case. There is no right or wrong point of view. You won't be penalized for taking an unusual or unpopular position, or for incorporating aspects of the other perspectives into your own. In fact, partial agreement with at least one of them signals that you have taken into account alternative points of view—a rhetorical technique that can strengthen your argument. But be most concerned about providing sensible, convincing evidence that your perspective is superior to the others.

Support your perspective with relevant, interesting examples and specific evidence. It's easy to write generalities. But the heart of an essay is its details. The development of specific supporting evidence reveals more about the depth of your thinking than almost anything else in the essay.

Be mindful of coherence. All parts of an essay should work together to make a single point. If the evidence you provide wanders from the main idea or raises additional issues that you don't have time to discuss, the effect of the essay will be diluted. Above all, don't let readers come to the end of your essay scratching their heads in puzzlement over what point you were trying to make.

The length of your essay is up to you, but quality should take precedence over quantity. There is no required length. Keep in mind that you are being asked to show your ability to think and express yourself. A short, well-written essay can produce such evidence. A brief essay allows you to devote more attention to choosing each word and crafting each sentence. Effective development of the main idea matters more than the number of words. Even an unfinished essay can earn a top score if it yields sufficient evidence of the writer's expertise.

On the other hand, beware of an essay consisting of a single paragraph. It may not give you an opportunity to fully develop your ideas. Expect to write at least two, three, or even more paragraphs.

Be sure to write only on the assigned topic. ACT topics are broad enough to give students of all abilities an opportunity to express themselves. The prompt won't trick or stump you. Nor is it apt to anger or excite you. In other words, it will be fairly innocuous, and your task is to transform it into a persuasive, engaging essay. Because you will be heavily penalized for an essay that fails to address the topic, read the prompt carefully. Read it twice or three times if necessary, underlining key words or ideas until you are confident that you know precisely what you are being asked to write about.

WRITE AN ACT ESSAY FOR PRACTICE

Time limit for reading the prompt, planning, and writing the essay: 40 Minutes

Prompt

The Perils of Praise

Virtually everyone appreciates praise, especially kids. Parents, teachers, coaches, and others know that paying a compliment to kids about their talents, brains, helpfulness, looks, skills, personalities, and almost anything else, will result in bursts of gratitude and pride. That may explain in part why in many places—homes, schools, playgrounds, or anyplace where adults and kids interact—children routinely receive praise, even when they haven't done anything overt to earn it. For example, participation trophies awarded to children just for showing up have become commonplace in sports and other activities. Steady diets of undeserved positive reinforcement, however, could have unintended consequences: Children may come to be addicted to praise and become quickly demoralized without it. Facing difficulty or failure, they may cheat, lie, or worse for the sole purpose of winning approval. These and other effects deserve examination. While many see value in freely giving praise to children, we should also be aware of the harm it may do.

Read and carefully evaluate the following perspectives. Each puts forth a specific way of thinking about questionable praise.

Perspective 1	Perspective 2	Perspective 3
The overabundance of rewards has significant negative effects on children. Young people should be praised only when they have legitimately earned it. Only then will they learn the value of hard work and effort.	In spite of adults' good intentions, pervasive praise deceives children by giving a false sense of themselves and keeps them from learning about defeat—a vital character-building experience.	Children need positive reinforcement in order to build confidence and enhance their self-image. Praise serves as motivation to do better, to strive, and to create.

Essay Task

Write a well-organized essay that assesses the three perspectives on excessive and often undeserved praise given to children. Be sure that your essay

- analyzes and evaluates the three perspectives.
- explains and supports your own perspective on the issue.
- discusses the similarities and/or differences between your perspective and those stated above.

Planning Your Essay

Plan your essay before you write. Use the space provided below to generate ideas. You may wish to consider the following as you think critically about the task:

Strengths and weaknesses of the three given perspectives

- What insights do they offer, and what do they fail to consider?
- Why might they be persuasive to others, or why might they fail to persuade?

Your own knowledge, experience, and values

- What is your perspective on this issue, and what are its strengths and weaknesses?
- How will you support your perspective in your essay?

ACT Essay by Tyler R., A High School Senior
(Printed just as it was written)

"Good job, Tyler." "Way to go, Tyler." "Great work, Tyler." I have heard these words for as long as I can remember. At some point, however, I began to realize that they sounded hollow, like when I put my cereal bowl in the kitchen sink. Or opening the front door when the doorbell rang. Or sometimes for not teasing my little brother that day, I was praised for doing things that really didn't deserve it. I was just being a kid, and doing what my family expected from me—not more or not less.

Has that affected me in ways that are described by the 3 statements in the prompt? The answer is mostly no, although I recognize that everyone's life and experiences are different than mine. Therefore, I would hesitate to say the perspectives are wrong, but they mostly don't describe me is more accurate.

Looking at "Perspective 1" the praise I got back when I was a little kid had no negative affects, as far as I can tell. Since that was a long time ago its possible that I felt proud after being complimented. But I don't think so. Putting dishes in the sink and opening the door was no big deal as far as I remember. The praise I received didn't influence me one way or the other. I know it didn't prevent me from learning "the value of hard work and effort" the prompt says.

Whatever "work ethic" I have comes instead from somewhere inside me. I happen to be lucky in that being a very good swimmer, competing in races since I was a little kid and now on my school's varsity swim team. I get satisfaction from swimming faster than others but I don't need trophies or praise to keep me going. My motivation comes from within to practice long hours, lifting weights, and watch what I eat. Winning ribbons and trophies is fine, but I'd swim even with out them because I love doing it. I get compliments all the time but it has not meant that much. They roll off me (if you'll pardon the expression) like water from a duck's back. I am motivated by the ecstasy of being in the water. That is where I belong, like a fish, It is where my body feels most comfortable. In my mind I solve problems and get some of my best thoughts while swimming. I would do it any time any place.

I don't want to sound arrogant, but I totally reject the statement in Perspective 2, that defeat builds character. It sounds like absolute nonsense to me. Defeat, like failure of any kind, is bound to hurt and makes you want to avoid it, if possible. But I doubt you become a better person as a result. In contrast. I can see that some children could develop a harmful "false sense of themselves" from too much empty praise. If a teacher gives high grades to a person's work which is not that good is an example. Basically, the teacher is lying to the person because she thinks that the student worked hard as he or she could and deserves a good grade. After a while that person may think that they are smarter than they are. But the day will come inevitably when they realize the truth, they've been misled. They discover that they've been tricked by false pretenses, and that could result in severe problems, from giving up trying any more, to dropping out of school or college or even something more worse—like self-destruction.

The third perspective makes the most sense to me. I base my opinion not so much on my own personal experience but on others, like my friend Vicki. She is an artist, and she tells the story about how in 6th grade art class the teacher whispered in her ear that 'You've got talent." Just that little compliment served as a motivation for doing more and more art, and now she is taking AP Art and doing very innovative and exciting paintings and collages. Other people I know have said the same thing. Support from a coach helped them alot, or a piano teacher made a huge impact on them.

Epilogue

As I wrote this essay, I kept wondering what the readers would think of me as a person. Do I sound like a creep, an egotist, a bore? I'll never know, of course. What I do know is that at age 17 I'm in a state of change. Ten or twenty years from now, maybe with kids of my own, I'll think about praise in a totally different way. Life is like a journey on river, and this essay for better or worse tells where I am now.

Comments to Tyler from an ACT Essay Reader

Ideas and Analysis. You clearly express your views on the issue and productively discuss pros and cons of the three perspectives stated in the prompt. The thesis of your argument, articulated in the second paragraph, that *everyone's life and experience are different*—although self-evident—is pithy enough in the context to generate a thoughtful discussion of the effects of undeserved praise on yourself and on others. Your analysis clearly addresses the complexity of the issue by taking into account not only the variety of responses that a single stimulus can elicit but also that people's assumptions and values inevitably evolve and change over time.
Score: 5

Development and Support. With only a brief time to write your essay, you made a practical and intelligent decision to focus on your own experience. By personalizing the topic you avoided falling into the trap of over-generalization—relying on broad statements about the human condition in order to build a convincing argument. Rather, you take a stand and develop your point of view using many engaging details—from *putting dishes in the sink* to describing *the ecstasy of being in the water*. When nothing in your own history supports your argument, you skillfully substitute meaningful experiences from the lives of Vicki and other people you know.
Score: 5

Organization. The heart of your essay is framed by an initial series of quotes, certain to reso-nate with readers, and a sensitive "Epilogue" which acknowledges that your views may change in the future. In between, you systematically and logically discuss strengths and weakness of each of the given perspectives, pointing out the few aspects of each that do—as well as the many that don't—pertain to you. In making transitions between paragraphs, you rely mostly on ideas rather than on customary transitional words and phrases, such as *in addition, in other words,* and *for instance*. For instance (ha!), the idea of "the value of hard work and effort" at the end of the third paragraph is carried almost seamlessly to the next paragraph by your allusion to a "work ethic." Such links help to build the essay into a coherent whole.
Score: 5

Language Use. Your use of language serves to convey your views to the reader. The writing style is informal and appropriate to the topic and to the essay's rhetorical purpose. Word choice is generally accurate, but with the exception of a single word—*ecstasy* in the fourth paragraph—is ordinary and uninspired. Grammar and usage throughout the essay adhere largely to the conventions of standard written English, but some obvious errors exist, among them:

Unrelated sentence parts: *Therefore, I would hesitate to say the perspectives are wrong, but they mostly don't describe me <u>is more accurate</u>.*
Punctuation: *Since that was a long time <u>ago its</u> possible that I felt proud . . .*
Comma splice: *But the day will come inevitably when they realize <u>the truth</u>, <u>they've</u> been misled.*
Lack of pronoun-antecedent agreement: *that person may think that <u>they</u> are smarter than they are*
Parallelism: *My motivation comes from within to practice long hours, <u>lifting weights</u>, and watch what I eat.*
Nonstandard usage. *. . . even something <u>more worse</u>—like self-destruction.*

Such errors reduce the overall quality of the essay. However distracting, they don't substantially interfere with its meaning.
Score: 4

Index

A

ACT essay
  description of, 231–232
  evaluation of, 233–234
  length of, 236–237
  prompt used in, 234–235, 237
  sample, 237–239
  scoring of, 233–234
  writing strategy for, 235–237
ACT Writing Test, 231–239
Active sentences, 72, 107
Active voice, 72
Adjective(s)
  adverbs versus, 43
  comparisons using, 37–39
  compound, 36–37
  definition of, 36
  function of, 36
  misusing, 106
Adjective clauses, 37, 62
Adjective phrases, 37
Adverb(s)
  adjectives versus, 43
  comparisons using, 43
  function of, 41–42
  misusing, 106
  in sentences, 42
Adverbial clause, 42, 62
Adverbial phrase, 41
Analytical thinking, 232
Antecedents, 10–12, 101
Apostrophes, 16, 85
Appositives, 86–87
Article, 5
Awkwardness of sentence, 77–78, 107

B

Being verbs, 7

C

Capitalization, 90–91
Claim, 224
Clauses
  adjective, 37, 62
  adverbial, 42, 62
  coordinate, 63, 105
  definition of, 62
  dependent, 49, 62, 65
  independent, 49, 62, 86–87, 104
  nonrestrictive, 17
  noun, 62
  relative, 17
  restrictive, 17
Collective nouns, 4, 12
Colon, 87–88
Comma, 17, 85–87, 102–103
Comma splices, 67, 102
Common nouns, 4
Comparative degree, 38–40
Comparisons
  adjectives used for, 37–39
  adverbs used for, 43
  degrees of, 37–39
  double, 38
  faulty, 102
  in pronouns, 8
Compound adjectives, 36–37
Compound sentences, 48, 63
Compound subjects, 32–33
Compound-complex sentence, 63
Conclusions, 226
Conjunction, 46, 48–50
Contractions, 85
Coordinate clauses, 63, 105
Coordinating conjunctions, 48
Correlative conjunction, 49

D

Dangling participles, 66, 104
Dash, 88
Declarative sentences, 75
Definite articles, 5
Demonstrative pronouns, 20
Dependent clauses, 49, 62, 65
Diction
  definition of, 77
  faulty, 82
Direct object, 61
Double comparisons, 38
Double negative, 79–80

E

Em-dash, 88
Emotional language, 227
Essay writing. *See* ACT essay; SAT essay
Exclamation point, 89
Exclamatory sentences, 75

F

Facts, 226
Faulty idiom, 78–81, 106
First-person pronouns, 9–10, 232

G

Gerund, 4, 16, 66
Grammar
  importance of, vii
  pitfalls, 99–107
  usage versus, vii
Grammar questions and tests
  ACT, 163–217
  SAT, 109–162

H

Helping verbs, 22
Hyphens, 37

I

Idiom
    definition of, 78
    faulty, 78–81, 106
Idiomatic usage, 78
Imperative sentences, 75
Indefinite articles, 5
Indefinite pronouns, 10, 34
Independent clauses, 49, 62,
        86–87, 104
Indirect object, 61
Indirect quotations, 88
Infinitives
    description of, 31, 66
    splitting of, 42
Interjections, 5
Interrogative pronouns, 19
Interrogative sentences, 75
Irregular verbs, 28–30

L

Linking verbs, 7, 43
Logical thinking, 227

M

Misplacing modifiers, 104
Mood, 31

N

Nominative case, 6, 46
Nonrestrictive clause, 17
Noun(s)
    collective, 4, 12
    common, 4
    definition of, 3
    plural, 33
    possessive, 85
    pronouns and, 8
    proper, 4
    singular, 12, 33
Noun clauses, 62

O

Object(s)
    direct, 61
    indirect, 61
    of predicate, 61
    of preposition, 46, 61
    of verbs, 7, 61
Object pronouns, 6–7
Objective case, 6

P

Parallel structure, 68–70, 101
Participial phrase, 66
Participles
    dangling, 66, 104
    description of, 16, 25, 66, 104
Parts of speech, 5
Passive sentences, 72, 107
Passive voice, 72
Past tense, 22–23, 23
Personal pronouns, 6, 8
Phrases
    adjective, 37
    adverbial, 41
    participial, 66
    prepositional, 7, 46, 64, 69
Plural nouns, 33
Possessive nouns, 85
Possessive pronouns, 16
Predicate, 59–60
Predicate nominative, 7
Preposition, 45–48
Prepositional phrases, 7, 46, 64,
        69
Present tense, 22–23, 23
Prompt
    for ACT essay, 234–235, 237
    for SAT essay, 222–223
Pronoun(s)
    antecedents of, 10–12, 101
    "case," 6–7, 46, 105
    in comparisons, 8
    definition of, 5
    demonstrative, 20
    first-person, 9–10, 232

indefinite, 10, 34
    interrogative, 19
    noun and, 8
    object, 6–7
    personal, 6, 8
    possessive, 16
    reflexive, 19
    relative, 14, 16–18, 101
    second-person, 9–10
    subject, 6–7
    subject-verb agreement and,
        33–34
    third-person, 9–10
    usage of, consistency in, 10–11
Pronoun person, 9–10, 105
Pronoun references, 13–15, 101
Pronoun shift, 12
Proper nouns, 4
Punctuation
    apostrophe, 16, 85
    colon, 87–88
    comma, 17, 85–87, 102–103
    dash, 88
    exclamation point, 89
    question mark, 89
    quotation marks, 88–89
    semicolon, 87, 103
Punctuation questions and tests,
        168–169

Q

Question mark, 89
Quotation marks, 88–89
Quotations, 226–227

R

Redundancies, 83–84
Reflexive pronouns, 19
Relative clauses, 17
Relative pronouns, 14, 16–18,
        101
Research studies, 226
Restrictive clause, 17
Rhetoric, 222
Rhetoric questions, 169–170

Run-on sentences, 66–67, 104–105

S
SAT essay
  analysis element of, 225
  criteria for, 223–226
  evidence used in, 226–227
  preparations for, 221–222
  prompt used in, 222–223
  reading element of, 223–225
  sample, 227–231
  scoring of, 223–226
  writing element of, 226
Scoring
  of ACT essay, 233–234
  of SAT essay, 223–226
Second-person pronouns, 9–10
Semicolons, 87, 103
Sentence(s)
  active, 72, 107
  adverbs in, 42
  awkwardness of, 77–78, 107
  "bare bones" of, 64–65
  compound, 48, 63
  compound-complex, 63
  declarative, 75
  definition of, 59
  exclamatory, 75
  faulty diction in, 82
  faulty parallel structure, 68–70, 101

imperative, 75
incomplete, 104
interrogative, 75
mixed construction, 106
parts of, 59–61, 102
passive, 72, 107
preposition at end of, 47
problems with, 64–73
redundancies in, 83–84
run-on, 66–67, 104–105
simple, 63
varying of, 75
wordiness in, 83–84, 105–106
Sentence fragments, 62, 64, 104
Sentence structure
  description of, 74–75
  faulty, 68–70
Simple sentences, 63
Singular nouns, 12, 33
Splitting infinitives, 42
Statistics, 226
Subject
  definition of, 60
  shifting of, 74
Subject pronouns, 6–7
Subject-verb agreement, 32–36, 100
Subjunctive, 31–32
Subordinating conjunction, 49
Subordination, 63, 105
Superlative degree, 38
Syntax, 77

T
That, 18
Third-person pronouns, 9–10

U
Usage
  grammar versus, vii
  idiomatic, 78
  pronoun, consistency in, 10–11

V
Verb(s)
  being, 7
  definition of, 22
  helping, 22
  irregular, 28–30
  linking, 7, 43
  objects of, 7, 61
  subject-verb agreement, 32–36, 100
Verb forms, 27–31, 100
Verb tenses
  guidelines for, 25
  shifting of, 24–25, 100
  types of, 22–24
Verbals, 66

W
Which, 18
Who/whom, 18
Wordiness, 83–84, 105–106